Understanding
CRISIS
THERAPIES

An Integrative Approach to Crisis
Intervention and Post Traumatic Stress

HILDA LOUGHRAN

Extract from Roberts 2005 on p.72 is reproduced by permission of Oxford University Press.

First published in 2011
by Jessica Kingsley Publishers
73 Collier Street
London N1 9BE, UK
and
400 Market Street, Suite 400
Philadelphia, PA 19106, USA

www.jkp.com

Chapters 1, 4, 5, 6, 7, 8, 9, 10 Copyright © Hilda Loughran 2011
Chapters 2, 3 Copyright © Jessica Kingsley Publishers 2011

Printed digitally since 2014

Library of Congress Cataloging in Publication Data
Loughran, Hilda.
  Understanding crisis therapies: an integrative approach to crisis
intervention and post traumatic stress / Hilda Loughran.
      p. ; cm.
  Includes bibliographical references and index.
  ISBN 978-1-84905-032-6 (alk. paper)
  1. Crisis intervention (Mental health services) 2. Life change events. 3.
Post-traumatic stress disorder. I. Title.
  [DNLM: 1. Crisis Intervention--methods. 2. Life Change Events. 3. Stress
Disorders, Post-Traumatic--therapy. WM 401]
  RC480.6.L676 2011
  362.2'04251--dc22
                              2010053441

British Library Cataloguing in Publication Data
A CIP catalogue record for this book is available from the British Library

ISBN 978 1 84905 032 6
eISBN 978 0 85700 555 7

To my parents Frank and Geraldine Loughran who showed me all I needed to know about strength and resilience.

Also to my dear friends who passed away in 2010: Sheila Lyons, Gabriel Kiely and Connie Loughran.

Acknowledgements

In the late 1990s I was approached by a group called Community Response who wanted to work with their local community in developing responses to the social issues troubling that community. They recruited me to develop and deliver a module on Crisis Intervention to a group of 12 people who were facing crisis every day in communities struggling with serious drug problems as well as problems around housing, welfare, health and education. With the support of my colleagues in the School of Applied Social Science we established a number of partnerships with community groups and continue to work in innovative educational programmes based in communities and linked with the university. In particular I would like to mention the staff and students who are connected with our three current partners Urrus, An Cosan and Merchants Quay. The students who engage with these programmes tend to be mature adults with a keen interest in community issues and incredible commitment. I have learned a lot from them and their experiences and also from the astute questioning that is a feature of every class we have together. I would also like to thank the students who have completed the Masters in Social Work programme over the past 20 years. They have made my work enjoyable and rewarding.

I am grateful to my colleagues and friends in the School of Applied Social Science for their support and encouragement. In particular I would like to mention Martina Reidy, who keeps the show on the road and is always there to back me up whatever the project; my research group: Mary Ellen, Muireann, Mary, Brian, Rosemary, Anna, Valerie and Suzi; my irreplaceable colleague Valerie Richardson who worked with me on some chapters in the book; my colleague, mentor and friend Gabriel Kiely; also my much loved friend and fellow 'scooter' Sheila; and finally my sister Gwen and the rest of my family and friends who are a true social network and are always there for me.

Contents

List of Tables and Figures

Chapter 1

Introduction to Crisis Theories and Therapies

Introduction

There is general agreement that the origins of crisis intervention emanate from the work of Lindemann in the 1940s. Starting with the classic work of Lindemann (1944) the notion that crisis created an opportunity for change has been adapted and changed to accommodate and be informed by a range of theoretical influences. Crisis intervention as a therapeutic approach dates back to these early works by Lindemann (1944, 1956) and later his colleague Caplan (1964).

The work of Lindemann and Caplan in developing crisis intervention is acknowledged across many disciplines, for example nursing (Clemen-Stone 2002), psychology (Brown, Shiang and Bongar 2003) and social work (Walsh 2006). According to Satin (1984) Lindemann was a pioneer in social and community psychiatry. In his work on exploring normal life stressors and their consequences Lindemann looked to the availability of community resources that could protect the individual. These ideas ultimately led him to consider ways of preventing the negative effects of stressful events on the mental health of individuals (Satin 1984).

James (2008) suggests that the benchmark for the development of crisis intervention is the Coconut Grove nightclub fire in 1942. Lindemann and Caplan worked together with victims and their families. They identified a common emotional response among survivors and the need for assistance and support. It was from this experience that Lindemann began to build a theory of crisis. While Lindemann (1944, 1956) focused on the resolution of loss as central to mental health, Caplan (1964) expanded these ideas to encompass the total field of traumatic events (James 2008).

Interventions based on the principles of crisis theory have been among the most enduring in the therapeutic field. This is attributable at least in part to the responsiveness of crisis work to new developments. In the same way that Caplan added to Lindemann's original ideas about crisis, so too, others have adapted and expanded both the ideas around crisis and the applications of these ideas to practice.

One of the most striking aspects of Lindemann and Caplan's contribution is that in spite of the dominance of long term psychoanalytic therapy at that time they were able to conceptualise and defend what can be seen as the first brief intervention. The basic premise of the crisis intervention model was that crisis created a time of instability and uncertainty (often referred to as disequilibrium) for those involved. They believed that this sense of uncertainty left a person more open to accepting help and so an intervention at the time of crisis could bring about change while at the same time helping to restore a person to a state of equilibrium or stability. This opportunity for change was seen as something that was short term and so the intervention was designed to support and work with the person in crisis over a brief period of time directly around the crisis event. It was devised as an intervention lasting usually no more than six to eight weeks.

Aims of this book

This book sets out to provide the reader with a comprehensive understanding of crisis therapies by tracing the developments in crisis intervention across its different phases. Each phase will then be presented as a set of theoretical ideas which will be identified and considered in separate chapters. The central ideas from each of the theoretical influences on the development of crisis thinking will be discussed. The final chapter will consider the implications of the various theoretical positions and present these as an integrative framework for practice.

The book presents this integrative framework for considering not just 'crisis intervention' but the more comprehensive construct of 'crisis therapies'. This different term is significant in that it indicates a change from the parameters of the original crisis intervention model to a broader approach, encompassing new ideas about dealing with disasters, post traumatic stress and the use of crisis informed strategies in other therapeutic approaches.

The book will provide students with a clear framework for understanding the multiple influences on crisis work and assists them in associating specific interventions to the related theoretical framework. Each chapter can stand alone in terms of offering an explanation of one particular crisis orientation and the book as a whole provides a comprehensive account of the many ways crisis work has been adapted over time.

Since crisis work crosses many disciplines including social work, psychology, psychiatry, counselling and nursing, this interdisciplinary nature of the subject is reflected in the book. The book should ensure that the reader develops an appreciation of the complexities of crisis theory and therapy while at the same time assist in making these complex influences more accessible.

While the book will serve as a useful introduction to crisis work, it also goes beyond that to facilitate both students and professionals to explore in more depth the application of crisis theory in practice and in particular to provide readers with a more analytic and investigative approach to considering crisis work as a range of strategies that have developed beyond the scope of the original notion of crisis intervention.

It will be a resource to students and professional workers interested in brief therapies in general as it will help them to make the links back to crisis intervention and also to make distinctions between the various intervention options offered in what will be formulated as crisis therapies.

While each chapter has its own theoretical focus some comments will be made about the compatibility of the different approaches and about a move toward integration. Finally the book will draw on the diverse ideas presented in each chapter to formulate an integrative framework for understanding crisis therapies. It is important to work with such a framework as it will inform both assessment and intervention strategies for helping people dealing with the impact of crisis events in their lives.

Defining crisis

Although there are many definitions of crisis it is actually a difficult concept to capture when attempting to use in practical applications. This may be because it is best understood as a *broad spectrum* of possibilities. The spectrum can go from an apparently minor incident which is experienced by an individual as a crisis but not easily recognised as a crisis to someone else; for example losing a valued possession or missing a family celebration; to an event that others see as a crisis but which is not experienced as such by the person/s involved; for example losing a job or having a problem with alcohol use. This leads to at one end the possibility that we miss the significance of the event and therefore do not see the crisis to, at the other end, the decision to intervene in such a way as to make the crisis more obvious to the person, in some cases to actually heighten the crisis until it is recognised as such by the client. This is illustrated in Figure 1.1 below.

The broad spectrum nature of crisis in some ways can be compared with the notion of treatment with broad spectrum antibiotics. We know that antibiotics are needed but are not sure what the real problem is so take the approach of dealing with the problem in general. While this may be somewhat effective it is less effective than a definitive diagnosis with a targeted and specialised antibiotic. In a similar way crisis intervention type approaches may be used to deal with what appears to be a crisis related issue but this is less likely to be effective since the target for change is ill defined.

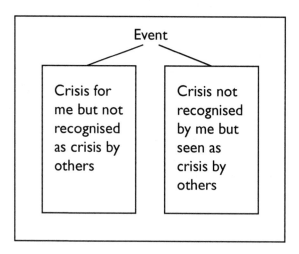

Figure 1.1: Differentiating crisis perspectives of an event

Attempts to define crisis are a challenge; however, Parad and Parad (2005a) state that:

because the stress-crisis sequence involves a complex set of biopsychosocial forces, crisis…is generally viewed as a configuration involving (1) a specific and identifiable stressful precipitating event, (2) the perception of the event as meaningful and threatening, (3) the disorganisation or disequilibrium response resulting from the stressful event and (4) the coping and interventive tasks involved in resolution, which may be adaptive or maladaptive. (p.5)

The idea of such a sequence is helpful in setting a context for consideration of different theoretical ideas, all of which deal with the elements of the sequence in different ways and with different emphasis.

Crisis: The event or the response?

Everly (2000) helps to clarify a question which is to some extent at the root of crisis therapies. When we think of crisis are we more concerned with the nature of the stressor event (the crisis event) or are we concerned with the response to that event? Focus on the nature of the event suggests that it is possible to categorise some events that will be a crisis for all who experience that situation. Focus on the response shifts our thinking away from the detail of the actual event itself and refocuses us on how that event is experienced and handled. This second conceptualisation of crisis, with its explicit focus on a crisis response fits with a perception that a crisis is not a crisis unless someone thinks it is a crisis. This is a commonly held viewpoint but relates back to some of the different theoretical influences on crisis therapies and should not be taken as a definitive statement about crisis.

Many people experience stressful and even traumatic events and appear to deal with these situations very effectively. Others when faced with apparently less trying events cannot cope and experience extreme crisis responses. This highlights an important point in attempting to define what a crisis is and that relates to the individual's natural resilience. Everly (2000) in his editorial on crisis intervention cites Breslau's (1998) work in which he estimated that 90 per cent of Americans will be exposed to some form of traumatic stressor as defined by the American Psychiatric Association. Everly goes on to point out that a US HHS report in 2000 concluded that about 9 per cent of those exposed to such a stressor would actually develop PTSD. This type of data serves to highlight the point that natural processes for dealing with trauma are largely effective. The importance of recognising such natural and/or spontaneous coping mechanisms becomes crucial when assessing crisis responses for the purposes of defining the most appropriate intervention.

Theory and therapy

It might be useful to clarify briefly one of the confusing issues for people about therapeutic strategies in general and that is the relationship between theory and therapy. When we talk about theory we mean the wider conceptual premises which inform a particular orientation or way of seeing the world. Therapy can be distinguished from theory because it implies some interaction between people; it is about two or more people in a relationship where there is a goal of change of some kind.

How the therapist goes about making sense of what the key issues for the client are and contributing to identifying and achieving the goals of the therapy depends on the theory which the therapist adopts. One difficulty is that in reading about theory and therapy the terms are often used interchangeably. This book will attempt to clarify these terminological pitfalls by dealing with theory as a separate issue. When we talk about theory we will use terms such as framework, perspective or approach. Other terms such as model or intervention will be used as an alternative to therapy. If you look at Figure 1.2, you will see that we have placed the theories that inform our work at the base of the triangle. Gray and Webb (2009) define theory as:

> a more or less well argued explanation of reality. Collectively, then, theories are explanations of reality – or human behaviour or particular social phenomena, depending on the theory's central focus – that lead to particular interpretations of that reality. The set of ideas or concepts are put together to form a theory. Sometimes we talk about the whole set of ideas as forming a framework. When we adopt or use a set of ideas or theory to help us make sense of what we are observing and hearing we can be said to be taking an approach to the problem. In other words, theorists, offer particular explanations of reality that influence the ways in which people interpret situations or events. (p.10)

From these theories we can see the next level on the triangle. This next level represents all the words we use to describe the application of the theory to practice. We shape the ideas from the theory and use them to form a way of helping. In other words when we get a set of ideas and figure out a way to make them work for people in distress we call that a model, an intervention, or a therapeutic strategy. What can sometimes happen is that we become so familiar with a way of working (a model or therapy) that we lose sight of the theory which informs our work.

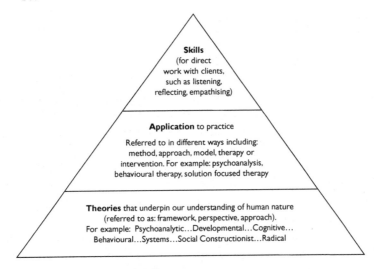

Figure 1.2: Theory, therapy and skills

Sometimes an approach can be such an integral part of how a practitioner works that it becomes like a belief system and it is difficult for the practitioner to consider alternative perspectives on clients' experiences. This is a debilitating way to work as it limits our ability to generate alternative ideas about clients and their lives and experiences and this in turn sets limits to the range of ideas we may have about how to be helpful. Theorising about life, events and experiences adds depth to our understanding and so enhances the chance that we will respond in the most appropriate and effective fashion. Adherence to a dominant discourse, in other words sticking with a set of ideas that are popular may create a barrier to our professional development and stifle our creativity. Neither are admirable qualities in a therapist/worker/helper. This is not to decry the commitment of therapists to one style of therapeutic intervention. In fact there is the suggestion that being expert in the therapy of your choice may be one of the most important attributes to working successfully with clients. This does not or should not deter from your ability to help clients make judgements about what works best for them even if it is not your preferred therapy style.

One of the most important things to remember about theory is that a theory is just a set of ideas. No one theory tells the whole story about what is happening. Think about someone telling a story in a newspaper or even telling a story to a friend. They often tell the story differently depending on who the audience is. So a story about a footballer and his wife told in a sports magazine may just mention the wife briefly but focus on the footballer and his football career while a glossy magazine may focus on the clothes they are both wearing or who they were with. It might be about the same event but it is told through a different lens. The same occurs when telling a friend about some incident that happened to you. Depending on the friend you may tell the story differently placing emphasis on different aspects of the same event. That is essentially how theories work; they tell a different story about the same event by placing emphasis on different aspects of that event or by giving more significance to one part of the event than another.

If you only use one theory to tell the story you will probably miss out on or ignore some aspects of what has happened. It is actually impossible to fully understand exactly everything about a particular event or story as there are usually too many aspects to take into account. We have to satisfy ourselves that we understand enough of what's happened so that we can be helpful to the people involved. If one version of the story emphasises for example the fact that the person is feeling overwhelmed and devastated and therefore reinforces a sense of helplessness then it may be important to know about another theory which directs you to look through another lens. Another lens might tell you to check out ways in which the person did manage some aspect of the situation better than others. Having an understanding of more than one theory provides both you and the client with a range of options about how to understand and therefore tackle the situation that is causing problems.

In order to illustrate just how different theories can enable us to see and tell a different story, each of the chapters in this book will adopt a different lens for telling the story of one case. The case concerns Susan and her family and the events surrounding her move out of her family home. We will take account of the worker or practitioner, and the theory and methods they bring to the situation as well as the client and the perception and response they have of the event (see Figure 1.3). In order to allow us to focus on what happens to the story when we switch lens or employ a different theory to help us understand the story, we are going to work with a relatively simple case. That should allow us to focus on the way the emphasis of the story changes rather than on the distress and emotion that is evoked in many more complex crisis type situations.

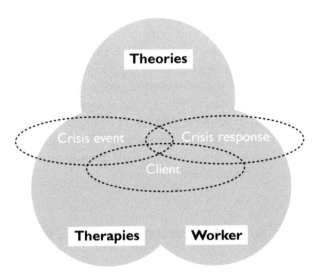

Figure 1.3: Worker/practitioner and client and the crisis event

Worker or practitioner perceptions

Theories about human nature are important in working in any helping profession. These are the basic tools we need to begin to make sense of how the people we work with experience the world. It is only through these notions or ideas or concepts about what makes us tick that we can gather clues about what might be useful in helping those people deal more effectively with life. The very notion of helping people does in itself raise some challenging questions. How do we know someone actually needs help, in particular when that person does not ask for such help and may actually appear to be resistant, resentful or antagonistic towards that help. How can we decide that someone needs help or needs to make changes? Therapy is about change but imposing change on another person has implications of power that have to be understood before we can make any ethical attempts to bring about change in or for another person.

Workers' own experiences

Even an introductory chapter on crisis would be seriously inadequate if it did not mention the role of our own experiences in colouring our views and responses to clients' crisis stories. Again different theoretical frameworks used to inform crisis therapies place different degrees of emphasis on this personal phenomenon but most do see connections. In my work with students and perhaps more particularly with mature students who have indeed lived life and experienced crisis, that experience has provided a useful backdrop to the discussion of preconceived ideas about crisis and about the assessment of preferred interventions to deal with crisis in clients' lives. In my experience as a trainer and counsellor I have always attempted to be reflective in relation to the impact of my own life on my interpretation of clients' stories. This is a good example of where supervision in any work with people in crisis, as with other areas of therapeutic intervention, is so important.

Timeline of the development of crisis intervention

Psychoanalytic theory is seen as the foundation of the brief intervention approach which is referred to as crisis intervention. Crisis intervention as presented here is the basis of the crisis therapies we are examining. One way to progress the exploration is to attempt to establish a timeline of theoretical influences on crisis intervention.

I developed what I think is a useful timeline model in relation to theoretical influences on alcohol and drug misuse (Loughran 2002). The idea of developing such a timeline is to place crisis therapies in the context of the broader influences of the day. There is no one fixed view of crisis and I think that is why it has survived. Ideas about using crisis as the basis for intervention have changed with the times (see Figure 1.4). As we become more familiar with alternative ways of knowing, the school of crisis approaches has absorbed these new ideas and engaged them to enhance our understanding of crisis.

1944	Lindermann – Ego psychology: looking at the symptoms and management of acute grief
1961/64	Caplan – Acknowledged family and sociocultural factors: in the field of primary prevention in mental health attempting to develop a unified theory of crisis
1971	Rapoport – Psychodynamic developmental life crisis (Erikson): crisis intervention as a model for brief treatment

1973	Eisler and Hersen – Behavioural and social learning approach to crisis
1978	Golan – Family and strengths approach
1980	Aguilera – Intervention based on systems theory of homeostasis/ stability
1991	Thompson – Behaviour and social learning approach
2004	Rechtman – Reformulated post traumatic stress (approach)
2005	Roberts – Unifying model: elements of behavioural/ cognitive/systems approaches
2007	Dattilio and Freeman – Cognitive behavioural approach.

Figure 1.4: Timeline of the development of crisis intervention

Even in the earliest iterations of crisis thinking it was recognised that there was a complex relationship between the outward sign of a crisis such as a crisis event and the response to that event. Parad (1971) one of the early exponents of crisis intervention cautioned 'it is important to note that the crisis is not the hazardous event or the situation itself, rather, it is the person's perception of and the response to the situation' (p.197). People interested in exploring crisis thinking began to integrate the basic ideas around crisis with other theoretical approaches.

The acknowledgement that perception and response were significant variables made it relatively easy to expand the thinking about crisis by adding the ideas from developments in such areas as cognitive theory, behaviour theory and later cognitive behavioural theory, social learning and systems approaches. In order to simplify the complex nature of these developments the strategy adopted in this book will be to look at each as though they were separate entities and only consider the interrelatedness of the theoretical developments in the final chapter.

The 50 years since Lindemann's breakthrough on crisis thinking could be viewed as a period of elucidating the theory or concepts underpinning the crisis approach, subsequent years are more noteworthy for the expansion of the type of events and incidents that were being incorporated into a crisis style model. This can be seen in the Roberts and Everly (2006) article on a meta-analysis of crisis intervention studies. The studies reviewed in the analysis included critical incident stress debriefing and family preservation (in-home intensive crisis intervention). They concluded that booster sessions may be required often several months to one year after initial crisis intervention indicating that they were looking at something beyond the original 'brief' intent of crisis intervention. They highlight the need for 'good diagnostic criteria' to assess the suitability of the crisis intervention modality. This variability in criteria for establishing the appropriate use of a crisis based approach will be considered as we explore the contribution of each of the theoretical approaches. We will keep in mind some of the central ideas behind the initial configuration of crisis in that it did place emphasis on the importance of crisis as an impetus to change.

Major crisis events and trauma

Understanding crisis therapies is underpinned by what could be viewed as a shifting focus of interest in the field of crisis work. There is a growing body of work within the crisis field that is concerned with 'major crisis' events and traumas. While these crisis events have a place in the 'crisis' world they do not necessarily fit with the intent inherent in crisis intervention with its focus on the crisis as an opportunity for change and a commitment to less intrusive but more focused brief interventions. In order to incorporate these developing fields of interest in disasters and traumas we need to re-conceptualise crisis intervention to include more extensive and longer term work. Rather than detracting from the essence of crisis intervention this book will consider post traumatic stress and crisis resulting in the need for social action within the expanded integrative framework of crisis therapies.

Crisis and opportunity for change

Caplan formulated a very simple definition of crisis in which he said that a crisis was 'an upset in a steady state' (in Rapoport 1962, p.212). The notion of a steady state seems to imply that the person was managing, at least relatively successfully prior to the crisis and that the crisis event had the effect of shifting the person into an unsteady state. In this state she finds that she is no longer able to cope. In a discussion of change and crisis this poses some very interesting possibilities. One of the well documented benefits of crisis therapy is the impetus for change that is created by having to face a crisis. So we need to ask three questions:

- *Who* needs to change?
- *What* needs to change?
- Change *to what?*

Asking these questions can help to formulate a clearer picture of what change needs to happen and also who or what needs to change. Let's consider first who needs to change.

Who needs to change?

This raises questions about who has the authority to say change is required and to define who it is that needs to change. The question of who says I have to change raises points about power and self determination.

For example is the target for change actually the individual at all or should it be something broader such as family, community or the social service system or some other organisation? Is the crisis situation induced or exasperated by someone or something outside of the individual? If this is the case then attempts made by the individual to change may be fruitless since the necessary change is outside their control. We will look at this question in more depth in Chapter 7 when we consider some of the power issues around crisis work.

What needs to change?

This question can act as a starting point for drawing on the theories that explain crisis. Assessment of what needs to change in order to deal with the crisis will depend on what theory you apply to your analysis of the situation. Each of the chapters will take one possible theoretical framework and explore how it shapes our answer to this question of what needs to change.

Change to what?

When a client experiences an event or situation as a crisis, 'an upset in a steady state', does that mean that a return to the steady state will be sufficient to resolve the crisis? Will restoration to prior coping levels mean that the client feels able to deal with the crisis, or will be able to see the crisis in a more manageable light?

Or, will dealing with the crisis demand the acquisition of new coping skills and strategies? In other words returning to established strategies will not be sufficient to restore the 'steady state', or perhaps the situation will have been changed so much by the crisis that returning to the prior state is not possible or desirable. This means that the change aspect of resolving the crisis will involve augmenting established skills and strategies.

Or, the crisis event may be such that dealing with it will involve a major change on the part of the individual. Will the resolution of the crisis involve not just additional skills but perhaps a transformation in many aspects of the person's life? If the pre-crisis 'steady state' was not particularly healthy or useful then maybe the level of change required is more in line with a transformation than a minor adjustment or augmentation to coping strategies. In a sense this opportunity to transform is at the core of crisis work.

Continuum of change

One way to think about these levels of change is to consider change on a continuum. Different degrees of change are possible and different degrees of change are necessary in response to different situations as illustrated in Figure 1.5.

Figure 1.5: Change continuum

We will consider this continuum as we explore the application of the various theoretical frameworks in each chapter.

Whose crisis is it anyway?

This is one of the questions that I find very useful when training students and workers in any crisis approach. Many people with work experience want to know what you do with someone who will not co-operate with you when you are trying to help them to deal with a crisis. Others ask what they can do to make the client see there is a crisis. Yet another related question is about helping family members who see that a loved one is in crisis who does not seem to be dealing with the crisis; or in some cases the family feels that the person who is in crisis is 'in denial' and so not accepting that she is in crisis. Many helpers and workers find dealing with crisis exhausting and emotionally draining. Sometimes I have seen that the worker is more overwhelmed than the client.

In all of the above situations I ask students to consider the question: Whose crisis is it? The theories underpinning crisis therapies all share a view that one must experience the crisis in order to evoke a crisis response and that this crisis response forms the basis of the opportunity to change and address the crisis in a helpful manner. Where it is the worker or the family who are feeling the crisis then there is no point targeting a crisis intervention at the 'identified' client.

We will look at this in subsequent chapters but just to clarify the idea behind the question of 'whose crisis is it?', consider the following scenario. A worker is seriously concerned that a client, June, is living in an abusive relationship. The worker knows that there has been yet another violent episode and decides that June is in crisis. June however has become so accustomed to the violence that she sees it as 'more of the same', or just part of the relationship. June is not in crisis even if the situation merits being seen as a crisis. The worker may experience a crisis response and feel he has to get June out of the situation or that this latest episode is an opportunity for June to change. The worker decides to use a crisis therapeutic approach. It will get nowhere because it is the worker's crisis not June's. Some alternative intervention will be required but continuing to employ a crisis model of intervention will be frustrating.

This issue can arise when working with families. One family member, Jim the 17-year-old son, is using drugs. Jim gets into trouble one night with a dealer and is beaten up. His parents arrive at a service because this is a crisis. Yet they cannot understand why Jim does not seem to be prepared to seek help. Whose crisis is it? It is a crisis response from Jim's parents and so may be an opportunity for them to change but the same does not apply to Jim. It's not his crisis at this time. Is it true to say then that a crisis is not a crisis until someone thinks it's a crisis?

A crisis is not a crisis until someone thinks it is a crisis

In my experience this is true. Part of the assessment process is to discover who thinks it is a crisis and attempt to understand what makes it a crisis for that person. This leads us into the next chapter where we can explore further this notion of a crisis as being dependent on someone's perception. But first we will introduce Susan and her situation so that we can follow her story through the various theoretical explanations in each of the subsequent chapters.

Case illustration: Susan

Each chapter will look in more detail at one theoretical framework for crisis interventions. In order to simplify what is potentially a complicated analysis I will introduce the reader to Susan. In each chapter we will consider how that particular theory might inform our thinking about Susan's situation. Working with a case to illustrate the differences between the theoretical ideas is useful for students and it seems that they enjoy this type of discussion. Feedback suggests that, in particular, students find it useful if we stretch the stories in different ways so that we can explore how Susan would be seen in different aspects of the crisis continuum. Hence, Susan will be someone who is experiencing a crisis response to an event that might go unacknowledged by many. In each chapter we will also look at other cases where more traditionally accepted crisis events will be considered.

Susan is a 25-year-old woman and single mother of five-year-old Jake. She continued to live with her parents and younger siblings after Jake was born. This arrangement facilitated Susan in continuing her education and training as a hairdresser. She got a lot of support both emotional and practical from her family and Jake is very attached to the rest of the family, in particular to his grandmother who has been his other significant carer. Susan now works for a well established large hair dressing company in one of its local branches. She has been quite successful and is viewed as one of the upcoming stylists. Susan recognises that she has good prospects in her current situation and appreciates all the help she has received from her family. Jake's father is involved with Jake but now has a wife and child and lives some distance away from Jake.

Because Susan was living with other family she had been living in one bedroom of the family home which she shared with Jake. This arrangement has never been totally satisfactory but they managed. When Jake started school it was obvious that he was realising that most of the kids in his class did not sleep with their parents – he started asking questions and acting up about wanting his own room. Susan too became more unsettled with the arrangements and made a decision to look into finding a place of her own. Within a short space of a couple of weeks from first considering the option of moving out of her parents' home she found a flat. It is ideal because of its situation in the same town as her parents and her work place.

Susan was very excited about the prospect of having her own place and it seemed that it was just the right time to make this move since Jake was now settled and well established in his school routine. Some people consider that moving house is one of the most stressful experiences. Skynner and Cleese (1984) in their book on families listed moving house as one of the top five most stressful events.

Susan had the help of friends and family. She made the move in what appeared to have been an organised and smooth transition. Her mother continued to be available as back up carer for Jake, her income was sufficient to meet the demands of maintaining her new arrangements. So where is the crisis?

Well Susan and Jake were living in the flat just two weeks when there was a flood in the kitchen. The flat had provided a washing machine and dishwasher. Something went wrong with the washing machine and one night after a long hard day at work Susan loaded the washing machine and sat down to do homework with Jake. Sometime later an irate neighbour knocked on her door to tell her that water was flooding into his flat from Susan's. When she checked on the wash the kitchen floor was a total mess, the water had already ruined the kitchen floor and had started to flow through to the neighbour's downstairs. Susan fell apart and became very distressed and was incapable of taking any action. She was in crisis. We will follow Susan and Jake in later chapters.

Outline of the chapters

The aim of this book is to work through the various theoretical influences on crisis intervention so that the reader can acquire a sufficient understanding to reach an informed decision about which theoretical framework fits best with any specific client situation. Following on from this the reader will then be able to assess the appropriate intervention within the crisis therapies repertoire or alternatively adjudge that the situation is not best served by a crisis based response. It may also serve to address one of my concerns that crisis therapies when misunderstood may be offered as an inappropriate response and result in an untimely or ineffective intervention.

The following chapters will deal with a range of theoretical frameworks and examine their relationship to crisis work. These include the following approaches:

- psychoanalytic
- developmental
- behavioural
- cognitive
- systemic
- radical
- social construction
- post traumatic.

In the final chapter we will consider what an integrated crisis approach might look like, and draw on the core aspects of the preceding chapters to highlight distinguishing elements of the crisis approach.

In an attempt to be inclusive the term worker has been used in this book. On some occasions it is used interchangeably with terms such as helper, practitioner, therapist, social worker, counsellor, crisis worker and/or mental health professional. While I am drawn to the term 'helper' I decided that in this case it was important to distinguish between a professional helper and helpers who may simply be part of the client's social network. In order not to confuse this important aspect or source of coping I use the term worker to distinguish those of us who are helping in a professional capacity not to underestimate the help we hope to provide.

Finally, although for simplicity I refer to the client, the intent is that the client is often not just an individual but may be a family or a community. Some of the chapters focus on this distinction more than others because the emphasis in crisis work can often be very individualised.

Clients and workers can of course be either gender; in acknowledging this point chapters alternate between he and she for the client. Where singular pronouns were required for both client and worker/helper the opposite gender was assigned to the worker (so odd chapters are 'he' and even, 'she').

Chapter 2

A Psychoanalytic Approach

Valerie Richardson

Introduction

This is the first of seven chapters which will explore a specific theoretical framework or school of thought attempting to explain human interaction. The chapters will progress in a sequence that mirrors the development of our understanding over time. Psychoanalytic theory, the subject of this chapter is a long established and some would argue the most influential of the theoretical frameworks of human nature emanating principally from psychology. As with each subsequent chapter we will start by looking at a brief history of the theory and connecting this to the theories and beliefs that were prevailing at the time of its development.

A brief history

Aguilera (1990) states that 'a broad range of theories of human behaviour including those of Freud, Hartmann, Rado, Erikson, Lindemann and Caplan' (p.2) have contributed to the development of crisis intervention as a therapeutic model and no one theory of behaviour can be cited as a primary influence on its development. However, the work of Freud (1900) was the earliest conceptual framework to influence the development of crisis intervention as a therapeutic process.

Prior to Freud's work psychology as a subject had been a static discipline based on concepts drawn from biology and physiology and which was slowly moving to include sociological ideas. Early understanding of personality was based on the mediaeval ideas of the link between the body and behaviour. The four humours of sanguine, phlegmatic, melancholic and choleric were based on four biological elements, blood, phlegm, black bile and yellow bile. Each of these elements represented a type of personality, sanguine being optimistic, cheerful and even tempered, phlegmatic being calm and unemotional, melancholic being despondent and depressive and choleric being mean spirited, easily angered and bad tempered. Work by Descartes in the first half of the 17th century (Cottingham, Stoothoff and Murdoch 1988) introduced the idea of dualism, where the mind and the body were two separate entities that interacted to form the human experience.

Wilhelm Wundt (Hall 1912) was the earliest psychologist to study human thought using scientific methods in order to describe the connections between the science of physiology and the study of human thought and behaviour. These early psychologists relied on observing and describing behaviours and stressed the importance of conscious thought processes which influenced behaviour. In contrast Freud saw the need to explain behaviour based on the unconscious workings of the mind. He recognised the importance of understanding emotions and behaviour which arise from crisis situations and how crisis situations affect subsequent behaviour.

The later work on crisis by Lindemann (1944), a psychoanalyst trained in the Freudian tradition, was developed based on Freud's theoretical and clinical work. He saw crisis through a psychoanalytic lens based on his clinical training. Later work by Parad and Caplan (1960) and Rapoport (1962) followed and were also based on the primary Freudian tradition. For example Rapoport (1962) provided a synthesis of psychoanalytic ego psychology, social system and role concepts together with social work practice propositions. As Rapoport (1965) puts it 'the crisis-theory framework… makes use of ego psychology as well as newer social science concepts now being incorporated into social work theory' (p.31). Since much of early crisis theory and crisis intervention was Freudian based, this chapter will take as its starting point an examination of the key concepts of psychodynamic or ego theories followed by further discussion of how these theories have served as a basis on which crisis theories have evolved. An understanding of crisis from the perspective of these theories will be discussed and case illustrations will be given. Conclusions will be drawn at the end of the chapter pointing to how the ego theories of human behaviour have been built on in the further evolution of crisis intervention therapies.

Key concepts of psychoanalytic theories

The key concepts of psychoanalytic theories derive from the original work of Freud (1900) and were subsequently developed by the post-Freudians (Adler (Ansbacher and Ansbacher 1956) Jung (Stevens 1994) Erikson (1950) and Klein (1927). Five major assumptions underlie the concepts of psychoanalytic ego psychology:

- people are born with an innate capacity to adapt to their environment and the capacity develops over time through learning and psychosocial maturation
- social influences on psychological functioning are significant
- individuals possess basic drives towards pleasure and aggression
- mastery and competence are important motivators
- problems in psychological and social functioning can occur at any stage of development due to the person-environment and physical development.

(adapted from Walsh 2006)

Structure of the personality

Freud postulated that the personality is made up of three parts, the *id*, the *ego* and the *superego*. He argued that the individual is born with basic animal drives and needs, such as survival needs, aggression and sexual instincts which are governed by the pleasure principle and which are embedded in the id. The id is self-centred and acts as the motivating force of human behaviour. The id has no self-control and uses demanding and aggressive behaviour to ensure that its basic needs are met. When these needs are not met the id responds with rage and illogical and emotionally childlike behaviour. As the child interacts with his environment the ego develops out of the id and is, therefore, the part of the personality in touch with reality. It also works to maximise gratification but needs are met within a logical and emotionally controlled manner having learnt how to respond and behave appropriately within the social environment. It is the ego that is the 'self' of the personality, the part that others in the social world observe and to which they relate. It is the part of the personality which encapsulates the identity of the individual. The superego develops as a result of the socialisation process experienced within the real world. It acts as the conscience or the moral and value system of the individual which controls their behaviour and manages the instincts and basic drives in an appropriate fashion.

Stages of personality development

Four distinct stages and a period of latency are central to Freud's theory of development. Each stage is defined around a particular part of the body and is determined by physiological changes:

- *Oral stage* (circa birth to 1 year): centred on satisfaction through sucking and biting. The child's physiological need for food is combined with their need for comfort, warmth and psychological needs.

- *Anal stage* (circa 1–3 years): centred on the struggle to overcome bodily control independent of the caring adult.

- *Phallic* (circa 3 to 5–6 years): at this stage desires and needs are centred on the genital area. Sexual urges are directed towards the parent of the opposite sex and are resolved by identifying with the same sex parent in order to obtain the attention of the other parent. Thus Freud argued that the child identifies and learns to be either a man or woman by this identification process.

- *Latency* (circa aged 5–6 years to adolescence/puberty): this stage is one of relative calm in which the child forgets the fantasies and sexual urges of the earlier stage and concentrates on school, learning and play. This stage provides for the acquisition of cognitive skills and social and cultural values.

- *Genital* (adolescence): as a result of physiological changes of puberty the adolescent directs his sexual needs towards the peer group, it is less self-centred love and the adolescent develops an adult approach to sexuality.

The way in which needs are met during each stage will determine how individuals relate to others and how they feel about themselves. Characteristic attitudes, defences and fantasies are developed and unresolved conflicts in any stage can influence how an individual will deal with crises in the future. Thus, in times of crisis individuals may return to the kind of behaviour exhibited during a period of development which was particularly satisfying of their needs. Individuals in a state of extreme stress may for example, be observed to return to curling up in a foetal position or may return to behaviour exhibited during the developmental period when they were the most comfortable and stress free, such as thumb sucking. (These developmental ideas will be considered in the following chapter.)

The unconscious

The basic tenet on which Freud built his theories was the presence of the unconscious element of the personality which motivated subsequent behaviour and influenced the development of the personality. He argued that the mind was divided into the conscious and unconscious, the former involving thoughts, perceptions, moods and self awareness. The unconscious involves the parts of the mind of which the individual is unaware such as drives, needs and events which may have been suppressed or hidden because of the painful emotions which they arouse. The unconscious, therefore, is a place to store events and memories which the conscious part of the individual wishes to avoid facing or dealing with. However, certain subsequent events may trigger the hidden thoughts and feelings bringing them to the surface and in so doing acting as a motivating factor for what might appear to be irrational behaviour patterns. Thus, a subsequent event may bring memories of past painful events to the surface or consciousness to which the individual may react in what appears to be an inappropriate manner in relation to the current situation, but which might be a delayed reaction to an earlier event which had been suppressed.

This insight is of considerable importance when considering the nature and meaning of a crisis to an individual. Freud believed that mental health problems or irrational behaviour was the result of either ego anxiety or defence mechanisms which have been unconsciously set up to prevent the anxieties becoming conscious.

Defence mechanisms

Traumatic events that occur at a particular developmental stage may lead to the individual's behaviour patterns being fixated or 'stuck' at that stage. Consequently, when faced with a similar crisis in adulthood they may revert back to the infantile behaviour of the previous developmental stage at which the original crisis occurred. For example, when a crisis occurs an adult may revert to extremely childish behaviour such as crying, thumb sucking, returning to the parental home, bed wetting or exhibiting over-dependent behaviour.

The function of defence mechanisms is to prevent recognition of the hurt and subsequent anxieties that were experienced at an earlier stage (Freud 1966). Some Freudian defence mechanisms are: repression, regression, denial, projection, displacement, reaction formation, sublimation, intellectualisation, rationalisation and conversion. These are summarised in Figure 2.1.

Repression: blocking threatening emotions, thoughts or behaviours from consciousness

Regression: behaving in a manner more appropriate to an earlier stage of development

Denial: preventing threatening material from entering consciousness by denying its existence

Projection: attributing one's own unacceptable thoughts or actions to another person

Displacement: changing the object of an unacceptable behaviour usually to a less powerful person than one's self

Reaction formation: expressing the exact opposite of an unacceptable desire

Sublimation: using symbolic actions to express an unacceptable wish or emotion

Conversion: dealing with unacceptable feelings, beliefs or actions by developing psychosomatic disorders

Intellectualisation: avoiding unacceptable emotions by thinking or talking about them rather than feeling them directly

Rationalisation: using convincing reasons to justify ideas, feelings or actions in order to avoid facing the true motivation.

Figure 2.1: Defence mechanisms (adapted from Freud 1966)

Therefore, Freud's whole thesis centred on the belief that present behaviour is predicated on earlier experiences which provoke sufficient anxiety to be suppressed by any number of defence mechanisms. However, some defence mechanisms are more mature and useful than others. The more mature ones can facilitate the individual in dealing temporarily with conflict situations allowing them to deal with the crisis over time and to grow through the resolution of the crisis.

Transference

Freud used his insights about the structure of personality to develop his method of therapeutic treatment of clients presenting with anxiety neuroses. The nature of the relationship between the worker and the client was central to any intervention. He argued that the interaction between the two parties needed to be understood in terms of the effect each had on the other. He labelled this interaction as transference and counter-transference (Freud 1912). Transference as a phenomenon in clinical work is the process by which an individual unconsciously redirects or projects the feelings he had for one person, with whom he has had a previous relationship, onto the worker thus relating to her as if she was the original object of his feelings. The worker/practitioner does not actually possess these characteristics but the client acts as if she does. Racker (2001) has defined transference as 'the inappropriate repetition in the present of a relationship that was important in a person's childhood'. However, more recent theorists have broadened out the definition of transference to refer more generally to all reactions that the client has to the worker. These reactions may be based on interactions with similar types of people in the client's past or on the actual characteristics of the worker. Thus, if the client has had difficulties with authority figures in the past he may anticipate a similar authoritarian attitude from the worker and thus relate to the worker as if she were being authoritarian rather than according to how the worker is actually behaving.

Counter-transference relates to the worker/practitioner's unconscious reactions to the client's projections. Thus, if the client places the worker in a role of 'mother figure' and relates to the worker as if she were his mother then the worker/practitioner may unconsciously take on the role of mother with the client leading to encouraging an over-dependence of the client. Therefore, in any clinical situation workers need to be sufficiently self aware to take into account these reactions in order that their clinical judgement and intervention are not influenced by the transference and counter-transference.

In any relationship individuals tend to relate to each other in both an objective way and also in terms of how they wish the other person to be, or fear they might be. In these terms the clinical relationship is not that different from any interpersonal relationship although in the clinical situation it is imperative that the worker is aware of the possibility of such transference and counter-transference occurring to prevent inappropriate intervention or relationships developing. Through the strength of the clinical relationship the process of ego sustaining can help clients become mobilised to resolve their crises and to understand their motivations and actions more clearly. Such techniques can be particularly useful for clients who present with dependency needs and require a highly supportive relationship and an opportunity to process their distress through ventilation and reflection.

From a Freudian perspective, therefore, an understanding of how an individual reacts to a crisis needs to be seen in relation to past experiences, the types of defence mechanisms normally exhibited by the individual in dealing with threatening situations and the way that individual relates to others in times of stress. Individuals will interpret and understand the crisis in relation to their own past reality and their own unconscious or subconscious mental representations.

Psychoanalytic theory and crisis

A crisis can be defined as an emotionally significant event or radical change of status in a person's life which is disruptive of his usual mode of adaptation. From a psychoanalytic perspective any definition of a crisis needs to include reference to social, intra-psychic and somatic factors. This is described by Jacobson, Strickleer and Morley (1968) as being the bio-psychosocial field. They note that 'a complete characterisation of any crisis must include references to social, intra-psychic and somatic factors' (Jacobson *et al.* 1968, p.338). In these terms the intra-psychic aspects are conceptualised as referring to changes in a prior sense of equilibrium between the three parts of the psyche or self. This involves unconscious as well as conscious processes. A number of factors will influence the outcome of any given crisis. These will include experience with other crises encountered earlier and the revival of memories or unconscious material which may have been suppressed in the past but may now influence the current response to the crisis. If one is working from a psychodynamic perspective the importance of the present and future are not denied but it must also include some dealing with the past. It is argued that in crisis counselling from this perspective some concentration on the past is not only needed but is essential. Working from a psychodynamic perspective relies on the belief that the cause of a current crisis lies in some previous pattern of thought, affect or behaviour (Jerry 1998).

Malan's (1979) depiction of the triangle of person and the triangle of conflict can contribute to an understanding of the dynamic of crisis from a psychodynamic perspective. His idea was that in relation to both the person and conflict there are three dimensions that should be considered. In the case of the triangle of the person, these are present others, transference and past others. In relation to the triangle of conflict, the three dimensions are anxiety, defence and hidden feelings. The triangle of conflict represents the likely scenario that a client in crisis will present, with anxiety and defences (usually depicted as two points on the top side of the triangle) often overlaying hidden feelings which the client is trying to avoid facing (usually the bottom or base point of the triangle). The triangle therefore represents deeper feelings that are the drive towards the anxiety and are defended against through the use of unconscious defence mechanisms. The defences play the part of keeping the anxiety at bay and the hidden feelings out of consciousness. The triangle of the person adds the interpersonal dimension. In the triangle of the person it is past others that are more likely to be hidden at the base of the triangle. They may represent parental figures who have contributed to the psychological development of the individual. Malan (1979) argues that clients are often aware of single points in these triangles but not the interconnections between them. In particular, the link between the two aspects of the triangles that form the base points (hidden feelings and past others) is often not available to the client's consciousness.

In crisis, therefore, the habitual defences are not performing adequately and the risk is that the client experiences a breakthrough of the hidden feelings causing the crisis. In crisis intervention the aim is to link the client's current relationship patterns and coping behaviour with the hidden feelings and defensive patterns. In addition a link is made to the transference. How the client may be re-enacting relational patterns between past significant others, present significant others and the worker can provide some insight into the client's understanding of the current crisis.

Thus, from a psychodynamic perspective crises can be seen as situational mediators that place an individual's typical defences and resistances in question. This state can allow for dynamic change beyond the relief of symptoms typically expected in crisis work and provide behaviour change which can be employed when faced with future crises.

Susan and Jake: A psychoanalytic perspective

Was it a crisis? In the case of Susan the crisis was one that went far deeper than a crisis of a flood in the flat. When the flood occurred she immediately phoned her father who dealt with the situation and took Susan and Jake back to the family home. However, she remained living at home and found it impossible to return to the flat. She became very stressed and terrified to move out again as she was afraid to be left on her own with Jake and developed a fear that another situation or crisis would occur.

What happened for Susan was not just an inability to deal with a fairly simple crisis; the event awakened in her the fact that she had not managed to develop her independence from her parents. She regressed back to a time when she was happy and stress free in her childhood and when her father was the person who resolved all her difficulties for her. Susan returned to this period of early childhood behaviour which was one of total dependence on her parents because it was too threatening for her to make another attempt at independence.

It may also be that Susan was not able to deal adequately with the period of her adolescence. She has a very close relationship with her father and may not have resolved the sexual fantasies from the earlier phallic period. She is now a single mother living without the father of her child and it may be that she has placed her father into the situation of being her partner and the substitute father of her child. She allows her father to take over that role, to do homework with her son and is financially and emotionally dependent on him.

The crisis therefore is one of resolving the developmental issues that have not been satisfactorily dealt with at the appropriate period.

Application of psychoanalytic theories to crisis

All individuals have a propensity to crises which can be inevitable, during their lifetime. These crises can arise as part of the normal developmental process or be caused by an external event in the environment which an individual is psychologically unable to deal with. From a psychodynamic perspective the ability to deal adequately with these crises is based on the individual's personality traits, repertoire of defence mechanisms, adaptive capacities, ego strengths and unconscious conflicts (Harris, Kalish and Freeman 1963). Glick and Meyerson (1980/1981) have argued that 'crisis theory is an application of Waelder's principle of multiple function (Waelder 1936) by which the ego is viewed as constantly attempting to deal with the conflictual demands of instinct, superego, ego ideal and reality' (p.173).

Glick and Meyerson (1980/1981) go on to state that when dealing with an individual in crisis there is an opportunity to observe character patterns that contribute to the crisis situation and intervention can offer the possibility for an increased mastery of previously repressed conflicts. Through intervening at the point of crisis, improved adaptive capacity can result in a shift in defensive patterns from rigid and immature defence mechanisms to more flexible and mature ones, thus providing new ways of dealing with the conflicts which have led to the crisis and allowing the individual to deal in a more mature fashion with future crises. Thus Glick and Meyerson (1980/1981) argue that:

> repressed neurotic conflicts and defects in ego organization determine vulnerability to specific stresses. Selection of focus (interventions) follows from the recognition of those rigid defensive patterns and adaptive incapacities which have either partially failed or been overwhelmed by the current stress. Aiming at the old problem in the new situation allows crisis work to go beyond symptom relief to improved conflict resolution and coping abilities. (p.171)

From a psychodynamic perspective a crisis in an individual's life which is serious enough to require professional intervention cannot be understood by a mechanistic model in which an external event merely overwhelms a passive individual. Thus, crisis intervention from this perspective requires more than dealing with the outward symptoms but must address the internal conflicts between instinct, superego, ego and reality. Reality can be an unforeseen incident in the environment such as death, bereavement, 'act of God', or accident but such events stir up repressed conflicts and demand coping capacities which may be affected by internal struggles which are a result of earlier conflicts.

Crisis intervention and intervention techniques based on a psychoanalytic model are often regarded as being incompatible (Glick and Meyerson 1980/1981). However, Bibring (1954) outlined the techniques required for a dynamic crisis intervention strategy as suggestion, abreaction, manipulation, clarification and interpretation, all of which are methods drawn from traditional psychoanalytic interventions. Similarly, Glick and Meyerson (1980/1981) concluded that adequate crisis intervention requires the application of certain psychoanalytic concepts since crises generally reflect the emergence of unconscious conflict evoked by a current stress.

Glick and Meyerson (1980/1981) reported that efforts to apply psychoanalytic understanding to brief therapy produced an increasing body of literature but that the emphasis was more on the application of psychodynamic principles to brief therapy rather than to crisis intervention or resolution. For example, Selby (1963 cited in Darbonne 1967) argued that crisis therapy is brief therapy to help the ego in its cognitive, synthesising and integrating functions.

Aguilera (1990) differentiated psychoanalysis, brief psychotherapy and crisis intervention on the basis of goals. She argued that the goal of psychoanalysis is the restructuring of the personality through the freeing of the unconscious and the therapist's role is as a non-directive passive observer and interpreter. The goal of brief psychotherapy is to 'remove specific symptoms and to aid the prevention of developing deeper neurotic or psychotic symptoms. Its focus is on the genetic past as it relates to the present situation, repression of the unconscious and restraining of drives' (Aguilera 1990, p.25). In crisis intervention the goal is the resolution of an immediate crisis. The focus while being on the past is directed to the restoration of the pre-crisis state of functioning. The therapist's role is direct and as an active participant in the process of recovery.

Aguilera (1990) makes no attempt to show that one type of therapy is superior to another. Similarly, Talbott (1980/1981) concluded that crisis intervention as a method and psychoanalysis, while different are not antagonistic and in fact are extremely compatible. However, several aspects of crisis intervention seem at variance with psychoanalytic theory and practice. The expectation that the client will go through a number of 'normal' phases and recover promptly is a feature of crisis intervention. This is in strong contrast to patients in psychoanalysis who might spend long periods of time in therapy. Crisis intervention focuses very much on the 'here and now' and on the immediate precipitating event of the crisis. In addition, the client's social situation is of considerable importance being seen as playing a part in the presenting crisis. The psychoanalytic approach, however, is to confront not the immediate problem but the genetic, familial and developmental issues from the past together with the resulting personality traits, defences and relationship patterns. The irrelevance of the past is a feature of crisis intervention.

Similarly, an active role for the therapist or worker is seen as crucial to effective crisis techniques compared to the passive role of the traditional psychotherapist of saying little, asking few questions and never giving direct interventions into the thoughts and feelings of the individual. Talbott (1980/1981) has argued that:

if psychoanalysis is defined as…an insight oriented, intra-psychically focused psychological therapy aimed at personality reorganization through such techniques as free association, dream analysis and transference interpretation it would seem antithetical to crisis intervention as defined as a short-term symptom-oriented and environmentally focused therapy intended only to restore the individual to his or her previous adaptive level through a combination of individual, family and environmental interventions. (p.200)

However, he concludes that these types of intervention should not be mutually exclusive as each has something to offer where the resolution of a crisis situation is concerned.

More recent writers, while acknowledging the importance of ego psychology and psychoanalytic insights have adapted these ideas to focus on a social work theory for crisis intervention. Woods and Hollis (2000) and Walsh (2006) have explored crisis intervention as either ego-sustaining techniques or ego-modification techniques.

Ego-sustaining techniques

Ego-sustaining techniques are relevant where the worker/practitioner assesses the client's ego functioning to be relatively intact but temporarily immobilised by the present crisis. In this instance the techniques of intervention include sustainment, exploration/description and ventilation, structuring the problem and personality reflection. This group of interventions allow the client to develop a positive relationship with the worker in which the client is encouraged to express his feelings about the current crisis and gain some objectivity about the problems he faces. In addition the client is supported to see the problems as more manageable, become motivated to take action, develop some hope and motivation towards solving the problem and more clearly recognise and understand his emotional reactions.

The relationship is extremely important as the basis for sustaining the client in the therapeutic work and allows the client to develop a positive transference relation to the social worker and reduce defensiveness together with gaining insight into his own behaviour. It also makes it possible to reflect on his thoughts and feelings related to the presenting issue. The worker may also provide some education for the client about possible external resources and offer direct influence where the client is so immobilised he is unable to exercise rational judgement about self-care. Giving advice and guidance is not a practice generally advocated within the social work process. However, where the worker judges that such advice or guidance is appropriate it should be given only when it is considered that the client is assessed as unable to exercise good judgement.

Such situations may be where clients are considering self-harm or in such a serious crisis that they are at a point where they are totally immobilised within the problem solving process. Any direct influence must be given in the best interest of clients and not force them to behave in the way the social worker wants them to.

Structuring the problem is an important element within the intervention. Breaking down the issues into manageable units that can be addressed separately is particularly helpful for clients who are so overwhelmed that they cannot 'see the wood for the trees'.

By helping the client to deal with one part of the problem at a time it can build the client's confidence in problem solving.

Ego-modification techniques

When using ego-modification techniques the worker would have assessed the client as presenting with maladaptive patterns of functioning that require an exploration of past experiences and unconscious processes. In this situation the worker facilitates the client's self understanding by discussing past behaviour patterns and provides new interpretations of relationship patterns, confronting defences used, dealing with developmental deficits and leading the client to new insights. Through the use of interpretation the client is helped to understand past issues that may be unconsciously influencing present reactions to the current problem. By gaining some insight into his past experiences or developmental patterns the client can be helped to adjust his behaviour towards a more appropriate response to the present crisis and build sufficient ego strength to solve the issues and reduce stress levels.

Case example: Bereavement and the Browne family

Simon, aged five years, was referred to the child guidance clinic by the school principal because of his lack of involvement in school, inability to relate to other children together with his very poor speech development for his age and his refusal to speak to the teachers in the school. Simon was the youngest child in a family of two older sisters aged 10 and 12. He had been born as a twin but the twin sister Margaret had died at the age of two. The twins had been close and had just begun to talk at the time that Margaret died. Margaret had been the more dominant twin showing more independence for her age and had led Simon along with her. The family had been devastated at Margaret's death.

After the funeral the parents had removed all the toys and things belonging to Margaret, put away the photographs of her and did not talk to each other or the other children about what had happened to Margaret.

They behaved as if the child had not existed. The family lived in a small rural community and Mr. Browne farmed a small amount of land. Both Mr. and Mrs. Browne were quiet country people not inclined to discuss feelings or other issues. As Simon grew up he spent most of his time with his father who he followed around the farm while he was working. The two did not talk much to each other as verbal communication was not an important part of their relationship or within the family as a whole.

The crisis only emerged when Simon went to school and he was not able to integrate into his new environment. Simon, therefore, was seen as the problem and the person with the crisis. However, from a Freudian perspective the crisis was precipitated by the parents' unconscious denial around the death of their daughter and their inability to grieve for her. Their inability to talk about Margaret was an unconscious avoidance of the very painful fact of the loss. Simon had unconsciously picked up the message within the family that talking about things was not an important part of communication and was dangerous. From a Freudian interpretation it could be argued that unconsciously he had linked talking and learning to become more independent during the anal stage, with disappearing out of the family. That is, at the developmental stage the twins were at, Margaret just disappeared and Simon could have linked the learning to talk and communicate with the act of disappearing. Therefore, in order to deal with the painful thoughts and fear of himself disappearing he had stopped talking.

Simon was using a defence of regression, that is regressing back to a period of his childhood when he felt secure and this coincided with a period when he was not using speech to communicate. Initially, the presentation of the problem could have been interpreted as a crisis of a child not settling into school or suffering from a speech defect or an element of autistic behaviour. However, in reality the crisis was one of an unresolved grief reaction of the parents and their inability to address openly the loss of their daughter and how their behaviour had affected Simon. The focus of any intervention therefore would be on helping the family to deal appropriately with the bereavement and the very strong defence mechanism of denial, rather than concentrating on direct intervention with Simon.

Conclusion

The psychoanalytic approach offers a specific interpretation of events that seeks to understand how the past impacts on the present. It is often seen as a precursor to and related to subsequent developmental theories. The next chapter will explore these ideas and what they can tell us about understanding crisis therapies.

Chapter 3

A Developmental Approach

Valerie Richardson and Hilda Loughran

Introduction

The links between psychoanalytic theories and developmental theories has already been mentioned. Most would agree that these developmental ideas owe much to Freud. He was one of the first to hypothesise that there are predicable and 'normal' stages in human development. We will first consider these links and then outline some of the key concepts in developmental theories before looking at what they have contributed to our understanding of crisis.

A brief history of developmental theories

Developmental theories of human behaviour attempt to describe and explain how individuals grow and change over time in a range of psychological areas, such as emotional development, cognition, language, social behaviour and moral development. These theories originally related to early development in infancy and childhood but have since expanded to include total life stages. Freud's theory of development was a major contribution to understanding how an individual moved through a number of stages from infancy into adulthood. However, his theories were criticised on a number of fronts and there was further development from those psychologists who had worked with him.

These post-Freudians such as Adler (Ansbacher and Ansbacher 1956), Jung (Stevens 1994), Erikson (1950) and Klein (1927) developed different schools of psychoanalytic thought. Jung for example disagreed with Freud's idea that personality and neurosis are established in early childhood arguing instead that behaviour is motivated by future goals rather than past events. However, all these theorists based their models on the underlying tenets of Freud's theory. Erikson (1950) developed his ideas out of Freud's psychosexual stages. He used Freud's structure of the personality with id, ego and superego but rejected Freud's approach based on sexuality. He also rejected Freud's argument that all mental illness can be traced to early experiences in childhood and that personality traits formed during this period remain irreversible. However, he shared with Freud the importance of understanding how personality is developed and behaviour influenced after birth. While Freud believed that developmental stages were influenced by biological development, Erikson (1950) argued that while early childhood experiences were important the individual also developed within a social context and therefore the wider environment was important in personality development.

Other developmental or stage theories such as Piaget (1950) (cognitive development) and Kohlberg (1981) (moral development) are particularly relevant to the understanding of human behaviour. This chapter will outline these three developmental theories and then examine their relevance for crisis intervention.

Some key concepts in developmental theories

Psychosocial theory

Erikson accepted the basic notions of Freudian theory such as the structure of personality, the unconscious, basic drives and psychosexual stages which affect development and influence growth to maturity. However, he centred his ideas on the development of identity through the entire life span (Erikson 1950). He argued that without a positive sense of identity an individual cannot relate to others in an adult and mature manner. He also emphasised the fact that individuals do not develop within a vacuum but are living within a social environment which influences their formation. Unlike Freud with his concern with how people develop defences to protect themselves from unpleasant tensions, Erikson saw the main goal in life as to achieve a positive identity. His understanding was that throughout life individuals ask themselves 'Who am I?' and form a different answer at each stage of development.

Erikson divided the entire life cycle into eight psychosocial stages, each with its own ratio of positive and negative elements to be achieved. Each stage of development involves the resolution of a normal developmental crisis of two opposing emotional forces. For Erikson the use of the word 'crisis' relates to the internal conflict the individual must negotiate in order to grow and develop as a fully rounded personality. He constructed the elements to be achieved at each stage along a continuum which the individual resolves to a greater or lesser degree depending on the environment in which she is living. One end of the continuum he called 'syntonic' for the positive disposition and the other end of the continuum was 'dystonic' meaning the negative disposition.

Erikson perceived each stage as being a normal developmental crisis which the individual needs to resolve more or less positively, in order to achieve ego synthesis and ego strength. Each stage is linked to a corresponding life stage and has a central task with particular ego qualities being attached to the task. Thus each stage contributes to identity formation depending on the level of resolution of the crisis. The role of significant relationships is vital to a satisfactory resolution of each crisis. For example the role of parents or carers is of great importance during the first stage in that the child, to develop trust, must be able to depend on the consistency and stability of the carers. At each stage the radius of significant relationships will differ.

Erikson's eight stages of psychosocial development
Trust versus mistrust (birth to 18 months)
The central task is to acquire a sense of trust in one's environment and in oneself. Trust is obtained from living in a trustworthy environment where caregivers can be trusted to meet the needs of the infant. The quality of caregiving is the central element in facilitating a positive resolution of this stage. By developing a trust in others one can develop a trust in oneself. However, some element of mistrust is necessary since it is important for the individual to develop the ability to discriminate between good and bad within the environment and develop abilities to deal with such issues. The ego quality which arises from a positive resolution of this stage is one of hope and the belief that one can attain one's own goals and meet one's own needs. Where the infant does not develop a sense of trust they may find it difficult to form normal healthy long lasting relationships. The main question to be answered is 'Is my environment trustworthy?' and the goal for identity is 'I am what I can hope to be'.

Autonomy versus shame and doubt (18 months to 3 years)

As the toddler begins to develop motor skills he begins to develop a sense of autonomy. Autonomy is the independence from the caregiver that the child strives for. The child develops a will to be independent and to explore the world. However, there is also the need to place boundaries on the child for its own safety. If these boundaries are too strict the child will feel shame and doubt as to its own ability and remain dependent on others to control his life. Ideally caregivers will create a supportive atmosphere in which the child can develop a sense of self-control without a loss of self-esteem. The contribution to identity is the ability to become an independent adult but also to be able to become appropriately dependent on others when needed. So, for example, the understanding that it is not a sense of failure to ask for help at a time of crisis, and it is not behaviour to be ashamed of. The main question here is 'Do I need help from others or not?' The contribution to an individual's identity is 'I am what I can manage to do'.

Initiative versus guilt (4 to 6 years)

The child at this stage begins to identify with his parents who he sees as powerful and able to do things. Therefore, the child begins to take responsibility for himself. He develops physical dexterity, language, cognition and creative imagination. The success of this stage gives the child courage to imagine and pursue valued goals. However, on the other end of the continuum is the sense of guilt. Guilt results from being punished or ridiculed for actions resulting from taking initiative or failing in attempts to achieve something. Caregivers' encouragement and patience are important at this stage. Suppressing experimentation, play or activities because of time, mess or some slight risk to the child can replace initiative with a fear of being seen as stupid, a failure or guilty about trying out the activities or aiming too high. The danger in later life is not to attempt to do things in case of being seen as a failure. The main question here is 'Am I good or am I bad?' and for identity it is 'I am what I can do for myself'.

Industry versus inferiority (6 years to puberty)

This period is characterised by the development of competence and skills and the satisfaction of achievement. The child who experiences failure at school, failure in relationships with peers and is never praised for something she has done or tried to achieve or is not given the opportunities to develop her own capabilities and strengths will be prone to feeling inferior and useless which leads to lack of self-esteem.

The main question is 'Am I successful or worthless?' The contribution to identity is one of competence and ambition: 'I am what I can make work. I am what I learn to do'.

Identity versus role confusion (adolescence/puberty to adulthood)

Erikson (1959) quotes this period as providing a moratorium to deal with the issues of 'I ain't what I ought to be, I ain't what I'm going to be but I ain't what I was' (p.93). It is a time of trying out new and varied identities to find the one in which the individual is the most comfortable. The task or crisis for adolescents to resolve is the integration of all earlier tasks of trusting, becoming autonomous, learning to show initiative and being industrious. It is a period of rapid physical and psychological development during which time the adolescent needs to have formed a physical identity, a sexual identity, a work identity and sufficient independence to have her own thoughts and feelings separate from others and particularly from her caregivers. A strong sense of trust developed earlier in life is essential for the resolution of this period. Adolescents need to have learnt to trust adults in order to allow themselves to trust becoming an adult themselves. Young adults want to be accepted by their peers and affirmed but they also want to become individuals. They need to acquire a sense of self or individuality in the context of their own lives.

The other end of the continuum is role confusion. The individual is unable to place herself in her environment, fails to make relationships with her peers and may well withdraw into her own world. She may develop a schizoid personality, one that is unable to make meaningful relationships or to commit to any particular person or role in life. The danger also is that she becomes confirmed in an identity imposed on her by outside social forces with which she is uncomfortable. The main question is 'Who am I and where am I going and who am I going with?' The contribution to identity is the successful synthesis of earlier identities into a composite integration of the ego.

Intimacy versus isolation (19 years–35/40)

According to Erikson the young adult stage is marked by the resolution of the identity versus role confusion. The young adult should be sufficiently secure in her own identity in order that she can give herself to another person in an intimate relationship without losing her own identity within that relationship and maintaining her own integrity. The young adult should be able to manage appropriately dependent relationships. Appropriate dependency is the ability to remain an independent person but allow another person to be dependent on them and be dependent on another person at appropriate times. Therefore, this stage is about reciprocal love for and with another person. The young adult also needs to be able to master isolation, be able to be alone and comfortable with herself but also able to balance that with being able to manage committed close relationships.

Erikson argues that this is a pre-requisite to being able to manage loss, the challenge of break-ups in relationships, or loss of a partner through death (Erikson 1950). Isolation means being and feeling excluded from the usual experiences of life which is characterised by feelings of loneliness, alienation, social withdrawal and non-participation. The main questions are 'Can I commit to intimate long lasting relationship(s) without losing myself?' 'Shall I share my life with someone or live alone?' The contribution to identity is being able to maintain one's own integrity while simultaneously being able to relate to others in a meaningful way.

Generativity versus stagnation/self absorption (35/40–65)

The primary task is one of contributing to society and guiding and helping the future generations, either one's own children or younger colleagues or peers. The identity issue here is to see oneself as a person who is productive and accomplishing something worthwhile that will be left behind as a legacy. It is also a period for acceptance of the ageing process and not to compete with young adults who are at earlier life stages. The opposing end of the continuum in Erikson's terms is one of stagnation, dissatisfaction and a sense of self absorption.

The main question is 'Can I produce something or somebody of real value?' The contribution or goal of this stage is to be able to reach out to the younger generation in some form through the giving of oneself.

Ego integrity versus despair (65 years and over)

Erikson regarded this stage as being a review of one's life. He defined integrity as being at peace with oneself, with no regrets or recriminations. Older people who are coming to terms with their own mortality have a need to look back over their lives and review what they achieved. In order to acquire a sense of integrity they need to be able to look back on the good times with thankfulness and on the hard times with self respect and to forgive and forget past mistakes or hurts. If they are caught up in sadness, unforgiving of past wrongs and dissatisfied with their lives or feel that their life has been wasted they will despair and become depressed, looking inward on themselves and resenting others who they perceive to have had a more fulfilling life. The main question is: 'Have I lived a full life?' The goal for identity is to be able to look back on one's life and feel that goals and ambitions have been achieved.

Table 3.1: Summary of Erikson's eight stages of psychosocial crises

Psychosocial crisis	Significant relations	Central task	Psychosocial modalities	Ego quality	Definition	Age
Trust vs mistrust	Maternal person	Receiving care	To get, to give in return	Hope	Trust in oneself and others	0–18 mths
Autonomy vs shame and doubt	Caregivers	Imitation	To hold on /to let go	Will	Free choice and self control	18–36 mths
Initiative vs guilt	Nuclear family	Identification	To make, to make like	Purpose	Courage to imagine	3–6 yrs
Industry vs inferiority	Neighbourhood and school	Education	To make things	Competence	Skill to complete tasks	6–12 yrs
Identity vs identity/role confusion	Peer groups and out groups	Independence	To be oneself: to share being oneself	Loyalty and fidelity	Ability to know oneself and sustain beliefs and values	12–18 yrs
Intimacy vs isolation	Partnerships and friends Co-operation and competition	Commitment	To lose and find oneself in another	Love	Mutual and equal relationships	Early adulthood
Generativity vs stagnation	Shared household Work peers	Nurturing	To make exist To take care of	Care	Commitment to and concern for family and community	40/45–65 yrs
Integrity vs despair	Mankind	Introspection	To be, having been through To face not being	Wisdom and confidence	Trust in oneself and belief in meaning of one's life	65 yrs and over

Source: adapted from Erikson 1980

Erikson's psychosocial theory of development, while based on Freudian theory, modified it considerably to move the understanding of human behaviour from the abnormal to the normal. He identified important social influences on behaviour and the interaction between the child and her environment. In addition his major contribution to an understanding of the importance of identity focused on ego processes rather than on ego defences. He agreed with Freud that the first few years of life were critical in the formation of basic personality, particularly the importance of developing a high level of trust in caregivers and the stability of the environment. Without a level of trust in others the individual cannot trust herself and this lack of trust can undermine any further development. However, Erikson's theory is a very positive and optimistic one compared to Freudian approaches. Erikson argued that even if a particular crisis is resolved less well the individuals can continue to resolve earlier stages as they progress through the life cycle. This reworking of certain crises can be undertaken with therapeutic help or through subsequent relationships encountered through life.

It is this positive approach which provides for individuals to respond to interventions based on crisis theory.

Piaget's cognitive-stage theory

Piaget's academic background lay in the discipline of zoology which led him to develop his theory of stages of development which he thought of as similar to the levels of adaptation to the environment within other species. He therefore belongs to the group of philosophers and scientists within the school of *structuralism*. Piaget's theory is a comprehensive one on the development of human intelligence based on scientific enquiry and testing. Thus Piaget theorised that a small set of mental operations underlie a variety of thinking or cognitive episodes which build on and evolve from each other. He concentrated his research on seeing how parts of mental functioning are organised into a whole and how they change with age to combine in different ways to form further mental structures. Piaget's stage theory has five major characteristics:

- a stage is a structured whole in a state of equilibrium

- each stage derives from the previous stage, incorporates and transforms that stage and prepares for the next stage

- the stages follow an invariant sequence

- the stages are universal
- each stage includes an initial preparation and a final period of achievement in each stage.

(summarised in Miller 2002)

Piaget's four stages of cognitive development

Sensorimotor period (approximately birth to 2 years)
The child learns about her world through her own physical actions. The simple reflexes move through several steps into an organised set of schemes. Initially primary reflexes such as sucking and the palm reflex begin to become voluntary actions followed by learned responses such as putting thumb into the mouth. The child gradually learns that certain actions will produce a desired response and can differentiate between means and ends. Piaget argues that this stage begins the development of logical thinking. By the end of this stage the child should have developed the ability to use symbols to form lasting mental representations. Therefore, during this period the child learns about objects and relations between them, cognitive structures become more organised, the behaviour becomes intentional and the self is gradually differentiated from the environment.

Pre-operational thought period (approximately 2 to 7 years)
The child begins to use symbols, mental images, words and gestures to represent objects and events in her world. These symbols become more organised and logical over time. At this stage children learn through imitation and play. While there is enormous development at this stage the thinking is still limited. The period is also characterised by a number of characteristics. The child is egocentric in so far as she believes that the world is only related to herself and cannot see another person's point of view. For example, if the child is in a moving vehicle at night and sees the moon changing position in the sky as she moves she will believe it is following them. At the beginning of the period group play is difficult. While children may appear to be playing together they will in fact be working individually. Team games for children at this stage are very difficult. Children also experience only semi-logical reasoning at this stage.

Concrete operational period (approximately 7 to 11 years)
Children gradually acquire the ability to understand certain operations in the world such as the grouping and organising of size, colour and

shapes which are solid objects. The ability to add, multiply and order objects is achieved. Children at this stage can only solve problems that apply to actual concrete objects or events and not abstract concepts or hypothetical tasks. As Miller (2002) puts it 'they are dealing with what "is" rather than what "could be"' (p.56).

Formal operational period (approximately 11 to 15 years)
Mental operations are no longer limited to concrete levels and the child is able to manage concepts and problems at a mental level. She begins to think abstractly, use logical reasoning and draw conclusions from the information available as well as dealing with hypothetical situations. This allows the possibility of finding a solution to a problem at an intellectual level without the need to go through the process in a concrete fashion in order to find a solution. Maier (1988) offers a very detailed description of the work of both Erikson and Piaget while Miller (2002) presents an evaluation of Piaget's theory and also discusses the work of the Neo-Piagetians.

Piaget's contribution to child development lay in his demonstration of the discovery of intellectual development which was largely unrelated to learning theory. The latter had, up to that time, been central to understanding child development. In addition Piaget's work was developed out of a rigorous observation of children's behaviour which could be replicated many times. Piaget's theory focused on children's adaptation to the world around them, their assimilation of new behaviours and the ability to move towards further adaptation as they become older. The stage aspect of his theory was subsequently criticised as being too rigid in that children may not achieve everything in a particular stage until the stage has ended and that concepts or structures of a particular stage are often only loosely in line with a particular stage (Flavell 1971, 1982 cited in Miller 2002). However, the important issue for understanding subsequent behaviour is the contribution of cognitive thinking to subsequent problem solving. Thus, in terms of Piaget's theory, the ability to deal with a crisis situation may well be related to the ability to address the issue at the level of concrete operations or at a higher level of formal operations.

Kohlberg's theory of moral development
Much of Kohlberg's theory was based on an adaptation of Piaget's work but emphasising the development of moral reasoning. He argued that moral reasoning was the basis for ethical behaviour and its development can be

divided into six developmental stages, each stage being a more mature or ethical way of dealing with a particular moral dilemma. He developed Piaget's work beyond the period of adolescence or young adulthood arguing that moral development continues through life (Kohlberg 1981).

Kohlberg divided moral development into three main groups which are subdivided into two subgroups giving six stages of development. The authors have expanded on these below.

Kohlberg's six stages of development

Level 1: Preconventional

- Stage 1: this stage is concerned with obedience and punishment
- Stage 2: self-interest orientation.

These stages are characterised by self-interest or egocentrism. All actions have the purpose of serving the individual's own needs and interests. The judge of morality is what are the direct consequences of the particular behaviour. The individual is solely concerned with self and how the behaviour will affect herself and how others will view the individual. Therefore actions are seen as morally wrong because they are punished and the more severe the punishment the greater is the moral wrong. In addition there is a lack of understanding that other people may hold a variety of views which may be different or superior to her own.

Level 2: Conventional

- Stage 3: interpersonal accord and conformity – concern with social norms
- Stage 4: concern with authority and social order.

This period is typical of adolescents and young adults. It is characterised by an acceptance of society's conventions concerning right and wrong. Individuals try to be 'good people' and to live up to these expectations. The belief is that conforming to societal norms will make them liked. Kohlberg argued that most people will remain at this stage where they conform to the law as an obligation to society.

Level 3: Post-conventional

- Stage 5: social contract orientation
- Stage 6: universal ethical principles.

At this stage there is a growing realisation that individuals are separate from society and that the individual's perspective may take precedence over society. The individual views rules as useful but changeable and realises that she does not have to obey the laws or rules without questioning them. There is an acceptance that the world is made up of a variety of opinions, rights and values and that these variances should be respected. Laws are seen as contracts rather than edicts which are not inviolable. Those that do not promote general welfare such as life, liberty and human rights should be challenged as morally wrong. Moral reasoning is based on abstract reasoning using universal principles with a commitment to justice carrying an obligation to disobey laws which are unjust.

Kohlberg speculated that there may well be a seventh stage which links morality with religion and the wider universal views of rights and ethics. Kohlberg's theory has been criticised on the basis that it is not culturally neutral although he has argued that his stages correspond to underlying modes of reasoning rather than to cultural beliefs (Crain 1985).

Susan and Jake: A developmental perspective

Is this a crisis for Susan? In terms of Erikson's theory it could be hypothesised that Susan had problems in initiative versus shame and doubt. At a period when Susan was dealing with developing initiative and making first attempts at independence, her father may have been over-protective and at any time when she tried to do something herself or on her own he found it difficult to give her the chance to try out new behaviours or allow her to make mistakes. She therefore had problems with shame regarding trying to do things for herself. Therefore in this situation when she took the initiative to move out to be independent she was unable to deal with a fairly simple crisis such as the flooding washing machine. She immediately allowed her father to take over and reproduce the way things were dealt with in her childhood. Before she moved out to the flat her father had done much of the caring of Jake – like doing homework with him – so she had allowed him to take over her role and this kept her in a childlike relationship of dependency on her father.

Susan needs to be given an opportunity to explore with her therapist how her relationship with her father may have resulted from an earlier period and encouraged to see how she should try again to be independent of her parents and move back into the flat with Jake but perhaps use their help in a different less direct way.

If an interpretation of the difficulties are made from the view of Piaget's stage theory it could be suggested that Susan had not developed far beyond the concrete operations stage. In other words she was not able to use hypothetical-deductive reasoning which would mean that she was not able to think through solutions to the problem and decide on the best path to follow in solving the problem. She was left with a panic situation of the flooding washing machine which she could not solve because she had not encountered a similar problem before and could not work out how to solve it.

This situation could be a crisis for Susan because in Kohlberg's terms she was in the adolescent or young adult stage of concern for social order. She saw herself as having to be the 'good daughter' and 'good parent' in order to obtain rewards for conforming to social norms of being a parent, adult and independent. The crisis of the washing machine could put her into a panic situation where she returns to the family home to be rescued from the situation of non-conformity. The crisis was that she could not deal with being independent and therefore was not going to be seen as being a coping and good parent and therefore would not be receiving rewards from her parents or family for acting in an adult fashion.

Developmental theories and crisis

Crises, in terms of developmental theories, are part of the normal processes of growth and development particularly at times of transition from one stage to another. There may be increased feelings of confusion and disequilibrium but the development of defences is not part of the solution to the difficulties that may arise. The existence of such crises is a normal process which occurs as part of biological, maturational and social development.

As Aguilera (1986) has stated:

the hazardous situations that occur in daily life may serve to compound normal maturational crises. When a person requests help at these times it is necessary to determine what part of the presenting symptomatology is the result of transitional maturational stages and what, in turn is the result of a stressful event in his current social orbit. (p.204)

The underlying presumption in understanding a crisis event is that early childhood experiences and development are the explanation of why a specific event becomes a crisis. The disequilibrium which accompanies a crisis can be understood through gaining access to the individual's past emotional and social experience.

The theories of Erikson, Piaget and Kohlberg deal with distinctly separate but complementary approaches to human development. However, they each recognise that growth through the stages or phases of development is influenced both by internal forces and by the social environment in which the individual develops. As James (2008) has stated 'when an external environmental or situational crisis feeds into a pre-existing developmental crisis intrapersonal and interpersonal problems may reach breaking point and elicit a crisis' (p.13).

James (2008) refers to this approach as the *psychosocial-transitional model* for understanding crisis. This model, in comparison with the psychoanalytic approach, does not see crisis as emanating only from an internal state within the individual but from a combination of the individual in conjunction with the systems in which she resides. James (2008) has argued that few lasting gains can be made in crisis resolution unless the social systems that affect individuals are changed or the individual accepts and understands the dynamics of those systems and how they affect adaptation to the crisis.

Collins and Collins (2005) developed an ecological model of crisis intervention that integrates developmental stages within the environment in which the individual in crisis exists. Therefore, they argue that any intervention needs to assess both the developmental issues and the environment and the relationship between the two. Therefore, a situational crisis must always be considered in relation to the stage of development of the individual and how she has resolved her earlier normative developmental crises. The strength of the crisis will depend on how well there has been mastery of the tasks in earlier stages of development. Thus, the goal of intervention must be to assess both the internal workings of individuals and the ego strengths they possess together with the external difficulties which have contributed to the crisis. By doing this it becomes possible to assist individuals in choosing an appropriate way to adapt their current behaviour, their affect and their understanding of the crisis which will allow them to build on their ego strengths and the resources available to them in the environment.

Case example: Retirement and Alan and Louise

Alan (60) and Louise (55) have been married for 35 years. They have two daughters Jane (33) and Jill (31) both now married with children of their own. Alan has worked for over 40 years in a large multi-national company in information technology. He had worked his way up to the position of director of human resource management. Louise was 20 years of age and had completed two years in university when she married. She 'dropped out' to relocate when Alan got a promotion. She stayed at home to be a full time homemaker until her daughters were older and then returned to university.

When she completed her business degree she eventually opened a small business support service and has been very successful.

Both Alan and Louise have been hard workers but Louise often complained that Alan was a 'workaholic' and that he spent more time at work even when he was at home. He brought his work home, worked late and even in leisure time was often more focused on work problems than family life. Louise recognised that being a successful 'breadwinner' for his family was very important to Alan and he did indeed provide well for them all. It was his support that gave Louise the impetus to start her own business.

When their eldest daughter decided to join Louise's business it meant that Louise was able to hand over some of the responsibilities. Louise over the past few years began to be involved more with her grandchildren and had developed an interest in art through her involvement with her local art group. Louise has always been quite independent socially since Alan was so caught up in work.

The company that Alan worked for had come under increasing financial pressure. They decided to downsize and HR was an obvious place to cut staffing levels. Alan was offered a redundancy package and it was clear that he would have to take early retirement. Alan at 60 now finds himself with no interests or hobbies, a busy and successful wife and a family that have learned to get on with their lives without much involvement from him.

He has taken the forced retirement very badly. This was probably made more difficult by the way in which it happened. It was very sudden and to Alan it seemed that he was being told very clearly that he had nothing more to offer. He had little time to adjust as things moved very quickly. Within two weeks of the decision Alan found himself at home and no longer employed.

Louise thought Alan was a bit shocked but was relieved that he was no longer under pressure. She put his initial 'bad form' down to his annoyance with the company. As the weeks passed she began to be more worried as Alan seemed to be quite depressed, listless and complained of an increasing number of migraine type attacks. Things between them became tense and Alan snapped at her when she went out to work or continued with her regular social activities. Louise was angry since she had always accommodated Alan's decision to dedicate himself to work and now just because he was at a loose end he wanted her to slow down.

Alan became increasingly depressed and Louise noticed he had begun to drink a lot during his days at home. She discovered that he was doing nothing all day but watching television and drinking. When Alan began to neglect even his basic hygiene Louise demanded that he see a doctor. She was concerned for Alan's mental and physical health and for their marriage.

According to Erikson's thinking we all have to deal with issues about our sense of being contributors to society. Through resolving this task we feel productive (generativity), if it is not resolved we may feel dissatisfied or worthless (stagnation and self absorption). While Alan did succeed in making a worthwhile contribution to society he did so at a price. He may not have achieved the balanced resolution demanded in the life stage because he neglected some elements of family life. He probably did more to give direction to workers and had limited impact in terms of his role as father in providing guidance for his children. Now he finds himself removed from the key role in life as a worker and facing unresolved engagement with his family and his role as father.

Erikson hypothesised that 65 plus was the time for dealing with issues of ego integrity versus despair. However with changing societal norms about retirement and withdrawal from the workforce it is fair to say that Alan probably has to face the issues in this task as well. This life stage is about being at peace with oneself and having no regrets. It is also about coming to terms with one's own mortality. The extension in life expectancy probably has made some changes to this time frame but none the less retirement is usually seen as a period to make a shift in life goals and activities.

Alan may be experiencing regrets and self doubt about decisions he made during his earlier life. He may see that since his employer treated him so badly in the end that he had made bad choices about where to invest his energies. This hurt and realisation that he is somewhat outside of his family due to these choices may be contributing to his depression and ultimate despair.

The crisis for Alan is that he lost his identity as a successful working man who provided well for his family and is finding it difficult to identify himself as a retired person who may still have something to contribute to life but in a different form. In order to deal with this crisis Alan needs help to create a new identity for himself as a retired person. He needs help to see that there are other areas in his life to which he could successfully contribute. If he has regrets that he did not have as much involvement in his children's lives he could now compensate for this by being supportive and involved as a grandparent. His eldest daughter who now works in Louise's business might welcome his assistance with child minding. He could also begin to share his wife's interest in art or develop new interests that the two of them could enjoy together.

Conclusion

Developmental theories offer an understanding based primarily on assumptions that we can track our lives across a number of phases or stages. The theories have attempted to be quite prescriptive about these stages and this feature in particular has given rise to many criticisms of the perspective. It is seen to have created a belief in a 'normative' progression over time that may be neither helpful nor accurate. Others being dissatisfied with these explanations moved on to see the world through a different lens. We will now look at one of these alternatives, the behavioural perspective.

Chapter 4

A Behavioural Approach

A brief history of behaviour theory

Miller (2002) outlines the dissatisfaction within psychology because of what Watson in 1913 saw as lack of systematic and scientific study. Watson according to Miller (2002) declared that the goal of psychology should be to predict and control overt behaviour. The 1920s saw the establishment of a 'behaviourism' stream in psychology. This was solidly based on a 'scientific' psychology and influenced by Watson's 1924 research and theoretical formulations and the laboratory studies published in 1928 by Pavlov (Miller 2002). This shift in focus emphasised the need to understand behaviour in a way that was observable and measurable.

Pavlov's work caught the imagination of generations of psychology students. His study of dogs' reaction to stimuli (Pavlov's dogs) is probably one of the most widely known pieces of behavioural research. His research into the behaviour of dogs was allied to human behaviour and in conjunction with Watson and Rayners' 1920s work became the foundation of a way of explaining human behaviour known as *classical conditioning*.

So theories about behaviour have been around a long time but therapeutic applications based on these theories are a somewhat more recent development. Bellack and Hersen (1985) in tracking the development of behaviour therapy commented that 'the period between 1920 and 1950 saw an unmarked progress in the understanding of conditioning and learning' (p.4). They suggested that it was not until the late 1950s and early 1960s that behaviour therapy as a discipline really began. The theoretical framework underpinning this behaviour therapy was according to Bellack and Hersen (1985) learning theory, specifically the principles of classical and operant conditioning.

The connection between learning theory and behaviour therapy was central to Eysenck's 1964 definition of behaviour therapy. Writers such as Yates (1975) disagree about this relationship between learning theory and behaviour therapy. Yates (1975) in defining behaviour therapy emphasised that although learning theory may have a role in many behaviour disorders, learning theory is not the essence of behaviour therapy as Eysenck claimed. Reid (2004) in his discussion of operant behaviour theory suggests that classical and operant conditioning along with theories about learning and modelling behaviour 'formed what is known as learning theory, the foundation of behaviour therapy' (p.36).

This issue about the place of learning within behaviour theory is significant. In the early days of the behaviour movement the focus was on the observable and measurable aspects of behaviour. Intervention to change behaviour was therefore focused on manipulating stimuli (classical) and reinforcement (operant) to shape behaviour. One well known adaptation of these ideas was behaviour modification (which will be discussed later in this chapter). What distinguished this behaviour theory was that it did not attempt to deal with any processing that the individual might do which might in fact also have an impact on the way the individual behaved – as already mentioned it was only concerned with the observable and measurable.

Many writers have attributed advances in the adaptation of behaviour theory within therapeutic interventions to work in clinical psychology during World War II because of the efforts to deal with 'battle fatigue' in WWII – what was called 'shell shock' in WWI and what we later came to know as post traumatic stress disorder in the Vietnam War (Bellack and Hersen 1985, Dattilio and Freeman 2007). Yates (1975) suggests that the publication of four substantial summaries and interpretations of the status of behaviour therapy: Bandura (1969), Franks (1969), Kanfer and Phillips (1970) and Yates (1970), marked the culmination of the development of the approach. These works attempted to draw into behaviour theory some exploration of the process of learning that might be beyond the behaviour 'training' that typified early iterations of behaviour theory. Not everyone agreed to this expansion in behaviour theory and so establishing the place of learning in behaviour theory was contentious.

Returning to the discussion in the introduction chapter we can see that the debate about what is theory and what is therapy is relevant for understanding behavioural work. Overall it seems that many writers in the field have conceptualised the different theories or concepts about human behaviour and amalgamated them to inform a general theory of learning. Hence we are looking not just at describing human behaviour but at understanding how the factors that influence behaviour can explain how we learn and how we learn new behaviours, in other words, change behaviour. This then is the connection between theories of behaviour and learning theory. This may also explain why writers like Bellack and Hersen (1985) and Reid (2004) make the distinction between learning theory and behaviour therapy. They see the amalgam of theories about behaviour as a unified learning theory and see this unified theory as the basis for changing behaviour that is the business of behaviour therapy. They suggest that behaviour theory is not in itself a sufficiently comprehensive theory.

In spite of the fact that there may be some disagreement about the relationship between behaviour theories and learning, this chapter will deal with the more expanded behaviour and learning theory and consider cognitive theory in its own right in the following chapter. The central influences on behaviour therapy are then therapeutic interventions drawing on key ideas about behaviours from both classical and operant conditioning (behaviour theory) and observational and vicarious learning (learning theory).

Later in this chapter we will be looking more specifically at behaviour based therapies or approaches that attempt to link with assessing and responding to crisis. The ultimate unification of behavioural ideas with the cognitive perspective has resulted in the development of cognitive behavioural therapy (CBT). For the purposes of providing a greater clarity about the origins and therapeutic applications of CBT and since it is essentially a combination of the key features of two theoretical approaches we will explore each of the constituent parts separately and then comment on the combined CBT as appropriate.

Key concepts in behavioural theory/ learning theory

Bellack and Hersen (1985) suggested 'the work of Skinner, Wolpe and Eysenck combined to provide a beginning set of procedures, a theoretical framework, and a raison d'etre for behavioural revolution. The theoretical framework was learning theory or more specifically, the principles of classical and operant conditioning' (p.5). Classical conditioning and operant conditioning could be seen as the core concepts of behaviour theory. From the point of view of working with clients or therapy the almost passive role attributed to the subject in classical and operant conditioning undermined ideas of self determination, choice or even agency on the part of the client. The limitations of the purely behavioural school of thought became apparent and so theorists and clinicians integrated aspects of learning theory and more recently the integration of behaviour and cognitive theory into a cognitive behavioural therapy which have further contributed to how we can understand what makes us behave as we do. The concepts about behaviour and learning can be attributed to either behaviour or learning theory while the application of these ideas in the therapeutic field is generally seen as behaviour therapy. This iteration of behaviour therapy goes well beyond the early ideas of behaviour modification and incorporates aspects of behaviour change which engage with for example, problem solving, vicarious learning (learning from the experiences of others) and coping skills. We will now look at some of the key ideas from behaviour theory that can be applied to behaviour therapy.

Classical conditioning

Stepney and Ford (2000) offer a more extensive but very accessible discussion of the early development of behavioural work. They discuss the contributions of Pavlov, Watson and Skinner as the key proponents of behaviour theory. Chronologically the development of theories to explain behaviour started with Pavlov and Watson in the early part of the twentieth century. Drawing from Stepney and Ford (2000) we will look at Pavlov and his dogs. Pavlov demonstrated that a natural or innate reflex such as salivating when the dogs saw food can be associated with a different stimulus, in this case a tone/bell, and that eventually the dog will associate the noise with food and react (salivate) when the tone is heard even in the absence of food. Watson and Rayner (1920) explored the connections between Pavlov's findings and the human condition. They found that not only did humans have similar reactions to stimuli but that it was possible for responses to become more generalised. In other words a reaction of upset or panic may be evoked not just from the repetition of a bad experience but from an experience that was similar enough to make the connection to the previous negative experience. Think of the sound of an explosion creating a panic reaction and then later on in a different situation the sound of a car back firing or a balloon bursting creating the same reaction.

Operant conditioning

Skinner's (1953) research also involved animal studies. He was again making the case that his findings were equally applicable to human behaviour patterns. He experimented with rats in a box. He looked at the behaviour of these rats and how they learned to distinguish between behaviour that would lead to a reward of food versus behaviour that would result in getting an electric shock. It all depended on pressing the right button in the box and the rats soon figured it out. Operant conditioning offers a more complex view of human behaviour. This concept explores behaviour in a broader context. If we want to understand behaviour we need to look not just at the behaviour or actions themselves but also at the context and consequences of behaviour. Just like the rats our behaviour changes depending on the consequences. This introduces another dimension to understanding behaviour, that is, the connection between consequences and repeating behaviour. It also means finding out about the setting in which the behaviour occurs.

Operant conditioning also involves mechanisms that are seen to promote or eliminate repetition of behaviour. If you want to learn new behaviour then encouragement to repeat or practise behaviour becomes important. First let's look at how the mechanism works as illustrated in Figure 4.1.

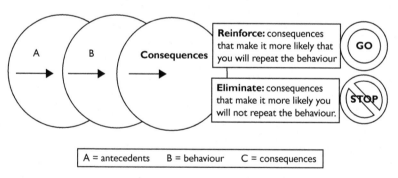

Figure 4.1: The ABC of behaviour

Figure 4.1 illustrates the relationship between antecedents, behaviour and consequences. It shows that reinforcing consequences result in repetition while non reinforcing consequences are more likely to eliminate the behaviour. What is helpful about these concepts is that they direct attention not only to the behaviour but to the context in which the behaviour has occurred (antecedents) and the result of that behaviour (consequences). Murdock and Barker (1991) emphasised that 'behaviour is thus functional and goal oriented rather than reflexive' (p.4). The theory helps us to understand that in certain situations we may be more likely to behave in a certain way. This may involve certain places or people or a combination of being with a particular person in a specific place.

For example for a young adult it may be more likely that he will smoke if he is out for the night with a group of friends than if he is at home with his parents. When working with someone to address behaviour it is useful to help him consider A (the antecedent) of the behaviour, this may even offer some ideas about what is more likely to trigger certain behaviours. The theory also draws our attention to the need to understand people's goals and what part specific behaviour plays in their lives i.e. what is the purpose or function of particular behaviour/s. Back to the young person and smoking: if one of the goals of smoking is to help him to belong then any attempt to change the behaviour that does not take this goal into account will fail.

Positive and negative reinforcement

The C is more complex but important to understand in behavioural theory. Consequences occur for all behaviour. If good comes of doing something you are more likely to want to repeat that behaviour so that the consequences reinforce your actions: *go*. If something bad happens you might not want to have that experience again and may not repeat the behaviour so that the behaviour is eliminated: *stop*. That all makes sense until you consider that sometimes we engage in behaviour that seems to have negative or bad consequences yet we cannot stop or choose not to stop repeating the behaviour. It is possible to have both negative and positive reinforcement.

Walsh (2006) helps us to understand this phenomenon: 'positive reinforcement encourages the continuation of the behaviour preceding it… negative reinforcement is the process by which an adverse event is terminated by the behaviour' (pp.111–112). Take smoking for example: if your friends are all smoking and you join in then you may feel that you are part of the group, enjoying the company and feeling you belong. These feelings are a positive reinforcement that smoking is good and a behaviour you want to repeat. Alternatively you may be under serious pressure at work and very stressed – when you smoke it gives you a short break from the pressure and you feel that the few minutes smoking helps you to relax, relief from the sense of pressure acts as reinforcement but negative reinforcement.

The example of smoking helps to highlight another important aspect of this reinforcement theory. Consequences for behaviour may be immediate or take a bit longer. If you are studying for a professional career, it takes time and while there may be more immediate rewards such as satisfaction and good grades the real reward is often seen as successful completion of the training or course. This may take time. It seems that sometimes the most immediate consequence is more powerful in shaping our reaction. So with smoking the immediate feeling of belonging or of stress reduction has more impact than the longer term medical complications that will ultimately be a consequence of continued smoking. This clearly has implications for behaviourally based therapeutic interventions since we want to use the reinforcement aspect of consequences to promote positive change.

Maladaptive behaviour

When behaviour which is problematic is reinforced this is sometimes referred to as maladaptive behaviour. The mechanism is the same but the behaviour that is reinforced and therefore repeated is not 'helpful'. Hence maladaptive behaviours have the same origins as adaptive behaviours. Sheldon (2000) in discussing this idea of maladaptive behaviour suggests that the most effective way to deal with this maladaptive behaviour is contingency management. He explains that contingency management involves changing reinforcement patterns to ensure that useful, pro-social behaviour attracts reinforcement and that negative self-defeating behaviour does not.

Observation and modelling

These ideas come from the expanded behaviour theory which includes attempts to deal with internal mechanisms which influence behaviour. Since these are not observable in the way valued by the early behaviourists some are reluctant to include them in behaviour theory and they may be more accurately assigned to the broader construct of learning theory. Jehu *et al.* (1972) offer this explanation of what they term observational learning:

> The client's observation of certain behaviour by other people and its consequences for them is another type of learning experience which may contribute to problem behaviour. One effect of this procedure is that the observer acquires new responses by imitating the behaviour of the model. (p.9)

There is another aspect of behaviour theory that explains how we can learn new behaviours by copying or imitating others. This involves modelling our behaviour on the behaviour of others around us. This modelling is also referred to as observational learning (Jehu *et al.* 1972). In some ways this helps to explain the importance of peers, especially for adolescents. Not only is there the behaviour mechanism of modelling our behaviour on those around us but combined with this is the adolescent interest in belonging and fitting in. This makes modelling among adolescents quite powerful and in the absence of 'good' role models it can leave an adolescent very vulnerable as well. This may also explain some of the concerns in debates today about the impact of video games and movies in terms of demonstrating aggressive behaviour. Jehu *et al.* (1972) pointed out that the evidence about this link between observation and imitation was mostly based on laboratory studies and this is still a contentious issue.

Behaviour therapy and crisis

Murdock and Barker (1991) in considering behaviour therapy comment that 'there are well-understood principles, a wide body of well-established facts, and theories about particular aspects of learning and behaviour based on sound research, but there is no single theory' (p.6). Behaviour therapy drawing on these principles of behaviour and learning theories designs interventions to facilitate behaviour change. The fact that behaviour theory is not a single unifying theory may explain in part why it has expanded and incorporated other ideas and is today more usually associated with a more comprehensive cognitive behavioural approach. For the purposes of this chapter however we will focus on the key ideas attributable to behaviour theory.

Behaviour therapy then involves identifying patterns of behaviour that already exist and making an assessment regarding whether the repertoire of behaviour is sufficient to meet the needs of the client in his current situation. It may be that current behaviour is causing problems and the client will need help to change his behaviour, it may be that the behaviour required is not familiar to the client and he needs help to learn a completely new way of behaving, or it may be that the client has some of the behaviour/skills required but needs to learn how to apply them to a new situation. As we discussed in the introduction this is a continuum of change behaviour so it may involve restoration to previous behaviour, augmentation to current patterns of behaviour or transformation. There are a number of mechanisms employed in this behavioural approach. Eisler and Hersen (1973) applying behavioural theory to crisis discuss a number of useful behavioural techniques such as modelling, behavioural rehearsal and problem solving. We will look at a few central techniques.

Behaviour modification

This involves finding out about the pattern of problem behaviour, in particular understanding the mechanisms at play that reinforce the problem behaviour. The goal then is to modify the problem behaviour by 'retraining' the client. Through employing conditioning and observational learning techniques the behaviour is relearned. What has been contentious about this approach has been disagreement as to whether such change in behaviour can be achieved without the client necessarily knowing or understanding the change that is being implemented. In other words the question is first, is it really possible to change another's behaviour by using conditioning techniques while not elucidating the procedure to the client? Second even if it were possible to change someone without him understanding about the change would that in any situation be ethical?

A classic case for behaviour modification might be training a child who is bed wetting. Can the child understand the problem and if he can does he need to understand the problem in order to change? Behaviour modification programmes can be based on modifying behaviour without necessitating full understanding on the part of the child. Yates (1975) draws attention to some of the criticism of behaviour therapy approaches and cites the work of Portes (1971) who was critical of behaviour therapy because of the lack of attention to what he thought of as important aspects of human behaviour, meaning and self-reflection. The place of understanding and meaning as well as thinking (cognition) and self-reflection in relation to dealing with problems will be further considered in the next chapter. This perceived deficit in both behaviour theory and then its application in behaviour therapy ultimately lie at the roots of what would become cognitive behaviour therapy.

Functional analysis/mapping behaviour/behaviour diary

The functional analysis approach to behaviour therapy acknowledges that the individual is not simply a passive respondent to stimuli or reinforcement and begins to engage with the idea that the individual is an active participant in establishing and maintaining the behaviour pattern. In order to understand the connections between antecedents, behaviour and consequences it is possible to conduct a functional analysis which enables the client and worker to map out the relationship between A, B and C. One example is where a client keeps a diary about specific target behaviours. He attempts to record the situations (A) he finds himself in, the actual incidents of the target behaviour (B) and keep a record of the consequences (C) of that behaviour in each example. This opens up the discussion about the role of reasoning and thinking, that is cognitions in influencing behaviour and again ultimately contributes to the cognitive behavioural approach.

Skills training

Target behaviours may relate to life skills training, relaxation training, coping skills training, assertion training, or desensitisation. All behavioural interventions are highly structured, which is helpful for people who feel overwhelmed and out of control (Walsh 2006).

Those who see coping as a state, or process, observe that coping strategies change depending on our perceptions of the threats (Walsh 2006). The function of problem focused coping is to change the stressful situation. This method dominates when we see the situation as controllable by action. In emotion focused coping the external situation does not change, but our behaviour or attitudes change (Walsh 2006).

Problem solving

Another aspect of behaviour that is important in behaviour therapy is the notion of problem solving. The accumulation of ability and skills to effectively solve problems is usually viewed as part of behaviour therapy and so we will include this as a feature of behavioural therapy. Given the discussion so far you can see that this problem solving approach is essentially built from a combination of behaviour and learning theory concepts. Problem solving necessitates engaging in cognitive processes to assess the situation and evaluate alternative responses. As such, problem solving is more correctly a formulation of cognitive behavioural therapy. Jehu *et al.* (1972) defined problem solving as a process that includes

> attending to and perceiving the relevant elements in a problem situation, storing these in short term memory and recalling other essential information, conceptualising the data into appropriate

categories and manipulating these by inductive and deductive reasoning to yield hypotheses, rules or principles which solve the presenting problem and others of similar nature. (p.11)

This is a far step away from Pavlov's dogs in terms of active involvement of the individual in shaping his behaviour.

Coping skills

Coping skills refer to a wide range of behaviours accessible to a person in order to assist in stressful situations or events. The notion of coping in itself is of course broader than response to stress. In reality good coping strategies may result in minimising experiences of stress or distress so that coping is not always a reaction to stress but may prevent or mediate the onset of stress. When we talk about coping in a therapeutic sense we usually mean that previous or accessible strategies for dealing with life are not effective in a particular situation and so it becomes necessary to learn new coping behaviours. This may involve revisiting old coping skills that have been forgotten so that the change is about restoring skills or it may involve adding some new dimension to an already established set of coping skills, in other word ameliorate or enhance present skills. In some instances it may be necessary to find completely new and untried strategies which may be transformative in nature. This transformative change may be required if the situation to be faced is so completely different from earlier experiences as can be the case in a crisis situation.

Modelling

Modelling can be used for skills enhancement. In the behavioural approach problems can often be attributed to a deficit in our repertoire of skills. For some reason we have not been exposed to opportunities to learn specific skills or we missed such opportunities or perhaps due to the behaviour of others we did not need to learn the skill at the time and now find ourselves with a skills deficit. One way of learning new skills or of developing required new social skills would be to have them demonstrated to us and then to imitate that skill. A good example of this can be found in group work. Yalom (1970) identified the opportunity to learn from others in a group setting as one of the curative factors in group interventions. Group therapy offers a chance to see someone else use a specific skill or set of skills to deal with a situation and then creates a safe environment in which you can practise. This modelling of a skill or set of skills can also work in a one to one counselling or therapeutic situation.

Role play

The notion of role play is a development of modelling and relates to this idea of practising a new skill. Eisler and Hersen (1973) referred to this activity as behavioural rehearsal where the client has identified some skills deficit and agrees that he wants to acquire new skills – it is often helpful to test out those skills in a protected situation. Working on new ways of dealing with situations can be very challenging and so it can often be encouraging and supportive to try them out first. This idea of playing out the new skill in a 'role play' situation also allows the learner to get feedback about how well he is employing the new skill and therefore have an opportunity to fine tune aspects of the skill so that he can be better equipped for a variety of situations.

Susan: A behavioural perspective

Let's look at a 'behavioural interpretation' of crisis for Susan. Susan finds herself responsible for running a household on her own. Up to now she has been living with her parents and may have been unaware of the day to day maintenance of a home, in particular more technical issues such as electrics or plumbing. In behavioural terms, if anything went wrong her mother or father ensured it was repaired or replaced.

You could say that the main skill Susan had acquired was the skill of identifying and reporting any household problems. The reinforcement element of this learned behaviour was that once identified the problem was handled by another so that she had no need to learn about the actual repair process. Some might consider that this is a form of learned helplessness but it may be simply that when one person in a home has a specific set of skills and others are not under pressure to develop the same set of skills they may contribute to the home by employing other skills.

The problem only arises when, as in the case of Susan, she finds herself trying to manage alone and so may need to learn more skills herself. Kfir (1989) in discussing some of the differences between stress and crisis suggests that for an event to become a crisis it can involve 'the confrontation of a totally new phenomenon (the situation itself may not be so terrible but the fact that it is confronted for the first time makes it a crisis)' (p.5). For Susan the reality is probably that she could actually continue with her previous behaviour because in all likelihood a quick phone call to her father would have the same results – i.e. he would come over and sort out the repair.

Susan: Crisis and change

Susan helps us to understand some of the aspects of crisis and change that can get clouded because of the emotive nature of many crises. The issue of domestic appliance failure would appear to be a safe topic and so we can track more easily the interaction between a range of responses and the likelihood that Susan will actually change. The question about whether Susan experiences a crisis is crucial. It offers a really good example of where an opportunity to promote new learning may or may not be followed through depending on the response of others to the situation. In order for this to be a crisis for Susan she needs to experience this as a domestic problem, recognise she does not have the skills to deal with it effectively and feel overwhelmed (we will deal with this feeling issue in the next chapter). The consequences of not being able to deal with it would also need to be quite significant for Susan otherwise she could just dismiss the problem and manage without her domestic appliances.

Not a crisis

If Susan has an alternative set of behaviours that would facilitate her coping with the situation then it would not be a crisis. Some options that would counteract a crisis might be: pay someone to come out and repair, check agreement with landlord and request that the problem be handled by him or her, call home and delay dealing with situation until father or someone else can come and sort it out.

- Calling a repair man is a different behaviour for Susan. How does she know to call a repair man? Is this something she has seen happening in her home and is she now replicating that or modelling the same behaviour in an appropriate way? It is new for her but she was able to call on behaviour she had seen before and was able to resolve the problem. The resolution of the problem would probably reinforce her confidence in herself and encourage further independent behaviours. It means she has to have skills for decision making about who to call, some communication skills about describing the problem and some organisational skills as she will have to be able to pay for the service.

- Likewise with calling the landlord, it is outside Susan's range of previous behaviour but she can connect the behaviour with her previous actions of calling those responsible and so the situation is sorted and she has begun to establish a behaviour pattern of dealing with issues without consultation with her parents.

- Calling her father who naturally comes to the rescue means that the potential crisis is handled and Susan's strategy to call home in a crisis has been reinforced. She has learned no new skill and is no better prepared for a similar event. Calling her father is a key aspect of her repertoire of skills for independent living. The parent's response to the news about the flooding is 'natural' but it does have the effect, in behavioural terms, of reinforcing her dependence on their interventions. Susan does not experience a crisis and so may be less inclined to see the need for change or skills acquisition.

It is a crisis

Susan wants to cope alone. She was confident that she had enough skills to manage her small flat without assistance. She was just getting used to the new situation when the flood happened. It seemed to Susan that suddenly the new found independence was threatened because she had no idea what to do. The washing machine was obviously at fault yet she did not know what had caused the problem and could not find a way to stop the flooding, her neighbours were irate and distressed and shouting at her to do something about the flood of water coming into their home. Susan was aware that her son, Jake, was listening to all the shouting and commotion and he was getting distressed. Susan was out of her depth, she knows nothing about domestic appliances and certainly nothing about how to deal with this flood coming from her kitchen neither did she have an experience of dealing with neighbours who were annoyed themselves. She could not make a decision about what to do and began to demonstrate her own lack of ability to cope by breaking into tears and screaming back at the neighbours.

Susan does not have the skills to deal with the practical or communication aspects of this situation. The pressure of this lack of skill leads to an escalation of the distress and whether or not the actual event was a crisis the level of skills deficit was creating a crisis for Susan. Lack of practical action further escalates the problem and things get worse. The neighbour calls the landlord to intervene and by the time she or he arrives there is substantial damage done to both flats. The neighbour says he intends to hold Susan responsible for it as it was down to her negligence.

Some resolution of the crisis possibilities:

- Susan gets over the trauma of the night once the water is stopped and the damage is reviewed. She decides that this was nothing more than a rocky start to life alone and recognises that she needs to find out more about basic household management. She gets her father over to give her a few hints on the basics.

- Susan calms down and discusses with her landlord what her responsibilities in running the flat are. Once she has clarified the extent of support she can get from him/her she sets out a plan of action to deal with the repairs and get the flat back in order. She talks to her neighbours and explains her situation and they are supportive. Susan is more confident about managing alone. She has found reassurance that even in difficult situations she can sort out her problems.

- Susan calls her parents and is distraught at the situation. She cannot make a decision about what to do next and in the end she returns home and accepts that it is too difficult to cope alone. She rationalises that she needs the support of her parents. Her parents are relieved to have her home as they were very worried about her coping skills.

What this case illustrates is that sometimes when we encounter a person in apparent crisis it seems better to intervene and relieve the crisis by taking action ourselves. This is where crisis theory and change become more complex. If you intervene and dispel the crisis completely you may also dismantle the impetus for change completely. On the other hand if people are so overwhelmed that they cannot engage the skills they actually do have to help deal with crises then the crisis will prevail and the situation will be exasperated. It is this intricate balance between support and resolving the crisis that lies at the heart of crisis therapy. In the case of behaviourally oriented crisis this means looking to the skills individuals have at their disposal to deal with crisis and not underestimating that coping, while at the same time making a reasonable assessment of the level of distress they can sustain without becoming completely immobilised.

Behavioural theory and crisis

In behavioural terms then what is a crisis? It is clearly connected to the idea that a person with inadequate skills to deal effectively with a particular situation may experience this as a crisis. Many definitions of crisis refer to some aspect of skills deficit. Caplan (1961) in defining crisis said 'that people could be considered to be in a state of crisis when they face an obstacle to important life goals, an obstacle that is, for a time, insurmountable by the use of customary methods of problem solving' (p.18).

Roberts in his overview of crisis discusses the difference between someone who faces a stressful situation successfully and one who experiences the same situation as a crisis. For Roberts (2005) the 'two key factors in determining whether or not a person who experiences multiple stressors escalates into a crisis state are the individual's perception of the situation or event and the individual's ability to utilise traditional coping skills' (pp.5–6). The perception aspect of this relates to cognitive theory and will be discussed further in the next chapter, the coping skills piece relates to behaviour theory as discussed in this chapter. The combination of these two elements forms the basis for the cognitive behavioural crisis approach. What is interesting is that although the cognitive aspect of 'perceiving' something as a crisis will be seen to be important and is often critical in making an assessment that someone is in crisis, the therapeutic interventions to crisis situations often focus on the aspect of skills enhancement which is a behavioural focus. A crisis in behavioural terms then draws attention to failed coping mechanisms, inadequate problem solving and/or inability to use known behaviours to deal with the event or situation.

In considering the more purely behavioural ideas a crisis might also result from an unexpected or different consequence to a familiar behaviour. For example a young person returns home intoxicated and usually enters the house and goes to bed and expects that next morning things are business as usual. On some occasion the consequence is different, perhaps he is locked out or his parents are up and waiting to confront him or next morning they deliver an ultimatum about his drinking behaviour. A different response may in itself be the start of differentiated reinforcement which aims to change the behaviour or it may elicit a crisis reaction which again may create the need for a different set of behaviours to deal with the crisis. A crisis then may be the result of a change in reinforcers.

It may also result from a situation that is actually familiar. For example an older woman has had her home burgled some time ago. This caused serious distress, even a crisis, and she has never quite been herself again. One night she hears a loud noise outside and it sounds like someone is trying to break in. She is in crisis. This crisis reaction to the noise may happen regardless of whether there is actually a break in or not. It may be someone making noise on the street but the impact on her is just the same.

A behaviourally based response or intervention then seeks to work with clients to build or restore their coping strategies and ameliorate their problem solving skills to meet the challenge presented by the 'crisis' evoking event. Because skills enhancement is seen as an important way to resolve any crisis then some behavioural training or retraining is usually a part of all crisis interventions regardless of what theoretical framework is used to understand the crisis experience. This recognition of the importance of learning new responses to what is a crisis makes the behavioural approach to crisis very important even if it does not offer a complete picture of what is happening when a client experiences a crisis.

Some examples of the inclusion of a behavioural component to crisis intervention include Roberts's (1991) seven stage model and James's (2008) six step model.

1. Plan and conduct a thorough assessment (including lethality, dangerousness to self and others, and immediate psychosocial needs).

2. Make psychological contact, establish rapport, and rapidly establish the relationship (conveying genuine respect for the client, acceptance, reassurance, and a non judgemental attitude).

3. Examine the dimensions of the problem in order to define it (including the last straw or precipitating event).

4. Encourage exploration of feelings and emotions.

5. Generate, explore, and assess past coping attempts.

6. Restore cognitive functioning through implementation of an action plan.

7. Follow up and leave a door open for booster sessions three and/or six months later.

(Roberts 2005, p.21)

James (2008) also proposes a number of progressive steps toward resolving a crisis. Again the steps relate to creating a working relationship and ensuring the client's safety before examining alternative choices, making a plan and obtaining commitment to the plan. The examining of alternatives or options according to James should involve consideration of three elements: situational supports, coping mechanisms and positive and constructive thinking patterns. This demonstrates the integration of cognitive and behavioural ideas as well as systems (to be explored in Chapter 6). The attention to coping takes account of the behaviour and action aspects of crisis resolution. The plan refers to following up on these three areas and so involves learning new skills for coping and problem solving.

Case example: Marital breakdown and Jack and Kate

Jack (43) and Kate (41) had been married for 15 years. They have three children: a boy Jay aged 14 and two daughters Allie (13) and Jenny (5). The couple have lived in a comfortable three bedroomed home in reasonable area for the past ten years since they moved because of Jack's work situation. Both Jack and Kate work outside the home and have demanding professional jobs. Kate had taken some time out of her career to have the children but had returned to build a successful career in business when she became pregnant with Jenny. Although this proved a difficult time trying to keep up with demands of a new baby and a career Kate was determined and Jack was supportive. By that time Kate was in a position where she was earning the higher salary and so Jack became more involved in child care issues and they had moved closer to his workplace so that he was more adjacent and accessible for sorting out the practical needs of the children. Jack handled school runs, shopping and general finances. Kate, who had a long commute, usually handled some meals and homework activities and they shared bedtime tasks.

Twelve months ago Jack was offered a new position and was keen to take the opportunity as it was a significant promotion for him. Although he was pleased with this development it put extra pressures on them as a couple. Jack thought that maybe Kate could ease up on her job and so be more available at home. This seemed to increase the tension between them and six months ago they had a major row which resulted in Jack walking out of the house. He remained out of the home for several days and Kate became very distressed when he made contact to say he would not be returning to the family home.

Is this a crisis and for whom?

A crisis for Jack but not Kate (one story)

Jack had been more and more dissatisfied with the arrangements at home. While he had been happy to take on more domestic responsibilities to facilitate Kate's career he had not envisioned that it would have such a detrimental impact on his own career. He was very committed to the relationship but during the row it became clear to him that Kate was completely unaware of his feelings. She was happy for things to remain the same and even seemed more distracted by her own work issues. He thought she had little or no appreciation of his contribution and this really came as a shock, it was the first time he felt so taken for granted. Up to this time Jack had experienced Kate's responses to his contribution in a very positive and reinforcing way and so had continued his family management activities. This new and clearly critical reaction was unexpected and he did not know how to respond. Even when he walked out after the row he had not decided to leave the relationship. However Kate did little to respond to his anger and her reactions indicated that she was OK with the separation. This change in reinforcement was sudden and unexpected and Jack had no ready response. In addition Kate had adopted a new reaction to him which was hostile and negative and so his normal pattern of behaviour, reinforced by Kate's positive regard was in turmoil.

The behavioural aspects of the crisis are further intensified by Jack finding himself living alone in strange surroundings and with extra financial pressures. His normal routine is completely changed and he has a lot of free time, something he has not experienced for at least 12 years. The absence of a normal schedule and his poor skills for coping on his own have contributed to his being overwrought and overwhelmed. He had no idea that his marriage was so vulnerable and so had few skills to deal with the disputes that were arising daily nor the apparent complete withdrawal of Kate's support.

Kate on the other hand had actually been dissatisfied with the relationship for some time. It worked for her because Jack took care of most of the domestic issues so that she was free to concentrate on work. She would have left things alone except she felt that Jack was becoming more demanding and wanted her to do more at home. Kate had thought about separation but dismissed it so that when the row happened it was not a shock for her. She had been feeling tense and dissatisfied for some time in the relationship. The row and subsequent separation actually brought a sense of relief. She had already emotionally distanced herself from Jack and the ties that kept her in the marriage were mostly of a practical rather than emotional or even sexual nature. She is financially independent and the children are all of school going age and Jack is still involved in their care so it all seemed manageable. She could afford to buy in extra help if necessary. So the separation did not evoke a crisis response from Kate.

A crisis for Kate (a different story)

Kate had been so busy with work that she was unaware of Jack's distress. During the row some things were said that she found very hurtful but at the same time she did realise that the arrangements had become imbalanced. Kate was still committed to the relationship so although she was upset she thought that the row would clear the air and they would sort things out. When Jack declared his intention to stay out of the home Kate was still optimistic. However during the first few days of the separation the children became very distressed. Neither Allie nor Jenny would go to school for her and she had to make emergency arrangements at work. Her company were not very helpful and she quickly began to feel overwhelmed both by the demands of her job which was falling behind and the new tasks of dealing with the practicalities of her family's day to day activities. She had developed little or no expertise in coping with the children's routine and this was exasperating because they were also very emotionally distressed. Kate was out of her depth and the problem solving skills she relied on in her work setting were proving inadequate at home.

Crisis and behavioural change

Examining this crisis situation from a purely behavioural perspective does place emphasis on particular aspects of crisis development. It draws attention to those elements of the situation which look at patterns of behaviour and disruption of those patterns. Crises arise when learned responses such as automated responses or reinforced behaviour and skills are not sufficient to deal with the changing circumstances. The impact of a change situation may be lessened if the client has had some time to anticipate such a change, such as with Kate becoming less emotionally dependent on Jack. Kate in the first scenario does not experience crisis because she had, at least to some extent, used behaviourally based skills to anticipate the 'crises'. She had rehearsed at least internally some of the coping strategies she could draw on should she have to face coping alone. Because of this she was in a position to react more effectively to the changed situation at home.

In the second scenario Kate was completely unprepared for the change. She became overwhelmed very quickly and that in itself made it more difficult for her to draw on the type of managerial skills that might have assisted her in sorting out at least the practical problems she faced at home.

Restorative change

One of the first considerations in crisis interventions is always to explore the possibility of restoring clients to their previous level of coping. This may be an interim measure if the coping strategies that were being employed are no longer sufficient for the demands of the situation. Restoring Jack and Kate to their arrangements might only be a very short term measure as the dissatisfaction about the arrangements would not be solved by simply reinstating the original behaviours. At some stage the dissatisfaction would re-emerge and another crisis event would occur. Remember that crisis is an opportunity for change so that restoration to previous levels of coping is often just one step to resolving the crisis. Sometimes restoration of previous skills is enough to allow the crisis to abate and to allow clients to engage their problem solving skills or develop new skills. If the crisis is resolved by simply a restoration to the earlier behaviours then an opportunity for learning new behaviours may be lost. The motivation to learn new responses is more likely to be present in the acute phases of the crisis. Once some degree of coping is restored then the impetus for change may be diluted.

Ameliorative change

In terms of working with Jack and Kate in their crisis it would be important to assess just what skills they already have that could be useful in handling their new circumstances. Reconnecting with already familiar skills that can be employed and developed to address the crisis is a good step since it does not mean starting from scratch with learning new skills but rather means ameliorating their skills set by learning to broaden the application of the skills with which they are familiar. For example Jack is very familiar with organising schedules for the children and arranging activities and dealing with practical problems. Many of these skills will assist him in reorganising his own schedule. The crisis intervention is about re-establishing familiar skills.

Transformative change

For Kate in her crisis it may be more transformative change. If she remains the primary caregiver then she will have to develop new skills in dealing with teenagers and setting boundaries and implementing discipline without the face to face support of her husband. These may be new skills for her and may demand more long term intervention work until she is confident that she can respond to the children in new and appropriate ways.

Concluding comment

While the behavioural approach may have limitations in terms of giving us the tools to fully understand the development of a crisis reaction it does demonstrate the importance of learning new skills as part of the resolution of the crisis. We have already seen that even in behavioural theory there is dispute about the place of thinking (cognition) so we will explore theories related to these processes in the next chapter.

Chapter 5

A Cognitive Approach

A brief history of cognitive theory

The place of psychoanalytic theory as the dominant discourse for therapeutic interventions from the 1930s onwards was discussed in earlier chapters. It is not surprising then that its influence has persisted even into the new millennium. However not all of the therapists and psychotherapists who were trained in psychoanalysis were completely convinced of its merits. Theorists and therapists began to augment mainstream psychoanalytic thinking as propounded by Freud and are often referred to as post Freudians. Some of these were discussed in the chapter dealing with developmental approaches. Even the advances in thinking offered by post Freudians did not satisfy everyone.

Two key thinkers whose work contributed to the shift away from psychoanalytic thinking to a consideration of cognition are Albert Ellis and Aaron Beck. Therapists such as Ellis and Beck in particular went on to explore alternative ways of understanding human nature and then of course developed therapies that built on their ideas. They both focused on different ways in which they saw our thinking impacting on our lives. Ellis (1969) developed an approach linking emotions and thinking called rational emotive therapy while Beck (1976) focused on the cognitive aspects with his cognitive therapy. Both in later years did add the behavioural dimension to their work and we will look at that later.

Reflecting on his career in 1995 Ellis said 'I was always sceptical of orthodox psychoanalysis, mainly because I read all the major works of Freud, Jung and other leading analysts between my sixteenth and twentieth years, and found them interesting but unhelpful' (Ellis and Blau 1998, p.337). Both Ellis and Beck share the belief that the traditional psychoanalytic approach did not address sufficiently the here and now of clients' experiences. Nor did it give sufficient attention to mechanisms that link thinking and emotions with problems or distress. Ellis went on to explore another influential therapist of the day, Rodgers (1957, 1980). Again he was not taken by the Rodgers approach to therapy. For Ellis the client centred therapeutic model developed by Rodgers did address the unconditional acceptance that he believed was central to successfully working with clients but Rodgers's model lacked the active direction that Ellis preferred (Ellis and Blau 1998).

It is worth considering then the development of these cognitive based theories. The development of cognitive theory is usually attributed to the work of Ellis and Beck. The chronology of these developments as tracked by Corey (1996) suggests that Ellis began his work on what he termed 'rational emotive therapy' as far back as the 1950s. The term rational-emotive indicated Ellis's concern not just with thinking or cognition but with the connections between cognition and how the cognitive processes interrelate with our feelings or emotional well being. Later on Ellis added into his configuration the element of behaviour. He published a piece on rational emotive behaviour therapy in 1995. While Ellis may be the grandfather of cognitive-behaviour therapy (Corey 1996) he is not the name most associated with the term cognitive therapy. Ellis's rational emotive terminology was largely superseded by cognitive-behaviour discourse. Ellis, while thanking Beck for comments that placed Ellis at the forefront of the cognitive movement acknowledged Beck's efforts to research and promote cognitive therapy (Ellis and Blau 1998).

Beck himself saw the roots of cognitive therapy in the earlier writings of the 'ego analysts' but suggested that this early iteration of cognitive therapy was more dependent on the insight approaches of psychoanalysis (Beck *et al.* 1990). He attributes the development of cognitive therapy primarily to Ellis and himself. In spite of his accounts of the differences between the cognitive and psychoanalytic and behavioural approaches he comments that behavioural aspects of problems were always emphasised by these cognitive therapists and that what would now be seen as behavioural interventions formed part of cognitive approaches from the beginning. Beck did recognise links with behavioural approaches which would later form the basis of the cognitive behavioural approach.

For the purpose of this chapter initially we are going to consider cognitive theory and cognitive therapy as a separate entity from cognitive behaviour theory and therapy. As we can already see, this in some ways has now become an artificial divide. However the separation is useful here because it allows us to explore the development of each aspect of the more comprehensive cognitive behavioural combined theory. It allows us to clarify the significance of the two sets of ideas, cognitive and behavioural, and so facilitates discussion of the ways in which both impact on the complex nature of crisis therapy.

We will now look at the issues related to cognition as a separate aspect of the clients' world to ensure that we give it sufficient consideration without becoming engaged by behavioural elements of the problem. Since cognitive and behaviour therapies developed separately the history of the amalgamation of the theories to produce a more synthesised theory is a topic in its own right and is best understood through an appreciation of developments in both cognitive and behaviour theory which led up to that synthesis. In fact behaviour theory was well established by the time Ellis and Beck emerged with their rational emotive and cognitive formulations. We will look at behaviour theory and therapy in another chapter. The amalgamation of the ideas of both the cognitive and behavioural schools of thought will be commented on where appropriate.

Some key concepts in cognitive theory

Returning to our earlier consideration of the relationship between theory and therapy we will first take a look at what this means for a cognitive approach. In this case cognitive theory is the set of ideas, concepts and hypotheses that underpin a particular understanding based broadly on ideas about 'thinking' and including ideas about how our thinking processes actually function and influence our experience of life. Cognitive theory privileges this 'thinking' aspect of our nature and so pays less or sometimes even no attention to such things as social networks or behaviour which other theories consider to be important. Cognitive theory offers a specific template for understanding people. Cognitive therapy is essentially the application of that theory (set of ideas, concepts and hypotheses) to working with people to help them deal more effectively with life. An oversimplification of this would be if we accept the theory that negative thinking is the most important factor in preventing us from achieving our goals (theory) then working on our negative thought processes and transforming them to positive thoughts or at a minimum neutralising them would be the most appropriate way to change (therapy). Cognitive theory as we have already established gives preference to ideas about human interaction which privileges our mental processes, thinking and understanding.

Self-esteem and acceptance

Blau summarised the key elements of Ellis's rational emotive therapy (which by the 1990s had become known as REBT – Rational emotive behaviour therapy). He highlighted that REBT teaches an explicit and coherent philosophy for thinking and living more rationally, it discourages conditional self esteem and encourages unconditional acceptance of self and other, it often focuses first on the disturbance of being disturbed rather than the 'reason' for the disturbance, it works on the basis that imposing shoulds and musts leads people to negative picture of themselves, it encourages people to get better with long term changes, it helps people to distinguish between unhealthy and healthy negative emotions and finally it helps people to work on developing better tolerance for frustration. (Ellis and Blau 1998)

Making meaning

Beck (1976) believed that the particular meaning assigned to events determines our emotional response and it is meaning therefore that is at the core of emotional disorders. Based on this theoretical framework that our thinking or how we make meaning of events dictated our response, Beck developed what he termed cognitive therapy – a therapy which sought to redress unhelpful ways of thinking and interpreting our world.

In discussing the importance of meaning within the cognitive approach Beck (1976) clarified that 'the behavioral and psychoanalytic models are similar in that they minimise the importance of meanings that are accessible to introspective observation and report. The behaviorist rejects meaning totally and the psychoanalysts emphasise unconscious meanings' (p.52). For Beck (1976) on the other hand 'the person's report of his ideas, feelings, and wishes provide the raw material for the cognitive model' (p.52). Furthermore, his various interpretations of events are accepted as basic, rock-bottom data – not as a superficial screen over 'deeper' meanings.

Misinterpretation

Beck's idea was that people who experience difficulties may be misinterpreting their experiences, perhaps not recognising all the aspects of an event and only noticing the negative points. He defined a range of 'thinking' mechanisms that might contribute to emotional upset or distress. Scott (1989) summarises some of these mechanisms: 'adverse experiences are over selected, over magnified and attributed to personal deficits. Standards are set too high... success is likely to be minimised or discounted' (p.2). In common parlance we set up a 'no win' situation.

Rational and irrational thinking

At the centre of cognitive therapy are some ideas about rational and irrational thinking. Dryden and Yankura (1995) in their introduction to rational emotive behaviour therapy as expounded by Ellis offer a helpful summary of Ellis's ideas regarding rational and irrational thoughts and beliefs. They identify a number of characteristics of 'rational' thinking and beliefs saying that

> rational beliefs are: flexible, consistent with reality, logical, promoting psychological well being, and help in the pursuit of personally meaningful goals. On the other hand irrational beliefs are: rigid, inconsistent with reality, illogical and interfere with psychological well being and pursuing meaningful goals. (p.vii)

These five characteristics can serve to illuminate some of the connections between cognition (thinking) and crisis experiences which we will explore in the next section of this chapter.

Corey (1996) agreed with this and summarised the focus of REBT as 'transforming an unrealistic, immature, demanding, and absolutist style of thinking into a realistic, mature, logical and empirical approach to thinking and behaving' (p.322). Ellis and Bernard (1986 cited in Corey 1996) described the key components to dealing with irrational beliefs as: detecting the irrational thinking or belief then debating it with the client and finally helping the client to discriminate between rational and irrational thinking about any particular situation.

Beck and Freeman (1990) draw out some of the key elements that differentiate cognitive therapy from psychoanalysis. One of the most significant differences is that while psychoanalysis does indeed see the importance of identifying 'core' problems it sees the nature of this core structure as unconscious and not easily available to patients while cognitive therapy holds the view that these are largely in the realm of awareness (Ingram and Hollon 1986 cited in Beck and Freeman 1990). Because they are in the realm of awareness they are readily accessible.

Automatic thoughts and schema restructuring

According to Beck and Freeman (1990) problems such as 'dysfunctional' feeling and behaviour are largely due to faulty thinking such as 'biased judgements and cognitive errors' (p.5). Corey (1996) suggested that the goal of cognitive therapy as developed by Beck was to change the way clients think by using their automatic thoughts to reach the core schema and begin to introduce the idea of schema restructuring. This is done by encouraging clients to gather and weigh the evidence in support of their beliefs. The technique of cognitive restructuring is particularly useful in application to crisis situations.

Attribution

Cognitive theory attempts to explain the ways in which we understand responsibility and cause. In some cases it may be that when a problem arises people's automatic thought is to take the blame themselves (attribute responsibility to self), or it may be the opposite, that is, to blame someone else (attribute responsibility to other). We will explore this notion of attribution further as it ties in with one of the interventions in this chapter, motivational interviewing. For the moment it is useful to consider work by Brown in 1986 discussed in Sheldon (2000) where it was suggested that 'women are more likely to look outwards for explanations of success (i.e. attribute to other) and inwards for explanations of failure (i.e. attribute to self). The situation is reversed for men. If this still holds true then there is clearly a gender bias present in the attribution mechanism that may be significant in terms of how clients understand their part in problems and solutions.

Cognitive theory and crisis

The centrality of 'thinking' and perception is evident in the earliest writings on crisis intervention. The work of Lindemann in the 1940s is generally seen as the beginning of crisis intervention. In his article on research into the grief reactions of those who suffered bereavements in the Coconut Grove fire he distinguished normal grief from what he termed the symptomatology of acute grief. One of the key factors underlying the symptoms he identified was the presence of 'distorted pictures'. These need to be transformed into a normal grief reaction in order to help in the resolution of the grief (Lindemann 1944). Rapoport (1962) in considering the state of crisis theory discussed the need for 'mental work'. In order to deal effectively with crisis reactions 'the mental work may be directed to correct cognitive perceptions, which means predicting and anticipating outcome through cognitive restructuring. The mental work may also entail rehearsal for reality' (p.29).

The link between cognitive theory and cognitive therapy and crisis is acknowledged by many writers in more recent literature on counselling, psychotherapy and social work such as James (2008), Walsh (2006) and Roberts (2005). The cognitive model of crisis intervention according to James (2008) is based on Ellis's (1962) premise that crisis is rooted in faulty thinking about the events or situations that surround the crisis – not the events themselves, or the facts about the events or situations. James (2008) suggests that crisis therapy drawing on cognitive theory is focused on helping people in crisis to become aware of and change their views and beliefs about the crisis. The basic tenet of the cognitive model is that people can gain control of the crisis in their lives by changing their thinking, especially by recognising and disputing the irrational and self-defeating parts of their cognitions, and by retaining and focusing on the rational and self enhancing elements of their thinking (James 2008). According to James (2008) the messages that people send themselves in crisis become very negative and twisted, in contrast to the reality of the situation.

Walsh (2006) outlines Beck's cognitive interventions which might be applied to a crisis situation. He offers three intervention approaches

1. Make an assessment of the client's cognitive assumptions and identify any distortion that may contribute to the onset of the crisis.

2. When the client does not function with cognitive distortion, educate the overwhelmed clients about ways of managing the crisis and implement directive approach work to problem solving.

3. When the client exhibits significant cognitive distortions, identify situations that trigger the critical misconceptions and determine how these misconceptions can be replaced with new thinking patterns.

Walsh goes on to summarise three categories of strategy based on cognitive theory that can be used to deal with crisis experiences.

- 'The first is cognitive restructuring, used when the client's thinking patterns are distorted and contribute to problem development and persistence.' (These include education, a review of event/thought/feelings, the point/counterpoint technique which is based on the notion of debating with the client the merits of their distorted thinking).

- 'Second is problem solving' for those who do not experience distortions but still struggle.

- The third is 'cognitive coping, where the practitioner helps the client to learn and practise new or more effective ways of dealing with stress and or negative moods (includes self-instruction and communication skills training)'.

(Walsh 2006, p.285)

Roberts and Yeager (2009) agree that a crisis can be viewed as 'an upset in a steady state' (p.2). For them however, the impact of the crisis on an individual depends on (1) the individual's perception of the event as the cause of considerable upset and/or disruption and (2) the individual's inability to resolve the disruption through coping mechanisms. Coping mechanisms include both behavioural skills for coping and cognitive skills. While Roberts's model of crisis intervention (2005) spans many of the theoretical considerations it is the cognitive aspects of coping that are of concern in this chapter.

Addressing the cognitive coping aspect of a crisis situation involves:

- willingness to look at a crisis from the client's perspective

- appreciation of the client's perspective

- assessment of the meaning that the individual has assigned to the event or situation

- consideration of the consistency between the event and the perception of the event for the client

- judgement of whether the response could be considered rational or irrational. This in itself is a major issue and involves exploration of context, power and social norms. It will be discussed in more detail in Chapter 7.

- support for the client in challenging any distorted perceptions which are contributing to the sense of crisis

- restructure of client's thinking to better accommodate the crisis and to enhance self-efficacy (belief in one's own ability to cope)

- facilitation of the development of more helpful thinking processes and beliefs with regard to the perceived crisis and the client's views about dealing with that crisis.

In some situations, working at a cognitive level will be sufficient to handle the crisis or at least put the crisis into a context that appears more manageable to the client. If this is not enough then it may be necessary to draw on some additional theoretical framework to assess and address the crisis.

Rational and irrational thinking: A difference of perception

As already discussed the concepts of rational and irrational thinking are key ideas in cognitive theory. This chapter will make a case that one's belief system about crisis is so central to both the acknowledgement and awareness of crisis that to a large extent it is true to say that 'a crisis is not a crisis until someone thinks it is a crisis'. If you follow through on the logic of this statement then it is important to take into account the perceptions and beliefs not just of the client but also of family members and of course helpers, workers and practitioners themselves. In many cases there is agreement that an event is indeed a crisis event and that the reactions of those involved are consistent with expected crisis reactions. They feel under threat and are no longer in a stable or steady state. But it is also feasible that the designated client does not think there is a crisis but that some family member thinks the situation has reached a crisis. On the other hand it is possible that the worker may be the one who thinks there is a crisis and again the client does not see things in the same way. Another option is that only the client is experiencing or perceiving the crisis.

The following diagram charts out these options and illustrates the relationship between the worker's perception and the rational and irrational perceptions of clients. There is a risk that the worker's perception will at all times be taken as rational and consistent with reality. It is vital to take account of the possibility that even the worker may at times misjudge situations. It is well documented that workers need to be cognisant of the impact of their own personal experiences on their perception and interpretation of clients' situations. There is probably no place where this issue is more vital than when making assessments about crisis. This is one of many important arguments for regular supervision and support for all people working with clients in crisis.

Apart from the need for objectivity with regard to the assessment of a situation as a crisis there is also the fundamental aspect of crisis work which looks to the experience of crisis as an impetus for change. It is this connection with the change process that underpins the importance of making sound judgements about who is really in crisis, illustrated in Figure 5.1 and Figure 5.2.

If the client is not experiencing crisis, despite the fact that the worker thinks there is a crisis, then it is unlikely that the client will engage in change. Golan (1978) pointed out that clients are more likely to be open to receiving help in a time of crisis. If it not a crisis then they may not be receptive to an intervention targeting change.

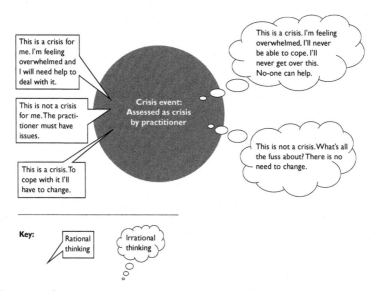

Figure 5.1: Crisis – rational and irrational thinking possibilities

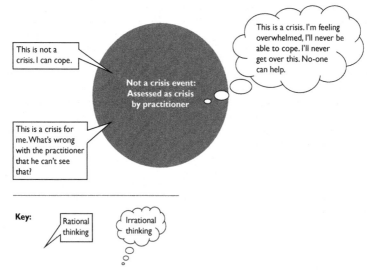

Figure 5.2: Non crisis – rational and irrational thinking possibilities

The following discussion of the case of Susan will be used to illustrate the implications of these ideas for practice.

Susan: A cognitive perspective

An appreciation of cognitive theory can help to make sense of Susan's situation. Susan is experiencing a crisis response to a domestic event. Cognitive theory directs us to consider if that response is consistent with the event. On the surface it seems that a crisis response is inconsistent with the event and so it is likely that Susan is thinking irrationally.

This is an irrational response to non crisis!

On the surface it seems that faulty domestic appliances should not have caused such an intense emotional reaction as to induce a sense of crisis. The event is not life threatening and may not even be seen by many as very challenging. Susan's reaction is not consistent with the nature of the event and so a cognitive approach would be very appropriate. The goal would be to help her to reconsider her distorted view that this is a crisis. This might involve cognitive restructuring where Susan can challenge her ideas that this event is unmanageable. Alternatively it might be useful to work on Susan's beliefs about herself and in particular her thinking that moving out of home was a mistake or even a disaster.

This is a rational response to crisis

It is important to explore one's own views as a practitioner in relation to crisis. Just because we might not consider this a crisis does not mean that Susan thinks and feels the same.

'This is a crisis for me – why can't you see that?'

Susan knows that she has never taken any time to learn about household management. She has never used a washing machine and she has no social network of friends who might be supportive of her in this or other situations in her new flat. She had misgivings about taking sole responsibility for her son and this event is a clear indication that she has a steep learning curve ahead if she is to redress the deficits in her skills. This is actually a realistic assessment on her part of the situation and the enormity of taking on single parenting has just been highlighted by the event. So while the event in itself may not fit with ideas of crisis the meaning of it for Susan does seem like a reasonable acknowledgement of what she has taken on in life. The crisis is more about being overwhelmed by the event than a total lack of self belief or insufficient resources to deal with the event. It is about inability to access this self confidence at the time of the event. When Susan knows that this event is a signal that she has to learn more about taking responsibility for a household she will be willing and able to change.

Dealing with irrational response to crisis

A helpful framework for assessing the meaning of the crisis for a client is to consider whether the event is sufficiently challenging to reasonably evoke a crisis response, or does the crisis response seem to be over reactive and indicative of an irrational response? On the other hand it may be possible to have an irrational response that dismisses an event as insignificant when others around do see it as a crisis. This is equally an irrational response to an event except that in this case it is a crisis that is not being perceived as a crisis. Earlier theoretical frameworks deal with similar examples in a very different way. Here in a cognitive orientation the focus is on the meaning being assigned by the clients and whether that meaning seems to fit with the magnitude of the event. The cognitive perspective also highlights the connection between experiencing a crisis and mental health issues. Sometimes the 'distorted' thinking that induces the crisis may have its roots in a long standing or for that matter newly emerging mental health problem. Since crisis intervention also has its roots in mental health concerns then a crisis therapy response may be indicated.

Worker perception

Apart form the implications for engaging in a change process the discrepancy about whether an event is a crisis may have significance for effective intervention. Where a worker thinks there is a crisis but the client does not it can be resolved in a number of ways:

- the worker through supervision reconsiders his assessment and recognises that the event triggered some crisis response in him but that it was not a crisis for the client

- the worker designs an intervention to help the client recognise the crisis situation and facilitates her to react appropriately.

It will be argued that this second option, designing an intervention to assist the client to reconsider her view of the event/s so that she can appreciate the crisis nature of her situation, forms a link between a cognitive approach to crisis and to motivational interviewing. In the final chapter we will consider this type of crisis work as a strategic form of crisis therapy. The following chart (Figure 5.3) tracks possible client views about change when she is having trouble engaging in the change process:

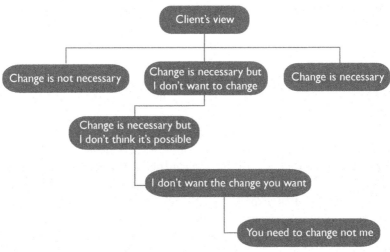

Figure 5.3: Possible client's views of change

Motivational interviewing, cognitive theory and crisis

Beck and Freeman (1990), in offering an overview of cognitive therapy, suggested that the basic premise of the approach is that attributional bias, rather than motivational or response bias, is the main source of dysfunctional affect and conduct. This means that a cognitive approach is more concerned with meaning that is given to situations, that is attributed to a situation by the client, rather than the presence or absence of motivation on the part of the client. Motivational interviewing addressed both attribution and motivation.

Motivational interviewing (MI) was developed in the early 1980s by a psychologist working in the field of alcohol addiction, William (Bill) Miller. He worked with a colleague Steve Rollnick to produce the classic text book on motivational interviewing (1991, 2002). Motivational interviewing, unlike Ellis, did recognise the merits of Rodgers's client centred approach. The value of positive regard for the client lies at the centre of MI. However Miller and Rollnick (1991) did also address the shortfall that Ellis found in the client centred approach. They developed an approach that married the unconditional regard for the client with the directive approach favoured by Ellis. MI is focused on the task of enhancing motivation to engage in change. As such it is a complex combination of cognitive and behavioural influences alongside ideas about relationship (the interaction between the therapist and the client) and motivation.

Miller and Rollnick (2002) identify the central principles of MI: expression of empathy, roll with resistance, avoid argument, develop discrepancy and support self-efficacy.

While all five of these form necessary ingredients for adopting an MI approach we will take a closer look at two elements, self-efficacy and discrepancy. Through these elements we will demonstrate the links to cognitive theory and a cognitive approach to crisis. Put simply it is suggested that expression of empathy, roll with resistance and avoiding argument are interactional guidelines for the development of a motivationally enhancing relationship. Supporting self-efficacy is viewed here as a bridge between the accepting and less directive attributes of the first three elements and the more directive aspects of MI. In supporting self-efficacy the therapist becomes more active in seeking out and highlighting both successes and responsibilities with the client. When moving on to developing discrepancies the therapist takes up a position where he is prepared to create or increase a level of discomfort for the client while attempting to hold the client in a safe and supported way.

The emphasis on cognition is particularly evident in these principles of self-efficacy and developing discrepancy and these are closely related to our concerns in cognitive therapy and more specifically crisis through a cognitive lens. Bandura (1997) has written at length about the importance of self-efficacy as one of the most central and pervasive mechanisms of personal agency. He emphasised the importance of people's belief in their ability to influence their own lives which is of course the basis of self-efficacy. Unless people believe in their ability to produce the desired effect from their actions then there would be little incentive to act. Belief in oneself, that is self-efficacy, influences the course of action people take, how much effort they make, how long they will persevere when faced with obstacles and their resilience in adversity (Bandura 1997).

In his first iteration of MI, Miller (1983) discussed the concept of cognitive dissonance and made a case for its centrality to MI. The importance of cognitive dissonance is associated with the underlying importance of ambivalence to the MI approach. This idea of dissonance relates to the view that Miller and Rollnick (1991) purport that ambivalence is a central concern in motivation. Ideas about this ambivalence in later versions of MI were also associated with the notion of discrepancies. A discrepancy occurs when, for example, behaviour and values are not consistent. The exploration of such a discrepancy can help to identify ambivalence. Miller and Rollnick's (1991) position is that most people do feel ambivalence about change: they want to change and don't want to change at the same time. It is this feeling two ways about change that both holds someone back from change but can also be used to propel someone towards change. For further debate on this topic Harmon-Jones (1999) offers an in depth analysis of the connection between motivation, cognitive dissonance and self-efficacy.

While we have already considered change as a continuum in the introduction there are many other ways to understand change. Before taking a closer look at self-efficacy and discrepancy we need to introduce the concept of the wheel of change. It offers a theoretical framework for understanding change informed by addiction research.

The wheel of change

Motivational interviewing is often associated with the notion of the wheel of change. In fact the two sets of ideas were developed separately. The wheel of change came out of a study on smoking cessation by Prochaska and DiClemente (1982). They wanted to understand the change process in relation to addiction to cigarettes. They formulated the concept of the wheel of change which proffers change as a process with six (sometimes presented now as five) stages. The idea is that people cannot engage in the change process when they are unaware of any need to change or have not given any thought to a need to change. This stage is pre-contemplation. Often the focus on motivating someone to change starts here with attempting to facilitate the client to consider change. Once the client has begun to consider the need to change she is in the contemplation stage of change. This does not mean she is making changes or that she has even made a commitment to change – simply that she is thinking about change.

The goal of the contemplation process for the worker is to support change if that is seen to be necessary and to work with the client so that the client will make a determination that she needs to and is ready to change (the stage of determination). Once this stage is reached then the client can go on to take action and maintain the change. In some versions of the wheel of change consideration is given to relapse as part of the change process in recognition of the fact that sometimes several attempts are made to maintain change before one is successful. Motivational interviewing is particularly useful in working in the early stages of this change process. Its non confrontational and affirming approach can create a non threatening environment in which clients can face some very difficult realities about their situation. The early strategies of MI concentrate on developing this safe environment and the spirit of MI emphasises acceptance, respect, empathy and affirmation.

Self-efficacy, discrepancy and crisis

For the purpose of this discussion we will look first at self-efficacy and then at discrepancy.

Self-efficacy and crisis

Self-efficacy is about helping clients to believe in themselves. This involves both taking responsibility for their actions and also accepting that they have abilities. This fits well with our earlier discussion about rational and irrational thought. If clients are unable to believe that they are in fact capable of change then it will be very difficult for them to undertake change. This lack of self-efficacy may in itself be the root cause of a crisis response. Inability to draw on this sense of self-efficacy leaves clients vulnerable and unable to recourse prior coping strategies. Lack of belief in oneself has the effect of deleting past successes.

Self-efficacy and the wheel of change

In the wheel of change approach self-efficacy can be used to create a level of confidence and belief in oneself so that consideration of change is possible. As one moves through the change process self-efficacy with its confidence and responsibility dimensions underpins the success of engaging with and maintaining change.

Self-efficacy and the continuum of change

Restoration of rational thinking which provides a realistic perception that a client can cope is a first step to resolving a crisis situation. However if coping prior to the crisis was already compromised then the principle of self-efficacy may be used to build up self-confidence not based on ability to resolve the current crisis but based on past success. Through appreciating oneself as having any success then self-efficacy can be supported and utilised as a basis for augmentation of coping strategies.

Discrepancy and crisis

Developing discrepancy is the second aspect of MI that we will consider in relation to crisis. Miller and Rollnick (2002) argue for the importance of recognising the relationship between discrepancy, and motivation to change. For them discrepancy 'underlies the perceived importance of change: no discrepancy, no motivation… The discrepancy is generally between present status and a desired goal, between what is happening and how one would want things to be… The larger the discrepancy the greater the importance of change' (Miller and Rollnick 2002, p.22). How does this concept of discrepancy help us to develop an understanding of cognition and crisis? We have looked at crisis as a perception or a way of thinking. One option we considered was when a worker or family member perceived a crisis but the person involved was not seeing the crisis.

Case example: Drug use and Jim

The relationship between discrepancy and the wheel of change and crisis can best be understood by looking at this case example. Jim is a young man who is using drugs and gets into trouble with a dealer and is beaten up. His family are terrified and in crisis but he sees no issue. From a crisis intervention perspective it is useful to make a clear assessment of who is in crisis… in this case it is the family. The family may feel that their attempts to deal with Jim's drug use have failed and they now feel overwhelmed. The sense of being overwhelmed comes not just from the risks to Jim but also to the potential risks for the other family members as Jim is involved with some very dangerous people.

The opportunity for change may be one that the family need to embrace at this point. Many services in addiction and substance misuse work directly with family members to help them consider new ways of dealing with drug use. Sometimes the family may have to make difficult changes to the support it gives to the person using drugs in a problematic way, perhaps even considering the withdrawal of financial and other supports. Return to the pre-crisis situation will usually result in a period of calm before some other situation or event arises and another crisis happens. Since the perception is that it is Jim who is in crisis it can often be difficult for the family to assess what to do. It may seem that nothing can change until Jim stops using. Of course this is true of the drug use aspect of the situation but the family may need to take a broader view of the situation. This focus on one issue can contribute to faulty thinking and therefore limit problem solving possibilities. Redefining the problem can be distressing as well as eventually helpful for the family.

However, given the risk to Jim it is worth considering if we can help to change his perception of his situation. The change in perception would facilitate him in taking a different look at his life and hopefully considering change in his drug use. This is where MI can be useful. MI can help Jim to consider (contemplate) the fact that his current behaviour is putting him at risk and causing distress to his family. Contemplation is a core cognitive mechanism. MI helps Jim build on this cognitive skill. It can then use the cognitive mechanism of challenging his perception that his use is harmless or perhaps harms only himself. This is a distorted perception and not consistent with reality.

In essence what MI does in developing this discrepancy is create a cognitive crisis for Jim such that it opens up an opportunity for him to consider change. It is important to offer support and affirmation as the goal of MI would be to enhance Jim's possibility for positive change. A cognitive crisis could also be resolved by changing one's value system. In Jim's case this would mean that he could resolve the discrepancy between his perception of his drug use and concern for his family by adjusting his value system to make family seem less important to him.

Discrepancy and the continuum of change

Following on with this case example we can consider the notion of the continuum of change. The type of change outlined for Jim where he begins to think about his drug use as a crisis and decides to address this might be considered as a transformation change. It is likely that he has been using for some time, perhaps since adolescence. Restoration of pre drug use strategies may no longer be enough and while there will be a need to augment his current coping skills it seems that this change in his life style will be very substantial. This may involve ongoing support and may be beyond the remit of a traditional brief crisis intervention. The crisis creates the momentum for change but the change process may take some time. Here is an example of the limitations of the simple crisis intervention paradigm. In Jim's case we are looking first at using crisis in a strategic way by working with Jim to actually recognise his drug use as a crisis. Then, following a short term crisis style intervention to help Jim make some decisions about responding to the crisis it may be necessary to engage longer term yet still crisis related therapeutic responses.

In the final chapter we will explore how the notion of crisis intervention may need to be expanded to incorporate this diversity of situation and make a case that the term crisis therapies is more all encompassing.

Conclusion

Cognitive theory offers a specific framework for understanding our clients. It places emphasis on thinking, perceptions and beliefs. Through a cognitive lens a crisis is only a crisis when you think it's a crisis and essentially it is only a crisis for whoever thinks it is a crisis. This presents a challenge to practitioners working with crisis as they have to be careful about the first phase of crisis work, assessment of the crisis. They need to take into account all the players in a possible crisis event and also take notice of their own perceptions and preconceived ideas. The cognitive approach to crisis focuses on techniques to resolve crisis that deal with changing thinking, building up clients' belief in themselves and helping clients to put crisis events into a manageable perspective. It is an important aspect of understanding how crisis events can create a crisis response and also of course, how events we might not see as a crisis may be experienced by others as a crisis.

We have already seen a flavour of some of the limitations of the cognitive approach and know that the most famous cognitive therapists did incorporate behavioural ideas into their work. In both the behavioural chapter and this chapter we have made some reference to the amalgamation of the two theoretical perspectives to inform cognitive behavioural therapy (CBT). CBT has addressed many of the limitations of the two theories by drawing on both in a more holistic manner. It takes account of the cognitive distortions we have discussed in this chapter as well as the need for enhanced coping skills associated with behavioural ideas. What is particularly interesting about CBT in general is the success it has demonstrated in terms of outcome research. It is one of the most researched therapeutic interventions and is often presented as the most successful (Reisner 2005; Hester and Miller 1995). More recent reviews of therapeutic interventions in general have questioned the focus on outcome measures and controlled experimental studies and highlighted the lack of attention to the process of therapy. A famous study (Project MATCH 1994, 1995a, 1995b) in the area of addiction treatment compared CBT (highly researched and demonstrated successful outcomes) with MI (also researched and successful) with a Twelve Step model (not researched and therefore no proven record of success). The three treatment models were found to have for the most part no discernible difference. So while CBT is obviously an important and useful therapeutic model there is still a lot we don't know about what works. The literature on crisis intervention clearly acknowledges that crisis work in particular had been little researched and this aspect of the work needs attention.

Chapter 6

A Systems Approach

A brief history of systems theories

According to the timeline outlined in the first chapter systems theory was applied to crisis thinking in the early 1980s but systems theories had been around for quite some time before that. Two important points will facilitate the discussion of systems theories. First you will notice systems is referred to as theories rather than in the singular, theory. This is because there have been numerous iterations of theoretical frameworks which have been informed by some basic systems ideas. Each of these has taken a slightly different perspective on the central idea that individuals are part of a system or systems. In order to understand human activity we must consider the individual and the systems within which they live and the interaction between them. This is the second important point. What systems thinking has contributed is not just another perspective on human activity it represents a fundamental shift away from individualising problems to contextualising problems within the social sphere.

For a systems approach the individual can only be understood in context. That context includes but is not confined to family, community as well as broader cultural and environmental factors and influences. Counselling and the helping professions have been caught between the tensions of psychology on the one hand and sociology on the other hand with the emphasis in psychology being on understanding the individual and in sociology on understanding the social context in which the individual lives. This might be challenged as an oversimplification since within psychology there is a discipline of social psychology but the point highlights the existence of competing discourses.

This shift away from the individual focus to the family/community/environment was not a completely new approach. For example, early social workers viewed community work and group work as their main focus and only engaged with casework (work with an individual) as the profession developed. What is perhaps different is that there is now a more widespread acceptance across a range of professions that attempting to understand and work with clients without reference to their wider lived experiences has limitations. This progression from the individual to the system view is akin to the shift in focus from the past (psychoanalysis) to focus on the here and now (CBT) or even focus on the future (as in solution focused work).

Some might refer to such a distinctive change as a paradigm shift. This shift is illustrated in Figure 6.1. The various theories are placed in a continuum under the banner of individual to social to suggest their position with regard to adopting an individual or a socially orientated perspective. Whatever terminology used these are significant markers in the progression of theories about human activities in that they represent dissatisfaction with and an openness to explore and critique the classic theories. They set the ground work for the post-modern era in which social constructionist thinking emerged. This will be the subject of Chapter 8.

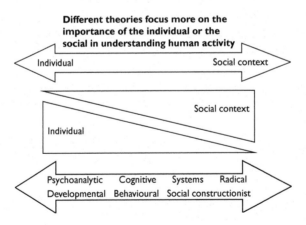

Figure 6.1: The individual and the social in theoretical frameworks

Systems theories like many of the other theoretical frameworks considered in this book grew out of the search for scientific objectivity. The influence of systems theory is generally attributed to the work of a biologist, von Bertalanffy, who was writing about systems from the 1920s, and Payne (1997) would suggest that the ecological school of sociologists in the US from the 1930s is also part of the antecedent to systems theory. This general systems theory views all organisms as systems, made up of many sub systems which are interconnected and interdependent. Change in one part of the system will result in changes in other parts of the system. This concept of a system within systems allows for an understanding of individuals in their environment. It could accommodate the internal systems of individuals as well as the external systems within which they live by considering the individual at a micro system level and social systems as macro systems.

Healy (2005) suggests that there were in fact three waves of systems theories: general systems theory, ecosystems, and complex systems theories. General systems theories although around in the 1920s were not articulated into an applied practice model until the 1960s. According to Healy (2005) general system theory did challenge the behaviourist view that humans were 'reactive automatons' and constructed a notion of psychological pathology as a product of social and cultural influences. In fact Healy (2005) comments that a criticism of general systems theory is that 'it maintained a relatively narrow focus on the interaction between the individual and their immediate environment and failed to address the impact of macro structures on service users' lives' (p.135). This concern about the macro systems becomes more central when looking at the world through the social constructionist and radical theories in Chapters 7 and 8.

If general systems theory failed on the macro front then the next wave, ecosystems attempted to redress this deficit. Through the 1970s the ecosystems theory promoted the view that problems arise not because of individual pathology but rather because of 'a poor fit between a person's environment and his or her needs, capacities, rights and aspirations' (Germain and Gitterman 1996, p.8). The development of a separate ecological systems approach helped to highlight the need to understand how the individual is affected not just by family but by the broader social context. Jack and Jack (2000) stress an ecological systems approach that 'incorporates appropriate analysis of the structural causes of disadvantage and includes full consideration of the wider social support networks that exist beyond the nuclear family' (p.93).

Sometimes it is this broader context that either heightens or modifies the experience of crisis. Jackson-Cherry and Erford (2010) explain that this ecosystem or social context is external to the individual and is composed of environmental factors that are usually outside of the control of the individual. 'Such external factors include historical, economic, developmental, hereditary and cultural contexts' (p.5). The ecological approach has gained new momentum with writers such as Myer and Moore (2006) returning to consider the importance of these ideas.

Healy (2005) did mention three waves of systems theory, the third wave she defined as complex systems. While some others have built on the ideas engendered in general system and ecosystems as distinguished by Healy there has been less evidence to support her idea of this third wave. Healy (2005) herself comments that this more complex view of systems was hampered in its development because of its links to the more technical and even mathematical background in science and sees this wave as being still in an exploratory phase.

Simon (2004) in a discussion on family therapy identified nine different forms of family therapy each informed by slightly different aspects of systemic thinking. These included the structural, strategic, collaborative language, solution focused, narrative as well as some of the earlier Bowen family therapy. We are interested in systems thinking in its broadest sense and so we will include some key ideas across a range of systems based theories.

Key concepts of systems theory

One of the organising themes of this text is the notion that our thinking about human activity has progressed incrementally from a position of focusing almost exclusively on individuals and their unconscious drives to viewing individuals as part of their broader environmental system. Inevitably there has been a lot of crossover between the various theoretical approaches with some systems thinkers demonstrating their earlier commitment to psychoanalytic approaches and others situating themselves firmly in a sociopolitical framework (this more radical approach will be considered in Chapter 7). For example Bowen (1959, 1978) who was among the earliest contributors to the application of system theory in therapy was influenced by ideas rooted in developmental theory, while Satir (1964) did take into account the cognitive dimension of communication. Goldenberg and Goldenberg (2004) discuss what they refer to as the behavioural and cognitive models of family systems therapy. It is possible for different theoretical frameworks to inform and complement each other.

For the moment we will consider some of the key ideas to come from the systems field. These ideas continue to be influential and useful even if critics now suggest that many were an over-simplification of complex phenomena. Like the other theories we have explored they each have their worth and their limitations and I would suggest they each have their place in the chronology of the unfolding understanding of human activity.

Some key aspects of this more complex systems thinking discussed by Healy include that:

- 'A complex system is one in which the behaviour of the whole system is greater than the sum of its parts' (Healy 2005, p.143).

- In general systems typically, social systems are viewed as stable; with complex systems theory change is a usual feature (Warren, Franklin and Streeter 1998, pp.364–5).

- Complex systems are extremely sensitive to initial conditions, that is, small changes at initial phases in the system's development can lead to substantial and complex changes in the behaviour of the system (Capra 1996, p.132).

- This sensitivity means that in practice 'sometimes a short term, and well timed, intervention can have a disproportionately positive impact on the capacity of the service user to achieve their goals' (Healy 2005, p.144).

- Complex theorists do not see people as victims of their social context or as entirely free agents (Healy 2005, p.144).

(adapted from Healy 2005, pp.143–146)

Let's move from these very general ideas to some more specific concepts emanating from systems theories.

Differentiation

Bowen (1978) wrote on the importance of understanding the purpose of family not just in providing a positive environment for children as they grow and develop but also as a place that they move on from to take up a more independent place in the world. He developed the concept of differentiation to capture the process of young people's journey to more independent life outside the family while maintaining links to the family of origin. This idea is quite reminiscent of the developmental phases that

Erikson proposed earlier. The key difference is that in Bowen's work he attempted to address the interaction processes between the individual and the family so that achieving independence and a sense of identity is a family and not just an individual task.

Homeostasis

Hoffman (1981) in her work reviewing the foundations of family therapy attributes the term family homeostasis to family therapist Jackson. She quotes Jackson where he described family as 'a closed information system in which variations in output or behaviour are feedback in order to correct the system's response' (p.18). Jackson was working with another key figure in the family therapy movement Bateson. Family therapy is one of the leading practice models associated with the application of systems theory to working with clients. Many family therapy practitioners have contributed to the elucidation of how systemic concepts can be employed in practice. According to Hoffman (1981) the Bateson group became identified with an idea of the family as an equilibrium maintaining entity because so much of the group's research was done with families that had an extremely restricted range of behaviour. This concept of homeostasis suggests that families and not individuals may resist change in an attempt to maintain this stability seen by Bateson as family equilibrium.

Boundaries

Minuchin (1974) another family therapist, also worked with this idea of families seeking stability. Minuchin utilised ideas about the structure and function of the family. He developed the idea that families as systems had boundaries. He believed that we could understand a lot about the individual in the family by observing the types of boundaries in the family. Families with 'enmeshed boundaries' were likely to be very caught up in themselves and closed to other outside influence while at the other extreme families with loose or unformed boundaries were vulnerable to too much influence from outside and had little sense of family unification to support or protect them.

Function

The early iterations of family therapy such as Minuchin (1974) were influenced by sociological ideas about structural functionalism. While the ideas that emerged from this era of family systems work are still around today successive thinkers were critical of the prescriptive and normative constructs underpinning the movement. Ideas such as the function of the symptom did not survive the metamorphis from system thinking to social constructionist thinking as we will explore in Chapter 8.

For now though it is useful to consider the impact of these systems concepts. The notion of function influenced how a problem was defined. As is characteristic of all systems thinking, the problem is viewed as embedded in the family not as a feature of one individual within the family. For the structural functionalist thinkers the problem was often seen as serving some organising 'function' in the family. This leads on to considering the part of the problem in maintaining family functioning and therefore asks the worker to address the fact that other family members may be invested in holding on to the 'problem' because it was helping to keep stability in the family (homeostasis).

This idea has great significance in formulating strategies to bring about change in the family as it means we have to look not just at what a change might mean for the individual but also what it might do to the family as a whole. The ideas about the problem serving a function offered some explanation as to the intractable nature of some problems. Workers may be in fact working against some aspect of behaviour or activity that the family is invested in keeping. One of the dangers of this is that it might promote a view that families are resistant and therefore that their ideas can be discounted. This concept sometimes referred to as the dysfunctional family is to my mind an unhelpful one and unfortunately one that seems to have persisted in spite of the fact that it later became clear (social constructionist thinking) that the notions of problem formation and retention as first developed in systems failed to capture the complexity of the issue.

Communication patterns and roles

Proponents of the structural ideas within systems (Satir 1964; Minuchin 1974; Minuchin and Fishman 1981) sought to understand communication patterns within families as a way of understanding individuals in families and the sort of problems that might emerge. Part of what they explored was the way in which families were structured so that each member had a role and that roles were understood by members in the family even if not consciously assigned or discussed. The family, according to this structural systems thinking, conveyed the expectations about roles through a set of rules. Rules were seen to be upheld through a system of feedback and sanctions so that each family member played their role and kept the system in this steady state.

Feedback

'Feedback' in systems theory means the same as the term in general conversation. It means a process through which we can find out about the effect our actions have on other people including family members and our broader environment. Feedback may be verbal but it can also be more subtle. Feedback may take the form of some reciprocal response in the form of action or even inaction. This systems idea as applied in family therapy helps to explore interaction between people where some actions are being maintained because of the feedback given to the individual. It is reminiscent of the notion of reinforcement that we discussed in behavioural theory. This relationship between action and feedback results in what systems theory refers to as a feedback loop. This is a systems way of understanding recurring or circular patterns of behaviour. In the same way that we distinguished between positive and negative reinforcement in behaviour theory we can look at positive and negative feedback in systems.

Goldenberg and Goldenberg (2004) offer a helpful clarification when they note that negative feedback 'triggers those necessary changes that serve to put the system back "on track" and guards the system's steady state, maintaining homeostasis in the face of change' (p.81). Positive feedback 'leads to further change by augmenting or accelerating the initial deviation... positive feedback mechanisms are operating here as the family adapts to change by modifying its structure, and the systems stability is regained' (p.81). According to Goldenberg and Goldenberg (2004) 'systems require both positive and negative feedback – the former to accommodate new information and changing conditions and the latter, when appropriate, to maintain the status quo' (p.81). The place of stability or homeostasis within systems thinking has been much disputed with earlier thinkers seeing this as a central aspect of the system while social constructionist ideas are more likely to think that change is happening all the time.

Family life cycle

Other proponents of family systems Carter and McGoldrick also demonstrated a connection to the developmental movement of the 1950s. Carter and McGoldrick (1989) in their classic text articulated their ideas about the development of families over time. They suggested that families moved through a number of stages from forming a couple, getting married, having babies, then family life with young children, teenagers and ultimately young adults, children leaving home and parents restabilising their relationship without children. This like any model which attempts to capture a complex set of experiences can now be criticised as an over-simplification. The concept in its inception was probably overly influenced by a middle class, white American cultural concept of family life. The basic notion that we could trace stages in family life is however useful provided it does not err on the side of becoming prescriptive. Any attempt to draw on this family life cycle to establish what the 'normal' family should do would be unhelpful and possibly destructive.

Triangulation

Hoffman (1981) defines triangulation as 'a process that occurs in all families, all social groups, as twosomes form to the exclusion of, or against, a third' (p.29). A triangle is an essential building block for Haley's theory of pathological systems and Minuchin's structural approach to family theory. Triangulation is particularly interesting when working with couples as the worker has to be aware that in her interaction with the couple she is likely to be drawn into a triangulation situation. This can happen when one of members of the couple tries to draw the worker onto their side of an argument or where one partner assumes that the worker is on his or her side. This triangulation can result in creating a stability which makes change more difficult resulting in the couple becoming more entrenched in their individual positions. According to Hoffman (1981) Bowen's ideas about triangulation were more fluid. Ultimately any number of people could become involved in a series of triangulated relationships. Where tension between two people is mediated by the involvement of a third party then others may become involved siding with one or other of the parties and so multiple family members, and even outsiders such as professionals can get caught up in the interaction. This can often happen when family members are under stress. The tension between members results in them attempting to form alliances within the family or their broader social circle.

Hypothesising, circularity, and neutrality

Hypothesising

By hypothesising we refer to the formulation by the therapist of a hypothesis based upon the information she possesses regarding the family she is interviewing. The hypothesis establishes a starting point for the investigation as well as her verification of the validity of this hypothesis based upon specific methods and skills. If the hypothesis is proven false, the therapist must form a second hypothesis based upon the information gathered during the testing of the first (Palazzoli *et al.* 1980).

Circularity

Circularity is described by Palazzoli *et al.* (1980) as 'the capacity of the therapist to conduct his investigation on the basis of feedback from the family in response to information he solicits about relationships and, therefore, about difference and change' (p.6). Sometimes this is referred to as circular questioning where the therapist seeks to develop understanding and gather information about family dynamics by consulting with one member of the family about how he or she sees the relationship between two other members. This conversation happens in the presence of the other two so that communication is enhanced. Circularity captures the notion that interaction between family members is complex and multifaceted and that different participants in the interaction can have different perspectives on what appears to be the same event or situation.

Neutrality

This concept refers to the therapist's neutral positioning in the therapeutic encounter. The more the therapist assimilates the systemic epistemology, the more interested she is in provoking feedback and collecting information and the less apt to make moral judgements of any kind. This is what maintaining neutrality is about. No-one should feel that the therapist has taken sides and yet all should feel listened to and included. This involves what Palazzoli *et al.* (1980) called the creation of successive alliances with each family member as the therapy progresses. The end result of the successive alliances is that the therapist is allied with everyone and no-one at the same time. Therapists will observe and neutralise as early as possible any attempt towards coalition, seduction, or privileged relationships with the therapist made by any member or subgroup of the family.

Cybernetics

The term 'cybernetics' is associated with computer sciences and is used to explain the mechanisms though which the system is organised and regulated itself. Goldenberg and Goldenberg (2004) offer this distinction between first order and second order cybernetics. First order cybernetics 'direct attention to structure, patterns of organisation and control through feedback cycles. It is further assumed that the system being observed was separate from the observer, who could objectively study and carry out changes in the system while remaining outside the system itself' (p.14). Second order cybernetics seen as a construct within a post-modern theoretical framework 'insists there can be no outside, independent observer of a system, since anyone attempting to observe and change a system is by definition a participant who both influences and in turn is influenced by the system' (p.14). This concept of second order cybernetics becomes more central when considering the social constructions theories in Chapter 8. For now it is sufficient to note that the notion of cybernetics helps to draw attention to the relationship between stability and change which we will now look at through the concepts of first and second order change.

First and second order change

These concepts in systems theory are particularly important because they describe the theoretical position on change. In the introduction we asked questions about change. Who needs to change, what do they need to change, who decides on these issues and how does change occur? The concepts of first and second order change add another dimension to the question of change: At what level is change taking place?

Watzlawick, Weakland and Fisch (1974) delineated 'two different types of change: one that occurs within a given system which itself remains unchanged, and one whose occurrence changes the system itself' (p.10). Goldenberg and Goldenberg (2004) explain that 'first order changes are superficial behavioural changes within a system that do not change the structure', while 'second order changes require a fundamental revision of the systems structure and function... changing the rules of the system and consequently reorganising the...system so it reaches a different level of functioning' (p.245). First order change is then easier to achieve but more unlikely to be maintained. The type of change involved in second order change because it actually changes the system itself, makes it more likely that the change will be sustained. This is a useful distinction for considering change in response to crisis situations. Second order change is more related to the concept of transformative change outlined in the introduction to this book while first order change may relate to the restorative and augmentative change categories. However there is an important distinction as some theoretical perspectives (social constructionist as applied in solution focused therapy for example) support a view that a restoration to old coping behaviour and/or building on already familiar behaviour if it is appropriate may be easier to achieve and more sustainable than transformation.

Social networks

The ecological dimension of systems theory situates individuals in their social context. This context consists of a diverse set of social networks that together create the individual's macro system. The network can include extended family, neighbourhood, school, church, work, as well as actual social, cultural, economic and political environment. In Jack and Jack's (2000) definition of an ecological system they highlight the importance of addressing the structural aspects of social networks as these networks explain in part some of the factors that may influence disadvantage and vulnerability. This broader definition of social networks is operationalised to some extent in community social work and community development but is little seen in the general counselling field. While the concept can be attributed to systems theory the application of the concept in intervention is most likely to form part of a radical approach to working with clients and so we will return to this in Chapter 7 to consider its connection to crisis therapies.

Systems theory and crisis

Jackson-Cherry and Erford (2010) date the interest in crisis and family back to the work of Hill in the 1950s. They note that in his works of 1949 and 1958, Hill was among the first to conceptualise a crisis theory that applied to family. His work took account of the stress on families, their resources to deal with stress and the meaning of that stress within the family. While this work was interested in the impact on families it did not address the more complex structural and interactive aspects of family that were explored later by family systems thinkers. It was McCubbin and Patterson (1982), according to Jackson-Cherry and Erford (2010) who built on Hill's ideas and began to consider the impact of crisis on the family system where the system evolves and becomes more complex over time. They also took cognisance of an important aspect of crisis that we are interested in, that is the opportunity for growth and development that might evolve from dealing with a crisis. The more extended model of McCubbin and Patterson looked at crisis intervention as both a reduction of stress and an adaptation and growth. 'Adaptation is an outcome variable, involving changes in functioning and perception. More than the simple reduction of stress, adaptation is the degree to which long-term change has occurred in response to the demands of stressors and crisis events' (Jackson-Cherry and Erford 2010, p.5).

Crisis writers have applied the concept of equilibrium to understanding individuals in crisis. Caplan (1964) defined crisis as 'an upset in a steady state' (pp.39–40). Later Golan (1978) discusses crisis as 'a hazardous event that disturbs the individual's homeostatic balance and puts him in a vulnerable state' (p.8). Systems thinkers on the other hand use the concept of homeostasis or equilibrium to understand the tendency of the family to seek stability. In a system informed crisis approach the concept of equilibrium should direct attention not just to the individual seeking balance or equilibrium but to the processes within the wider family or even social system which tend to prefer the status quo. Individuals may experience crisis because they want change when the system/s they are involved with do not. A family life cycle example of this might be a child growing up in a family where he is not ready to accommodate the independence of adulthood or a couple who have separated where one of them refuses to accept that the relationship has changed.

Aguilera in her work on crisis builds on the idea that there are two distinct types of crisis, situational and maturational. The situational crisis for Aguilera (1990) is potentially any situation that is perceived by an individual as a crisis that is experienced as causing an imbalance in his life. The type of situations referred to include such events as loss of role or status, rape, physical illness, onset of Alzheimer's and suicide. She notes that available situational support and available coping mechanisms also play a part in whether or not any one situation becomes a crisis. So this means that Aguilera (1990) takes account of cognitive (perception), behavioural (coping), support and homeostasis (systems) in her elucidation of crisis. Aguilera is still focused on how the individual responds but the acknowledgement of the place of situational supports indicates an acceptance of the systems ideas that the individual cannot be understood outside of his social context.

The developmental or maturational crisis draws on some of the ideas in Chapter 3 (developmental crisis) as well as those included in the family life cycle concept in systems theory. Aguilera's (1990) view is that

> all people are exposed to a variety of stressors virtually all the time throughout the course of their life spans... the problem is in the degree and duration of these stressors and in the variable range of

personal responses and capacities to withstand and cope with such stimuli. (p.186)

She uses the concept of life cycle phases to capture the challenge to adapt that is faced at different, usually relatively predictable times in life and discusses the possibility that prolonged stress response may result in maladaptive or destructive outcome. Problems in working through these life transitions may be experienced as a crisis. Again in this aspect of her crisis intervention model Aguilera (1990) emphasises the importance of including situational supports in the assessment and sees the crisis as a loss of homeostasis which she calls equilibrium.

Roberts (2005) in his work on crisis tends to focus more on the individual than the systemic context although he has explored ideas about family crisis (Roberts 1991). Roberts's (2005) seven stage model fits more readily within the cognitive, behavioural theoretical framework already discussed. He (2005) does however acknowledge that 'the resilient person generally has sufficiently high self-esteem, a social support network, the necessary problem solving skills to bounce back, cope with, and thrive in the aftermath of stressful life events or trauma' (pp.23–24). Contributors to Roberts's *Crisis Intervention Handbook* (2005) such as Greene *et al.*, Yeager and Gregoire, and Granvold (2005) engage with the post-modern ideas emanating from social constructionist theory including the application of solution focused and strengths perspective to crisis. These will be explored in the next chapter.

Crisis intervention has its origins in the field of mental health. The emphasis on the individual to be found in the crisis literature is consistent with the chronological development in theory that informed mental health practices as we discussed earlier in this chapter. As we noted developments in theories to explain the connections between individuals' behaviour and the social systems in which they live are relatively recent. The family systems ideas have been applied, mostly through the family therapy movement within mental health. Application of ideas about the significance of wider systems is less commonplace. There is little emphasis on the ecosystem perspective within the crisis literature although a growing interest in natural disasters and the trauma associated with such events is likely to draw on that systems framework. Some theoretical frameworks that attempt to incorporate the interaction of the individual and wider systems will be examined in the chapter on radical approaches. However within the crisis literature writers such as Johnson *et al.* (2008) demonstrate the shift in focus away from the individual and towards capturing the importance of networks and systems. Bindman and Flowers (2008) in discussing the crisis resolution teams (CRTs) in the UK comment that all crises encountered by the crisis resolution teams (CRTs) arise in a social context. In most, problems in the social environment have a direct role in precipitating the crises. Bridgett and Gijsman (2008) examine the nature and importance of social networks and look at the place of family and social supports in their crisis work. Collins and Collins (2005) also employ an ecological systems perspective in their consideration of crisis and trauma.

Susan: A systems perspective

A crisis leading to restoration of homeostasis

Susan and Jake form a nuclear family, parent and child. Their extended family then includes grandparents, aunts, uncles, and cousins. For Susan and Jake this may not be such a clear distinction as they have lived with Susan's parents in a situation where the parents/grandparents had more of a parental role with Jake. The structural concept of boundaries might indicate that this lack of role distinction either created or reflected some boundary issues for the family. Susan and Jake as a family unit might be viewed as enmeshed with the extended family where Susan did not engage fully with her role as mother and moved fluidly between 'mothering' and 'daughtering'. Susan often allowed her parents to parent Jake while she identified more with her role as a daughter than a mother. Jake's arrival caused the family to make adaptations in the way it functioned and had an impact on all members of the family. Adherence to these new roles and the unspoken agreement with the allied rules of how the family operate had created stability within the family, a stability that was disrupted when Susan moved out.

Susan's parents, Bill and Kate have been in the role of parents for a long time. They did think that the opportunity to move on from these responsibilities might arise when Susan got pregnant but as it turned out Susan's relationship with her boyfriend, Jake's father did not last and so Susan and her baby moved back home to Bill and Kate. While there was no actual discussion of the arrangements it just seemed to happen that Kate took her role as carer/mother and postponed a renegotiation of a primary role as Bill's partner. Bill for his part continued with his interests and hobbies outside the home and again postponed plans to travel and spend more time with Kate. Having put their own lives on hold Bill and Kate were taken by surprise when Susan announced her plan to leave the home and set up on her own with Jake. While looking forward to the earlier opportunity to have more time to themselves, Bill and Kate had readjusted their lives to include Jake and found this 'enforced' separation very difficult.

When Susan called because she was in trouble with the apartment Bill and Kate were delighted to be needed again and were keen to have Susan and Jake return home. They wanted to be helpful but this incident reinforced their belief that Susan was not ready to manage alone. They took immediate action to bring them home and Bill handled the situation himself. This left Susan once again in a dependent role. The crisis was resolved because Susan accepted her parents' assessment and decided that the plumbing problem was a sign of things to come and returned home. The family was restored to equilibrium, Bill and Kate did not have to renegotiate their relationship, Susan has postponed taking on an independent mothering role.

This resolution in systems terms is likely to restore the equilibrium in the family. However the life cycle stage of becoming independent for Susan remains as a possible disruptive feature for the future and so it is possible that the restored state of play in the family will be less stable than before as all concerned realise that it has come about because of a sense of failure for Susan and not because of a rational choice. The opportunity for Susan to embrace a new challenge has been lost and with it the opportunity to learn new skills, create a new role for herself and establish new boundaries within her extended family.

A systems crisis leading to change

Susan was struggling to cope on her own with Jake. The experience of moving out of her home was very emotional and stressful. She was aware that she owed her parents a lot because they stood by her and helped without question when she came home with Jake. She was very grateful and had thought about moving out for a long time before letting Bill and Kate know of her plan. The move was stressful as was the reorganising of day to day arrangements for work and Jake's school schedule. Because Susan knew that her parents were upset she had made the decision to deal with the new arrangements without their involvement.

After a long day at work Susan often wondered if she could cope. On the day of the flooding Susan was particularly tired as she had had a bad night's sleep the night before because Jake had been upset. He sometimes woke up looking for Kate. Work had been busy and she was beginning to have reservations about this whole independence thing. The flooded apartment just sent her over the edge. It seemed to reconfirm her worst fears that she was not going to cope and in the panic of the situation she found herself screaming at Jake which she had never done before.

She called Bill to tell him about the flood and asked if they could come home. Bill got Susan to explain about the flood. While immediately reassuring Susan that of course they could come home anytime they wanted, Bill engaged Susan in a discussion about what might need to be done now in response to the 'crisis' of the flooding in the apartment. Bill let Susan know that he understood this was difficult and distressing and that he could call over as soon as he got back from his walk. In the meantime Bill talked Susan through the instruction about how to turn off the water. In reality Susan did realise that she would have to do something as she knew she had to stop the flooding before she left. Susan managed to turn off the main supply of water and stopped the flooding. Bill checked with Susan about the arrangements with the landlord about this type of problem. Susan remembered she had a number and with Bill's prompting she decided to call before leaving the apartment.

The landlord was not particularly helpful but when he realised that there was immediate damage being done to his property he gave Susan the number of an emergency plumbing service and she called the service and they agreed to send someone at once. Within the hour the flood situation was under control and Susan called Bill to say they might come over for the night but that the crisis was over. Once the flooring and damp was sorted Susan and Jake returned to the apartment and Susan was enjoying telling everyone about her first domestic emergency and how she had learned a bit about plumbing.

In the first scenario one could say that the decision to move out of home was simply a change in behaviour not accompanied by the necessary systems change (second order change) that could sustain Susan through initial problems. Bill and Kate it appears had not readjusted their relationship either and so the triangle that included Susan continued to be appealing as a form of stability to the couple.

In the second scenario Bill and Kate had already made adjustments and they saw their role as a support to her new life as they had with their other children. The family system had changed and was able to accommodate the separation while still offering support (second order change). Susan may have been testing out her place in the family and once reassured that she was still welcome calmed down enough to deal with the responsibilities she now had.

From the change perspective it is important to understand that the crisis did create an opportunity for Susan to grow into her new role. This opportunity came with some distress but if that had been resolved as in the first situation by immediately withdrawing her from the crisis event then the crisis would not have resulted in increased self-esteem and confidence and confirmation of a second order systems change.

Ecological systems perspective

This perspective draws attention to other factors such as neighbours, friends and broader social networks. Susan might not have experienced a crisis if she had been aware of a residents' association or building supervisor or even neighbourhood response that might have been an obvious source of support or service provision in the case of the domestic flooding.

Suicide as a crisis from a systems perspective

Suicide is identified by Aguilera (1990) as a situational crisis. It is a crisis that is outside of what one expects as part of the developmental process. A suicide is usually traumatic for those left behind. Suicide itself is often the result of some type of crisis. The type of crisis that results in suicide may not be one that is obvious to those around. Suicide is itself a very complex phenomena and this chapter is not going to attempt to deal with the full range of issues to be considered. For a more in depth exploration of suicide consult Bartlett and Daughhetee (2010); Jobes, Berman and Martin (2005); and Weiss (2001). In the context of the current work we will consider some of the factors that might be important when thinking of suicide from a systems based crisis intervention approach.

Suicide

Someone experiencing difficulties may turn to suicide for many reasons maybe because he sees no alternatives or because he believes that his suicide will be better for those around him. Suicide can be seen as the only option for many reasons ranging from a distorted view or understanding of a situation, distress in response to crisis, to serious mental illness. Aguilera (1998) reports that depression is the most common suicidal symptom. She also says that the majority of adolescent suicide completers exhibit symptoms of some psychiatric disorder before their deaths, although only a small percentage ever received mental health treatment (1998). On the other hand Jobes, Berman and Martin (2005) tell us that research indicates that most people who kill themselves give some form of prior warning.

What we do know is that completed suicide is much rarer than attempted suicide. This means that for some the failed attempt at suicide can offer the opportunity to get help in dealing with their suicidal thoughts. It also means that there is pressure on those working and living with potentially suicidal people to be able to observe and assess the signs in order to prevent a completed suicide. Aguilera (1998) comments that in relation to adolescents 'the focus for suicide prevention programs clearly must be on the ability of parents and teachers to recognise symptoms that indicate that the adolescent may be at risk for suicidal behaviours' (p.172).

A crisis therapy model may be helpful when someone has become aware of a risk of suicide. While a crisis approach may be helpful in mitigating the immediate risk of an attempt in some cases the final act of suicide may be the final part of a pattern of mental illness that is of long standing. Other more extensive long term and even medical models of helping a client with mental health problems may be more appropriate. A key aspect of crisis work with suicide, no matter which of the theoretical frameworks you apply, will be the assessment of risk. This is a priority in all cases of crisis and of course this means that a crisis worker must be familiar with the tools that are available to make good assessment of a client's risk.

Assessment of risk of suicide

There are many tools available to assess crisis and suicide risk. Teater (2010) mentions a number of useful resources such as the Beck Hopelessness Scale, the Beck Scale for Suicide Ideation, the suicide Potential Lethality Scale and the Modified Scale for Suicide Ideation. He quotes Roberts and Yeager's (2005) comment that the focus on suicide does not assess the extent to which individuals perceive a crisis or their ability to overcome crisis. This means that we should assess risk including suicide risk in all cases of crisis.

Bartlett and Daughhetee (2010) claim that

individuals who are considering suicide as an option have characteristics that can be recognised, and an assessment of risk can be made... By focusing attention on and evaluating the client's verbal and non verbal communication in terms of what the client is feeling, doing and thinking, the assessing professional is able to make an accurate judgement about the suicide risk that the client represents. (p.109)

However, according to Jobes, Berman and Martin (2005) attempts to construct inventories and use psychological tests to predict suicide have thus far failed. Here is a dilemma not just for the person experiencing suicidal ideas but also for all those around him. In the absence of accurate measures to assess risk we are likely to assess many more to be at risk of suicide than will ever complete the act of suicide (Jobes, Berman and Martin 2005).

The reality is that in spite of major efforts to develop accurate assessment protocols the World Health Organization (2007) reported that there was a 60 per cent increase in suicide over the past 45 years and that suicide attempts were 20 times more common than completed suicide among the general population. This means that although we as a society may be taking the crisis of suicide seriously we still have a long way to go to improve our management and prevention of suicide risk. This leads on to some ideas about what a systems framework had to offer in terms of considering the crisis of suicide.

Differentiating crisis leading to suicide and suicide as a crisis

Crisis intervention may then be most helpful in working with a number of aspects of suicide. First, crisis therapy may be useful when working directly with someone who is having suicidal thoughts. It may be possible to identify a person as vulnerable because he has experienced a crisis or even a series of crisis events. When these crisis events have depleted coping abilities and have led to self destructive or suicidal thinking then a crisis intervention may be helpful in dealing with the immediate risk of suicide. However such an approach is dependent on the person being able to talk about his suicidal thoughts or in some way express his extreme distress. It might otherwise be difficult to identify someone at risk of suicide. Detection and prevention are known to be very difficult in relation to suicide and often we have to be over inclusive, in other words err on the side of caution. This results in identifying many more people who are at risk than will ever actually commit suicide. In this type of incidence a crisis may lead to suicide. These factors are among many that make work with suicide challenging for professionals.

This leads to a second aspect of crisis and suicide that may benefit from a crisis therapy approach. Professionals who are working with crisis on an ongoing basis will need support and help in dealing with the emotional impact of this on their personal and professional lives. There is of course the more direct stress on workers who are in contact with clients who are at high risk of suicide. Bartlett and Daughhetee (2010) comment on workers' own anxiety associated with having a suicidal client.

Adams and Payne (2009) in a discussion of power, social work and mental health offer a case example where the social worker following agency protocol is asked to decide if a client who has already attempted suicide is still at serious risk. This is a weighty decision for one person to make about another when an error may result in a completed suicide. In light of the pressure of this type of work there are now well defined guidelines and procedures designed to be effective in managing suicide situations and also safe guarding those trying to assess risk and prevent actual fatalities. Ensuring compliance with such defined policies, protocols and guidelines can be in itself a further source of stress. So crisis therapies may be helpful in being diligent about taking care of those exposed to crisis through their work and also in acknowledging the risk that may be associated with the pressure of exposure to suicide situations. Thompson (1991) reminded us that the

> pressurised and emotionally demanding nature of crisis work can lead to poor decision making, unwise moves and a potentially disastrous impact on clients. This is one of the risks of crisis work: those who are brave enough to undertake it deserve the 'safety net' benefit of effective supervision. (p.117)

The family system
An important aspect of systems consideration of suicide refers to the family system. A crisis model may be helpful in working with the families and friends who are trying to come to terms with an attempted suicide or the loss of a loved one through suicide. The crisis here may result from the distress of a failed suicide attempt or from a completed suicide. The attempt and the completed suicide may each have a devastating impact on families and loved ones. Bartlett and Daughhetee (2010) estimate that 'in the US for every suicide, an average of six people are affected and left behind to deal with... the emotional tragedy' (p.106). In light of the fact that Aguilera (1998) pointed out that the focus of many prevention strategies is the ability of those close to someone to recognise the symptoms of risk then it is inevitable that this pressure may result in serious distress when their vigilance is not sufficient to prevent the suicide.

The broader social system
Systems theories also draw our attention to factors outside immediate family and considers the broader social systems that may be affected by a suicide. Friends, wider family members, work mates, school mates, in fact anyone who is connected to the victim. This mapping of the wider system can play a significant role in prevention of further tragedy. Through some of the eco mapping techniques a range of people may be identified who would benefit from crisis intervention to help them to deal with their distress, guilt, sadness and other emotions associated with their loss. Concepts such as family boundaries and roles within the family

can be useful in assessing who is available to the family as a resource as well as assisting in identifying who may need help and support.

In order to understand the full implications of a system interpretation of suicide it is worth looking to sociological attempts to develop a theory of suicide.

Theories of suicide

While we are concerned here about theories that inform crisis work it is important to note that most cases of crisis relate to some issue that in itself has a specialised body of knowledge. When this is the case it is useful to be familiar with these specialist areas of applied knowledge. Suicide as you can see is such a case. There is a vast wealth of theory and practice knowledge which can help to inform our practice. We will consider some of these ideas here.

Suicide is a very emotive subject. It highlights our worst fears of being powerless to help someone we love. This is evident in the discussion of suicide in the context of family systems. Certainly understanding suicide and its impact on the family system is an important aspect of systems theory. Systems theory however also challenges us to step outside the intensity of the interpersonal distress that accompanies suicide and consider some broader, systemic influences. One of the themes in the current book is the notion of an individual–social continuum. Suicide is often considered solely in its manifestation at the individual end of that continuum. Since this chapter is attempting to explore ideas of the 'social' end of the continuum it will not look in depth at the individual dimensions of suicide although it is acknowledged that these are very important and may even be the most significant aspects of many attempted and completed suicides.

For the purposes of making this shift from individual and personal concerns to social considerations we will first draw on some of the ideas emanating from early sociological theory. As we have already discussed systems theory is itself based within a sociological framework so it is consistent to look to these ideas to help us explore systems thinking and suicide. It was Durkheim in 1897 who drew attention to the social phenomena of suicide (Durkheim 1951). In his classic work on suicide the sociologist did not focus on the question of psychological motivation but rather attempted to make sense of rates of suicide. He developed the theory that two key variables determined the rate of suicide in any group. These variables he identified as the variation in levels of social integration and social regulation (Durkheim 1951). Based on these variables he postulated that there were four types of suicide.

Explained in simple terms one form of suicide resulted from a social attachment or belonging that advocates or promotes the act of suicide. In today's world this might include such experiences as terrorist suicide attacks. Suicide is for a cause perceived as being beyond the individual (high integration and regulation). At the other extreme of this is another form of suicide because of a feeling there are no other options (low integration and high regulation). Sometimes this type of suicide may be related to mental health, or distorted perception or even emotional despair and on the outside no-one might realise that the person was feeling so cut off. This social isolation (low integration and low regulation) can also lead to suicide. Durkheim also noted that suicide may have some type of social mechanism that is tied in with lowering the social taboo on suicide (low social regulation and social integration). Although Durkheim disputed the idea of suicide because of imitation this form of suicide does fit here. This form of suicide may be relevant in a situation where one person commits suicide in a particular geographical area and another one of two suicides happen in a relatively short space of time.

Not everyone agrees with Durkheim's theory. Johnson (1979) dismissed some of the ideas and suggested that Durkheim had over extended his theory. Yet Durkheim's ideas are still used in discussing social aspects of suicide (Kushner and Sterk 2005). Durkheim's ideas are considered by Kushner and Sterk (2005) in their exploration of the relationship between social capital and suicide. These researchers (2005) are critical of those who claim that social capital, inferred in Durkheim's work, is likely to result in a reduction in morbidity and mortality. They are cautious about the 'current enthusiasm for social capital as a core concept in suicide prevention' and warn 'that the health benefits of social capital should not serve as an occasion to view it as a substitute for other forms of capital and status' (p.1142). This discussion of social capital relates to the ideas about social integration and social regulation central to Durkheim's theory of suicide. The idea here is that Durkheim simplified his interpretation and that if we focus on social integration or social cohesion as a major contributory factor to suicide it may result in blaming the victim, in this case the community without reference to broader social issues such as disadvantage, oppression or class. Some of these issues bring us into a radical discourse so it is enough here to raise the points as we will explore some of these in Chapter 7.

A final concern about the social integration interpretation in Durkheim is that it did not take account of the place of women in families. More recent evidence contradicts the idea of Durkheim that integration into family protected women. Kushner and Sterk (2005) reference research that found women's submersion into family offered no special protection and further that women living in the most integrated societies had higher incidence of suicide than men (referenced Johnson 1979 and Rosenthal 1999).

Systemic ideas about suicide can also be found in the context of family therapy. Haley (1980) for example described ways in which young people in a family may attempt to restore stability in a troubled situation by acting out in some way. The notion of the function of the symptom is part of a structural functional interpretation of family systems as espoused by Minuchin (1974) and Paolino and McCrady (1977). In the context of suicide this may indicate that a family member may attempt or even complete a suicide with the intention of helping the family. Aldridge (1998) in a more extensive discussion of these systemic ideas references a number of authors who connect suicide to family conflict as well as the social disorganisation mentioned earlier. He also suggests that suicide may be a form of communication or an expression of hostility within the family system. Aldridge (1998) also reports on researchers who suggest that there is often a direct contact with such behaviour in a family history.

Case example: Suicide, systems and Jack

A young man Jack aged 17 years is found by his brother hanging from a rope in the local community sports facility. The family are devastated and both his parents blame themselves for not seeing the signs that he was troubled. Jack's brother, Joey along with Jack's school friends try to make sense of what seems to them a senseless death. It seems that Jack was under pressure in his school work. He had decided he wanted to go to university and knew that would demand high performance in his exams. He had been working hard and everyone thought he was on track to achieve a place in university. It may have been that Jack was not so confident and that as the time for exams approached he felt more and more unable to deal with the pressure and stress. The terrible thing is that no-one will ever really know what led him to such a desperate act.

One of his friends suggested that Jack had been interested in a girl at school but that recently he found out she was dating someone else. Did that trigger a further stress for him? He was at a vulnerable age for mental health issues and although his parents were not alerted by any signs of depression or more serious psychotic disorders they now are unsure of their judgement.

Since sadly Jack has already completed his suicide the focus of intervention/therapy shifts to others in his family and school system. One of the central tasks of any crisis approach is to assess risk. This will be discussed further in the final chapter. Of course the main concern will be for immediate family. Perhaps Joey is of particular importance since he not only has to deal with the loss of his brother but with the trauma of finding him. Loss through suicide will often bring feelings of guilt and self recrimination as well as despair and overwhelming sadness (see Worden 2002). The family will need support through this difficult time but crisis therapy will be a brief and focused response to help them through the immediate aftermath of the suicide, the family may need further help and this will be part of the crisis assessment. Sometimes those close to someone who has completed a suicide are seen as survivors. One concern might be that Joey or some of Jack's close friends may experience something like survivor guilt. This would be an important risk factor to be worked with.

Collins and Collins (2005) suggest a six step process that could usefully be adjusted in this type of crisis: be supportive and empathic with the client as this will help to foster a good relationship with him (in this case first Jack's family and then others as you become aware of their involvement in the crisis); work with the immediate needs of the family to help stabilise the situation; explore and assess the dimensions of the crisis and the family reactions; help identify possible actions and anticipate future needs and arrange follow up.

The connection between individuals and their social context is central to systems thinking so this social aspect will also be considered. Here we are looking at a systems interpretation of what needs to happen to manage this crisis. As a preventative strategy all those associated with Jack might be considered to be at risk. This means that starting with family and then working our towards school mates, the school in general, and those preparing for exams specifically, those involved in the sports centre and any others who may be identified as being affected by Jack's suicide should be offered support and be assessed for risk of further crisis responses.

This means that the crisis response goes well beyond the individual who committed suicide and reaches out to the many systems he was associated with. This represents a shift from the individual to the social aspects of suicide. Following assessment of risk the crisis should also result in opportunity. It may be useful for some of those wider systems to reconsider their support of young men like Jack and consider if there was anything that might have helped Jack seek help. The management of this crisis may involve placing some resources in the school for students who are in similar situations regardless of whether they were friendly with Jack or not. In some incidences crises similar to this case may be the starting point for developing not just local and community strategies to prevent suicide but also national strategies.

Realising that Jack is not only a victim himself but that he is part of a high risk group means that it is not enough to respond to Jack and his family but it should highlight the need for social action to address suicide as a social crisis. This is the importance of recognising that even in a case of suicide the issue of opportunity for change can be important. Change as defined in systems terms should address not just immediate stabilising change (first order change) but more extensive second order change such as national policy or even international research.

Concluding comment

The systems perspective draws a picture of a world where the individual is viewed not just as one person or personality dealing with his situation. Systems theories have as a core interpretation the individual as part of a social context. This paradigm shift changes not just what we see and understand, from the point of view of any intervention it changes the questions we ask and the perspective we develop about what needs to change along with the ideas about how that change might actually happen. In this chapter some decisions have been made to attribute key ideas to a broad exposition of what systems theories encapsulate. In reality it is more difficult to identify indisputable cut off lines between the theoretical positions informed by the shift of focus from the individual to the social. Certainly early systems thinkers lived in a 'modern' world where certainty and science prevailed even in relation to human activities. This certainty brought with it a confidence about the therapeutic strategies we employed. There is a certain comfort in working with the idea that we can define and identify what is normal while at the same time remaining objective observers. But not all those who were influenced by systems thinking were satisfied with this position. As we move into the thinking of more radical theory we will see how some professionals became concerned that seeing the individual as part of a social context was not enough. More steps were needed to address being organised to change the social and not just the individual. Later we will look at further developments among those who allied themselves with systems thinking but then began to see the world differently through the 'post-modern lens'. The links between systems thinking and what some might say was an inevitable progression to social constructionist influences will be explored in Chapter 8.

Chapter 7

A Radical Approach

Introduction

This chapter will look at a radical approach to understanding crisis. It will consider the development of radical theory and the place of ideas drawn from a radical framework in the counselling, social work and community field. The radical frame of reference is critical in highlighting the limitations of individually focused brief interventions where socio-economic and political issues may be overlooked or ignored.

A brief history of radical theory

There is no one radical theory but rather ideas, concepts and ideals that privilege an interpretation that places central importance on the socio-economic-political context within which events take place. Contributions from writers such as Marx formulated ideas about how everyday life is influenced by powerful economic and political imperatives. Freire (1970) applied these ideas about power and oppression in discussing the relationship between education and disadvantage. His ideas later influenced community development.

While it is possible to see the connections between the radical and community development the connections between these radical ideas and counselling is less obvious. It is possible to take account of the actions of others within a counselling framework. We have seen how 'others' can be significant in the psychologically based behavioural and cognitive approaches and of course in systems ideas. However most counselling interventions work directly with an individual and or family members and so they rarely consider an interpretation of problems through a sociopolitical lens. By taking a more all-encompassing view of radical thinking then you also would be justified in including anti-racist, anti-oppressive and anti-discriminatory approaches. These are of course very much part of any counselling or helping practice (Payne 1997).

Perhaps social work is or should be more centrally concerned with this radical perspective since the notion of the social is part of the profession's title. Social work even where it implements individual interventions should by definition always have an eye to the social implications of any problem situation. While the radical theory/ies may have come later social work itself was developed as a response to social as well as individually defined problems and issues. Social work has embraced some of the broader views of radical thinking in its attempts to engage with anti-racist, anti-oppressive and anti-discriminatory practice. One criticism of social work may be that over time it lost this focus and was persuaded by the developments in individually focused psychological theory. Even in relation to the interpretation of anti-oppressive practice Pearse (2009) points out that 'one of the debates is about the extent to which oppression is systematic and structural as opposed to primarily interpersonal' (p.196). In other words focusing on ensuring that as workers we engage in anti-racist, anti-oppressive and anti-discriminatory practice with our clients is not a sufficient response to the demands of a radical approach.

Ferguson (2008) echoes these criticisms of radical theory 'it is allegedly, a theory in search of a practice' (p.101) but also offers the counterargument of Langan and Lee (1989) in which they make the case that radical social workers are steeped in practice: 'Too often such theory is removed from reality, denying for example the impact of racism or the extent to which government legislation…is making social workers agents of punitive and repressive policies' (p.7). These elements of practice address the interpersonal relationship with clients but may overlook the wider sociopolitical environment and structural oppression that clients are subjected to. While acknowledging that these issues are not just important aspects of the interpersonal counselling relationship it is fair to say that ideas about anti-racist, anti-oppressive and anti-discriminatory practice are not exclusive to radical theory and have gained a wider acceptance as part of best practice. For this chapter we will focus on concepts underpinning radical thinking rather than best practice in its broader application. Radical theory is then an umbrella term for a range of ideas that move from the individual to the political. In reviewing the radical school of thought we will return to the field of social work to help us understand the developments that lead to an acknowledgement of the 'political' in the personal.

The paradigm shift in its move away from an emphasis on the psychological limitations of the individual and onto sociopolitical economic failings can be dated in the field of social work from the 1960s. Fook (2002) claims that from the earliest days the social work ethos of helping people included something to do with the social environment and never focused simply on the individual. She comments that those first social workers such as Jane Adams from 1910 worked in situations where disparity and discrimination based on social class were evident. The traditional ways of understanding human behaviour (as discussed in earlier chapters) reinforced the view that the individual could be held responsible for their situation. Fook (1993) suggested that the emergence of radical critique in the 1960s put the issue of social context back on the agenda and broadened it to include understandings of how the socio-economic structure and historical conditions also influence individual experience.

The notion that the structural aspects of the socio-economic and political world are important for understanding individual situations and events is consistent with the ecological systems view we discussed in Chapter 6. Langan and Lee (1989) over 20 years ago warned that radical ideas might be threatened by attempts to redefine social issues such as poverty and unemployment as personal problems. They were also concerned that adopting this narrow view of problems would support the development of responses based on 'reactionary' and 'punitive' ideologies (p.16). Economic prosperity may have contributed to complacency about both the definition of social problems and the acceptance of reactionary and punitive interventions.

The radical approach goes further in exploring issues of power and structure and includes a politicised awareness of oppression and inequality which is seen to be perpetrated and sustained through these structures. Gray and Webb (2009) identify a number of strands within an overall radical discourse in social work. In what might be considered a re-emergence of radical thinking for the 21st century they distinguish between what they refer to as structural, critical and feminist social work. All of these draw on basic radical ideology but stress different aspects of this ideology in their focus for change. In considering some key ideas in this radical discourse we will draw on these various strands of radical social work as well as taking account of the radical social work movement of the 1960s and 1970s.

Perhaps one of the difficulties in translating radical theory into a practice response is the fact that there is no one theory. In fact even in what appears to be one school of thought such as a feminist approach there are actually many strands all of which have a slightly different central concern or viewpoint. Orme (2009) distinguishes between liberal feminist theory, Marxist feminism, radical feminism and post-modern feminism. Each of these strands of feminism share a common concern that relates to gender as a focal aspect of discrimination or inequity. Orme (2009) suggests that

> the liberal feminism is more concerned with white, middle class women and takes a more individual approach while socialist feminism although also concerned with women and inequality takes both an individual and collective view. Socialist feminism is based on mainstream political thinking that focuses on individual rights and opportunities and champions the collective interests of working class people as a group. (p.67)

Critical social work in some ways represents the new face of radical discourse. Gray and Webb (2009) clarify that 'critical social work seeks to understand how dominant relations of power operate through and across systems of discourse and deconstruct and reconstruct these discourses' (p.80). They quote Fook (2002) who said that 'a post-modern and critical approach to social work is primarily concerned with practicing in ways which further a society without domination, exploitation and oppression' (p.18). Perhaps one of the most helpful aspects of this critical discourse is that it includes consideration of the power differential that exists between worker, counsellor, therapist, social worker, psychologist and their client. In general there is a commitment to reflective practice in order to keep this power issue in view while working with clients. The worker is not an objective outsider but in the same way that second order cybernetics in systems thinking took cognisance of the worker as an actor, so too the critical approach addresses the complexity of this interactive relationship.

Structural social work again with its radical roots moves on to focus on emancipation and social justice. 'Structural social work seeks the transformation of society towards values of freedom, humanitarianism, collectivism, equality, self determination and popular participation' (Hick and Murray 2009, p.86).

Keeping in mind that we are no longer talking about a unified radical theory but rather a diversity of approaches all of which are related to and informed by radical theory we will extract some key ideas that will later contribute to our unfolding story of radical influences on crisis thinking.

Key concepts in radical approaches

When looking at key terms in this approach it becomes evident that the approach has more to say about a theory or orientation than about a specific application to practice. At the centre of the radical framework is the principle that 'the personal is political'. All interaction with clients must take place with this in mind. It impacts on all interaction, assessment and planning. It influences defining targets for change and methods of achieving change. In this radical approach all professionals need to take account of the power differential that underpins their relationships with those they 'help'.

Problems

The key underlying concept in this set of theories is that the problems as experienced by individuals are social in nature. Problems are to a greater or lesser extent created as a result of some social inequity. In attempting to understand a problem from the client's perspective the worker/helper must keep this basic principle in mind. There is a risk that both the worker and the client may be so absorbed by their surroundings that they are unaware of the elements of domination and oppression highlighted in this radical discourse. This is the mechanism that supports a personalised definition of a social problem where the individual is held responsible. This is the opposite to the radical position.

Ferguson and Woodward (2009) comment on Midgley's account that the radical approach in social work was for America 'the road not taken' (p.16). Radical social work just did not develop in the same way as other aspects of social work:

> The reasons for this are not hard to see. Any approach that locates the sources of people's problems primarily in the structures of the society in which they live, and which encourages social workers to challenge these structures in their day-to-day practice, is likely to be viewed less favourably by governments and funding bodies than those approaches that instead highlight clients' individual

inadequacies, faulty thought patterns or stunted emotional development. (Ferguson and Woodward 2009, p.16)

Inequity

Problems may be derived from basic inequity in the distribution of resources in society. There are different ways of conceptualising this inequity; it may be seen as about class, gender, race, power and/or resources. Whatever the interpretation, problems arise for our clients because of some aspect of inequity which makes it more difficult for them to live than others. This inequity must form part of our understanding of problem formation and of course be the focus or one focus of problem resolution.

Change

Any meaningful change must incorporate structural change. This is reminiscent of the second order change we discussed in systems theory. The additional aspect of the radical notion of change is that the systemic change must occur all the way to a socio-economic-political level not just at a family systems or community level. Critical social work, Gray and Webb (2009) and structural social work, Hick and Murray (2009) for example seek social transformation and view individual problems in the light of economic and political domination. Some feminist approaches although concerned with individual issues look to collective change for the resolution of problems. From the worker perspective this means that investment in direct work with clients will always be seen as of limited value unless accompanied by some change effort that addresses the larger socio-economic and political factors that are contributing to the creation and maintenance of the problem as experienced by the individual client. This has implications for ideas such as resistance to change. If the client is in a powerless position as seen through the radical lens then it would be inevitable that she would struggle to engage in change negotiations with the worker since she is in fact not really the problem or at least is only one aspect of the problem.

Change then is not about restoration to a prior level of coping. It is not about simply augmenting prior skills – real change is transformative, not necessarily transformative of the individual but transformative of the social context in which the individual lives.

Client

The term client has been used in this book more out of convenience than conviction. It is seen as an improvement on the medicalised term 'patient' but does not go far enough to satisfy the radical discourse of this chapter. Camilleri (1999) in a related discussion commented that 'social welfare theorists have resurrected the notion of citizenship as a source of renewal for the welfare state. It is about developing a new "social contract" between citizenry and the state in the development and delivery of services' (p.34). The concept of citizen then might fit better with the radical framework. It certainly promotes the view that individuals have rights and that the state has some responsibility to address the needs of the individual.

But it may not be sufficiently empowering to satisfy radical ideals – perhaps the notion of customer goes further. The concept of customer again reinforces the notion of rights but may in fact detract from the social contract that is implicit in the term citizen. A customer while having rights is usually seen as someone with sufficient resources to shop around. Since one of the basic premises of the radical approach is that such resources are in themselves problematic, they are not evenly or fairly distributed then the customer notion may simply reinforce socially constructed inequalities. The customer term also does not help us to resolve the question of whether the customer is the person paying for the service or if the customer is the person receiving the service.

From a reflective or radical perspective probably what is most important is that we question this terminology and that we design interventions based on a presumption that the person we are working with may experience discrimination or oppression simply by being labelled 'a client'. Smith (2008) suggests that 'the challenge is not to redefine the object of concern, but to identify a more rounded and holistic approach to understanding the power dynamics which surround the individual distinctively and uniquely' (p.152).

Working in collaboration with or in partnership with people is seen as more consistent with a radical frame of reference. This too has its difficulties in that it implies an equality which may not be an accurate reflection of the relationship. Social workers and others in the 'caring' profession often find themselves struggling to reconcile a role of care and support with a role of control and monitoring. This is another dilemma for the radically orientated worker.

In essence the 'client' as viewed by other theoretical approaches to therapy does not really exist. The client, in so far as we are using the term to refer to the person in need of help and attempting to change, is not the individual at all but the socio-economic and political context in which our client is attempting to survive. Of course this radical definition of who is the 'client' probably results in identifying one of the most resistant and unco-operative 'clients' you will ever meet... all of us.

Discrimination, racism

These are complex and challenging terms. They are however very important in this radical perspective and have become more acknowledged in the world of professional helping in general. It is not acceptable to distract from these unfortunate realities because they are difficult to define, identify or address. Discrimination in this context refers to any act or situation which results in an individual or group being treated in a negative way because of gender, race, class or other perceived difference. Anti-discriminatory practice should be predicated on not just accepting but valuing this diversity. Concern with anti-discriminatory practice demands consideration of the individual in her social context because it is that social context which creates, generates, supports, maintains and ultimately must challenge discrimination.

Where the focus of the discrimination is a person's or group's ethnic origins or race then this is referred to as racism. Thompson (1997) highlights a number of the key elements of racism:

> racism is an ideology, it involves holding a set of values and beliefs, it relates to real or imagined biological characteristics, it is a negative term with strong connotations and is used as a term of abuse...discrimination and oppression, stereotypical assumptions are used to sustain this negativity and thus maintain dominance, power and privilege. (p.62)

Mullaly (1993) comments that early radical social work theory neglected patriarchy and racism as sources of oppression. Racism and discrimination are then forms of oppression. Social work and other professionals place a strong value on anti-racist practice (see Dominelli 1988).

Oppression and power

> Oppression is a structurally based phenomenon that affects individuals and communities. Oppression can lead to many negative outcomes, such as physical death, due to a lack of adequate healthcare, violence or forms of homicide and suicide, individuals more readily targeted for incarceration or even increases in general hopelessness leading to self doubt, despair or false beliefs. (Teater 2010, p.56)

Fook (2002) writes that 'the idea of a connection between knowledge and power is a postmodern one, in that it is argued that whatever group controls the way things are seen in some ways also have the power to control the way things are' (p.37). Oppression is then about a person or group using whatever powers or influence they have to create situations where they retain control. Oppression involves domination of others employing any source of power available. For those in the helping profession we try to acknowledge the risks of inadvertently taking advantage of positions of authority by committing to the principles of anti-oppressive practice (Dominelli 2002).

Burke and Harrison note that oppression is often seen through marginalising the oppressed (2009). They see

> anti-oppressive practice as a dynamic process based on complex changing patterns of social relations. It looks at the use and abuse of power not only in relation to individual or organisational behaviour...but also in relation to broader social structures, for example health, education, political and economic, media and cultural systems and their routine provision of services and rewards for powerful groups at local as well as national and international levels. (p.209)

Fook (2002) cautions that even as professional helpers we need to be cognisant of this. 'Professionals therefore stand to lose quite a bit of power if alternative perspectives are accepted, so a challenge to the exclusive knowledge of professionals is a direct challenge to their power base' (p.37). The risk is that professionals privilege their knowledge and this legitimates their superiority and power in terms of 'knowing' what the problems are and what needs to be done. This could then become the foundation of oppression perpetrated against clients. Professionals and workers need to be vigilant, and Fook (2002) sees engaging in reflective practice as a safe guard against misuse of knowledge or power by the professional.

Power has multiple origins. Power can have a personal or structural base. Depending on what is valued in a society, power may come from resources, position, knowledge, appearance, even celebrity. An interesting feature of power which Fook (2002) commented on, is that if you have power then you can influence what society values and therefore can ensure that you retain power. She also questions social workers' ambivalence about power. They feel uncomfortable with their own personal and structural power and so construct themselves as relatively powerless. This serves to highlight the point that people may not be powerful or powerless in all situations. The notion of power may in fact be relative. Thinking of power in the therapeutic context raises the question of empowerment.

Empowerment

Smith (2008) in discussing empowerment comments that 'the implication is that empowering practice must work not just at the level of individual concerns and needs, but also in the context of wider (cultural and social) forces which incorporate inbuilt oppressive tendencies' (p. 149). Empowerment is a contentious issue. It seems that empowerment of those without power should be a positive value and in its simplest terms it is. But empowerment implies giving power to someone who has no power. As workers is this the role we see for ourselves, giving away some of our power? Some of the points raised by Fook (2002) in her discussion of empowerment are worth noting here. She asks does empowerment mean taking power from one to give to another, is it true to say some people are powerful while other are powerless? Adams (2008) adds that empowerment is about self empowerment. He defines empowerment as

> the capacity of individuals, groups and/or communities to take control of their circumstances, exercise power and achieve their own goals, the process by which, individually and collectively, they are able to help themselves and others to maximise the quality of their lives. (p. 17)

Social justice and social action

If you begin to look at problems not as individual concerns but as created and defined in and through a social context then inevitably change will involve social action. Social action means targeting the social in the change process. Undertaking this ideological shift is underpinned by a commitment to social justice. Social justice is about creating a society where diversity is embraced and valued and where fairness, integrity, impartiality and honesty prevail. It is predicated on a view that justice is a social as well as individual construct and so is consistent with the radical theory world view.

We will consider some examples of crisis that illustrate the radical interpretation later in this chapter. But first we must face the challenge of looking at Susan and Jake as a political not personal crisis.

Susan and Jake: A radical perspective

Let's consider how Susan, Jake and their family might be seen when looking through a radical theory lens. Of course the first and most important point that it is not actually about just Susan and her family. The radical lens exposes the broader social context so it's about Susan, Jake and family as they live in the current social, economic and political environment. These broader issues translate the potential personal crisis into a potential social crisis.

Drawing on two of the radically informed theories we have mentioned we will reinvestigate the domestic problem described in the introduction. The first one we will consider is a feminist based perspective.

Not a crisis

Susan has been raised in a society with clearly defined male and female role descriptors. To fit in with the social norms of femininity it would not be expected that Susan should be given the education for living that includes information about a male engendered activity such a plumbing. This discriminatory assignment of role based information has left Susan inadequately prepared to deal with simple domestic situations without a male partner to turn to. In the absence of a male partner she can and does turn to her father. As long as Susan's father is available and willing to help out then Susan will not experience a crisis. She will however experience multiple limitations to her independence because her social context has created a definition of her role as woman and mother that precludes preparation for the type of task she faced in this scenario. As long as Susan is happy in her belief that this is 'man work' then she will simply turn to a male figure to handle the situation and not question the issue. The crisis is resolved. Of course it is quite possible that a male protagonist may experience the same or similar limitation however the gendered view of the scenario draws attention to the more intransigent social environment that creates this limitation rather than more personal preferences or choice that may lead to a similar skills deficit.

A feminist crisis

If Susan sees the domestic difficulty as an indication of what may lie ahead in terms of her thwarted attempts to become independent then she may experience a crisis. Susan recognises that she is a powerless woman faced with multiple domestic responsibilities and expectations. She has been raised in a patriarchal society where she was not equipped to deal with life without the support of a male figure. She realises that this is not just about her it is a much larger problem. Such subordination is not just a personal experience but reflects a social reality which embodies a patriarchal oppression of women. This support of women in crisis is portrayed as benign but actually is the embodiment of a fundamental inequity creating a female dependency.

A personal crisis

Susan has engaged in a tenancy agreement with a landlord and finds herself in a position where the landlord has supplied sub standard facilities. She has to deal with the immediate flooding problem since other neighbours are being affected. The danger is that because people are feeling vulnerable and threatened by the potential of damage to their homes they look to Susan as the problem. In a sense the neighbours get involved in a dispute because they address their frustration and anger at Susan. She is very distressed and this is exacerbated by the anger being expressed by neighbours as they too attempt to cope with the situation. She feels responsible for the difficulties her plumbing problems have created. She does not have a relationship with the other tenants and so cannot rely on a more impersonal system of communication to draw on mutual support. Susan finds herself faced in a crisis situation. She feels she cannot cope and sees herself as responsible.

A structural crisis

Susan is a tenant. Her landlord is engaged in the profit oriented business of supplying homes for rent. He has rented out an apartment to Susan without completing a check on the facilities. There was a fault in the plumbing system and this was not detected because no check was completed after the last tenant left. While the tenants in the building are looking to Susan as the problem they are not addressing their annoyance at the landlord who is in fact responsible. This creates a crisis that a radical take would interpret as a failure of collective action. A radical resolution would entail addressing the larger question of the rights of tenants. Resolving the crisis in a way that was transformative would perhaps involve the formation of a residents' group to negotiate with the landlord to ensure that any damage was repaired and that in future the tenants as a collective could deal with such issues. Susan is no longer the focus of the problem or target for the resolution of the problem, it becomes a collective issue. To further the radical view then some aspect of the inequality of resource distribution which supports the capitalist venture of property ownership where a landlord can neglect the welfare of tenants without penalty might need to be considered and representation could be made to support tenants' rights. Susan has been oppressed by the profit motivation of the landlord classes. Ultimately in a radically informed analysis the underlying political and economic structures that support the system whereby landlords can own multiple residences and Susan cannot afford one residence would be scrutinised.

Radical theory and crisis

There is no established radical crisis intervention approach. The dominance of the individual discourse around crisis may in some way account for the lack of a radical socio-economic political crisis intervention model. Crisis by its nature tends to draw those affected into an introspective place where immediacy and personal or family risk become of paramount importance. The ideas embedded in a radical interpretation of crisis would draw attention to factors that might have exacerbated the crisis but which may not have an immediately obvious connection. Structural issues such as distribution of resources or political orientation while creating an environment that might underpin the escalation into a crisis state can rarely be directly associated with the crisis. This indirect connection can be further obscured by the need for an immediate response to the crisis which precludes the longer term measures of changing established structural contributory factors.

Perhaps one place where we might expect the link between a crisis event and the broader or macro systems that are the focus of a radical viewpoint is in relation to a national crisis. This after all does draw attention away from the individual and onto the social and even political. We have discussed in Chapter 6 the notion of macro systems as the extension of a systems informed view of crisis. The systems perspective attempted to deal with an expanse of systems that covered the individual, the family, the community and then the socio-economic and political structures (macro systems). In the radical approach it is the last of these the socio-economic and political system that is of concern.

James (2008) in a review of disaster responses highlights the need to include local, national and international policies in a model for crisis assessment. The challenge for a radical crisis model is to enable the individual who is directly affected by a crisis event to turn their attention from the immediately relevant experience of the crisis to the more distant structural factors that may underpin the crisis. Often the macro system is only engaged at the level of ameliorating the crisis. Those dealing with a crisis event look to the political structures, national and international, for assistance. If assistance is delivered then the minute to minute dealing with the crisis will take precedence. By the time the crisis is resolved and post-crisis equilibrium is established there may be little or no change to the core macro systems structure. Radical perspective would demand that structural factors implicated in precipitating the crisis should be transformed not just restored or adapted.

One of the problems in applying a radical perspective to crisis intervention may be that it offers somewhat conflicting views on change. Crisis intervention was the original brief intervention. The idea was that when faced with a crisis old ways of coping were insufficient to meet the demands of resolving the crisis and so change was required in order to restore stability. Such changes were seen to take place within a short time of the onset of the crisis. In fact the mechanism for change is embedded in the momentum created by the crisis. Once the crisis is over then change becomes less likely and the challenge is to sustain the changes achieved in response to the crisis. The method does allow for the possibility of transformation where the change achieved was so extensive that it has encompassed new and hitherto unknown skills. In the systems chapter we talked about first and second order change in a similar way.

Within the radical framework transformative change is not just desirable but necessary. Restoration to the pre-crisis structures would mean that the next crisis was already inevitable. Adaptive or augmentative change would not be sufficient as these would probably only address the appearance of things and not the actual inequity that concerns the radical thinker. The changes envisioned by the radical thinker may require long term and sustained pressure. Sometimes a crisis event can draw attention to an injustice or inadequacy in structures. The onset of a crisis may highlight this and instigate the change process. More often structural change is incremental and slow. Perhaps crisis and a radical perspective are incompatible because they are set in different time frames and have different goals.

This analysis overlooks an aspect of the relationship between crisis and the radical perspective that is important. A crisis can draw attention to the association between structural problems and the crisis only if those involved are prepared to acknowledge that association. Often the structural response to a crisis is one that mirrors the patriarchy of the feminist critique. Adopting a helpful and caring stance by assisting with the crisis may have the effect of keeping attention away from the underlying structural factors that have contributed to the escalation of the crisis. If this underlying causal relationship is not understood and acknowledged then there will be no call for a radical change. Applying this analysis to crisis events supports a radical perspective of crisis. It suggests that the radical approach to crisis may be thwarted not by incompatible goals or time frames but rather by the success of the macro system in detracting attention away from its part in a crisis and focusing on the immediacy of an emergency response. Crisis intervention requires a balanced response. It is a priority that people are safe. So an assessment and a planned response are vital to ensure that safety. However if the response completely resolves the crisis then it is possible that the impetus for change is lost. This may be the key to the lack of development of a radical crisis model. Where crisis occurs enacting a response to resolve the immediate risk may have the fortuitous effect of neutralising the impetus to target structural change. At a time of crisis people may be simply relieved to return to 'normal', that is, the homeostasis discussed in the systemic approach. A return to pre-crisis equilibrium may as Hill (1958) pointed out imply that things are better than before but it might also mean things are about as good as before or even that things are less satisfactory than before the crisis.

Before we leave this discussion of crisis through a radical perspective it is worth noting a point about structural change. While radical theories are about addressing deficiencies in the socio-economic political arena the direction of the change is also important. Radical thinkers want change to be in the direction of more participative, collective action where people can have more of an influence on the environment in which they live. Langan and Lee (1986) warned against reactionary and punitive ideologies. Given that we are looking at the mechanisms through which change can be initiated by a crisis event we should also consider what type of change. From a radical perspective then one of the dangers inherent in crisis driven change is that it may offer a rationale for the implementation of exactly the reactionary and punitive changes that the radical thinkers feared the most. It is possible that people in a crisis state will be accepting of changes that are presented as vital for their safety even where such changes would have been unacceptable prior to the crisis. From the radical perspective such changes should be viewed with at the very least caution and possibly with trepidation. For example there have been criticisms levied at governments for implementing more intrusive infringements on civil liberties in response to the threat of terrorism. Such changes might not be tolerated or supported if it were not for the fear educed by crisis, an inevitable response threat.

Case example: A natural disaster as a radical crisis

Thompson (1991) included in his work on crisis a chapter on the concept of a disaster as a crisis. More recent books on crisis seem to have followed this lead and now often include a chapter or more on aspects of natural or man-made disasters: Roberts (ed.) 2005, James 2008, Jackson-Cherry and Erford (eds) 2010. These works are very useful because they not only raise awareness of the connections between disasters and crisis but contribute to the debate about how best to work with such situations. Roberts in his edited text (2005) has an eight chapter section covering aspects of disaster and crisis such as terrorism, community disasters, and the impact on 'first responders' and their families. James (2008) covers a wide range of situations including hostage negotiation, disaster response to terrorism and human-made disasters and burnout among those who work with such disaster events. McGlothlin, Jackson-Cherry and Garofolo (2010) deal with emergency preparedness. These texts are a resource for anyone attempting to plan and deliver an emergency crisis response. The current text is concerned with these issues but is focused more specifically in helping to present some challenging ideas that the radical approach we have been considering brings to our understanding of disasters and crisis.

A community crisis

Since we were interested in the small scale flood in the last case example (Susan) let's look at what can happen when a large scale flood hits a whole community. As with other cases this is not a real case but an amalgam of ideas drawn together into the experience of this Riverside community. Riverside is a town built as you might guess in and around the river Blue. It is mostly a commuter town for a nearby large industrial town. Developers have been working in the area during 'good' economic times and so the population has almost tripled in the past 15 years. It has managed to keep a small town feel but the fact that most people have to travel to work has limited some opportunities to build community cohesion. For the most part the residents work in industrial jobs in the larger town, with some being employed as tradesmen in the developments in the area while others work in the service industry. Before the surge in development there were a number of large residences in the surrounding area, but these tended to be away from the centre of town.

Richard and Avril moved to Riverside about three years ago. They had been living in rented accommodation but when they had their second child they decided to stretch themselves and try to buy a home. Riverside with its expanding development of low cost housing seemed like a wonderful opportunity for them. They bought a three bedroomed semi-detached house near the local park with access to the Blue river.

In the winter of their third year a crisis hit. That month had recorded heavy rainfalls in the Riverside area. A few residents had been watchful as they could see that the river was rising and that the rain was lodging in the park and it seemed that the ground could not absorb the water. They did not have any plan in place as no-one really believed that it would become a major problem. But that is what happened. One night following days of heavy rain the river burst its banks and within minutes the homes by the river were under feet/metres of water.

By midnight the water had risen and all the homes in the Riverside Park were under water. People were in panic as they tried to rescue their families and some possessions. Although the rescue and emergency services responded as soon as possible it became clear that they did not have the resources to deal with the extent of the flooding. With the water continuing to rise rescue operations were hampered. The first causalities were reported and the panic increased.

It took 24 hours for the flood to stop rising and several days for the water to recede. Four people died and several more were seriously injured. Over two hundred people were made homeless. There was extensive damage done to their homes and most of those in the Riverside Park lost all their possessions in the flood. Richard and Avril were among the families who lost everything. They had been trapped in their home on the first floor for several hours waiting for rescue services to get to them. Avril had been particularly distressed because of the baby. She was terrified that somehow in the attempt to get out of their home the baby would be hurt. She also became fearful when she realised that the waste treatment plant nearby had also been affected and the water was already contaminated. She thought the baby would catch an infection and be too weak to survive. Richard tried to keep calm for Avril and their other child but as time passed he too became panicked. When the rescue teams finally got to them they were distraught. Other neighbours were calling out to each other trying to reassure each other that services were on the way.

Richard, Avril and the children were rescued along with their neighbours and were given shelter and food in the next town in the community centre. It was several days before they were able to get back to their house to see the damage and both were even more distressed when they saw the extent of the damage, not just for themselves but for their neighbours. They did have insurance cover but even that did little to comfort them in the crisis.

This type of community disaster demands immediate crisis response. The priority is of course the safety of those people involved in the crisis event. For a more detailed account of the crisis planning and emergency response consult Jackson-Cherry and Erford 2010, James 2008, Thompson 1991. James (2008) highlights that we must consider multiple systems in this type of environmental or eco disaster. That means taking account of the individual involved in the disaster, their families, the community, organisations within the community, larger national and international services and organisations and of course the environmental system. He also draws attention to such issues as the importance of communication systems, 'for crisis intervention agencies, fast, effective, clear communication is at the centre of everything they do' (p.571). Some have suggested that flooding disasters are different from other types of disaster because while losing everything to the flood your home and possessions are often visible and still in place even though they are destroyed.

Any flooding event will test the national planning and strategies for crisis response as well as the actions of the emergency teams. Unfortunately the nature of this event is often that there are unexpected aspects to the disaster that we are not prepared for, there are always lessons to be learned from each event.

While acknowledging the priority as the safety of those involved not just in the immediacy of the actual crisis but also in the aftermath as they attempt to get their lives back in order we want to take a few minutes to consider the additional perspective of the radical approach to this event. A number of elements to the event may be considered. First a radical look at the failure to prevent the crisis and then some thoughts about dealing with the actual event and the aftermath.

The radical approach as we have already discussed looks at the individual as political, so that we are not only looking at the experience of Richard and Avril and their family. Let us add some more information to the case that would be of concern to the radical approach.

Some time after the flood as Richard and Avril were attempting to salvage what they could, Richard happened to get chatting to some locals who had lived all their lives in the other end of what was then a village. They were discussing how surprised they were that someone had decided to go ahead and build in what they called The Shallows. He discovered that the area around their home was locally named as The Shallows because it was known to have experienced build up of water sometimes during a severe winter. Some of the older people from the original village told stories about the area being underwater during the winter months. It seemed that somewhere in the planning of Riverside Park this local information was at best forgotten or at worst ignored.

A radical thinker would turn attention to such things as planning regulations and ask whether the fact that this was a low cost project have any impact on the decision to build in what may have been unsuitable land. It is true that development often happens in areas that have previously been unsuitable and that some form of land reclamation is normal and usually successful when handled correctly. This raises other questions about the steps taken to ensure that land prone to flooding was suitably prepared for housing development. This may add cost to development and so again the radical thinker will be interested in these processes.

Kutak as far back as 1938 wrote about the sociology of flooding. His article is interesting in that it highlights many points about a flood crisis that have resonance today. He summarises key points that we still consider to be essential when he discussed the importance of communication and transportation in a time of such a crisis. He also made a comment that would be controversial today but which fits well with some of the considerations of the radical approach. Kutak (1938) reflected that in the case of a flood in Lousiville many local people were eager to help and quickly volunteered to assist those in the flood area. His comment was 'in the first place, all of those whose homes were on dry land rushed to volunteer to work in them, and, because the homes of business executives and professional people were more likely to be in the dry-land areas, there was an overabundance of executive talent' (p.69). For a radical approach this question of socio-economic inequity in terms of the burden of the crisis would be of central importance.

At another level the crisis would be considered in light of the resources available to the stricken community. Again socio-economic and political factors may have some implication for the availability of resources to deal with the actual crisis and probably even more significantly resources to prevent the crisis in terms of preparedness and prevention. Are some areas better prepared because they can prioritise investment in an infrastructure to deal with a flooding crisis? What factors may influence this allocation of resources?

James (2008) in commenting on the Katrina disaster summarised some of the factors that contributed to the extent of that disaster. He reports that such factors as lack of efficient communication, poor coordination plans, personal and community preparedness (or lack of), and what he terms as the geography of poverty. With regard to this last point he says (2008)

> while race became a factor due to the majority of the poor in New Orleans being black, the fact is that disaster plans as they are currently formulated put the poor, the elderly, the sick, and other disenfranchised individuals who are not financially or physically able to evacuate, relocate, or rebuild at extreme risk without regard to race, creed, color, national origin, religion, sexual preference, or any other distinctive human quality. (p.590)

These are the issues that would be raised in a radical debate on any crisis event. Are the poor more vulnerable to either experiencing the crisis or in the aftermath will the fact of their economic disadvantage mitigate against a recovery or resolution of the crisis?

Some of these considerations draw attention to the response from local community, regional, national and international services and organisations. All of these levels of systems would come under the lens of the radical approach. All of the levels of systems should be examined and their contribution if any to the disaster itself or to the problems in dealing with the disaster should be taken into account. The radical approach to flooding as a crisis would probably demand that steps beyond helping individuals and their families be taken. These steps may target change at any or all levels of systems.

Finally since a radical approach encompasses all levels of systems it might include some reflections on flooding as an aspect of international issues about climate and general environmental concerns.

James (2008) has addressed some of these socio-economic and political points in relation to the Katrina disaster. Of course the nature of the crisis is important in any assessment. In many cases the natural disaster is not preventable and so the radical analysis will take account of that. However in all crisis situations some thought is given to the wider dimensions of the response and resolution to the crisis. It is interesting to note that Kutak (1938) all those years ago warned that

> the rain cannot be prevented from falling, but its course from the time it falls upon the earth until it empties into the sea can be controlled in such a way as to prevent harmful social consequences from ensuing. Reforestation projects, dams which will hold back the water, sea walls about the cities may control floods in such a way as to prevent them from becoming social disasters. In considering this approach, it is necessary to balance the cost of flood control projects against the possible losses due to floods. Again, flood control projects must be carried on over a number of years, and there is a possibility that the acute distress felt at the time of the flood will be forgotten, and the projects never carried through to completion. (p.70)

Chapter 8

A Social Construction Approach

Introduction

It is consistent with developing a chronological guide to the theoretical influences on crisis to finish with social constructionist theory. This theory sits well following both systems and radical theory. Hedges (2005) links this social constructionism with earlier systemic thinking. He credits Boscolo and Cecchin (systemic post-Milan practitioners) with having embraced social constructionist ideas in the late 1970s. Burr (2003) gives similar recognition to Gergen when she says that

> in psychology the emergence of social constructionism is usually dated from Gergen's paper in 1973 entitled 'Social psychology as history', in which he argues that all knowledge, including psychological knowledge, is historically and culturally specific, and that we therefore must extend our enquiries beyond the individual into social, political and economic realms. (p.13)

This returns us to some of the ideas we explored in the radical chapter.

Radical theory with its emphasis on critiquing 'accepted' realties shares some tenets with the social constructionist approach. This commitment to critical thinking which is embodied in radical theories may have contributed to an enthusiasm for social constructionist theory which of course shares this commitment. After a brief history of social constructionist theory we will discuss some of the key concepts emanating from this theoretical framework. The links between social constructionist and social constructivist will be commented on given they are both aligned with the post-modern era. The chapter will then go on to consider the connections between social constructionist thinking and crisis work. This will include an exploration of one of the therapeutic interventions associated with social constructionist thinking, solution focused work.

A brief history of social constructionist theory

Social constructionist ideas in themselves have been around in sociological perspective for some time. Most would attribute the development of the social constructionist movement to the work of Berger and Luckmann in 1966 with the publication of the classic 'The social construction of reality'. They (1966) started from the position that the sociology of knowledge is concerned with the social construction of reality. This debate about the relationship between knowledge and reality is central to the theoretical framework. One important aspect of the theory is the shift away from the certainty that previous theoretical approaches conveyed to highlighting the lack of certainty that is essentially a post-modern position. Berger and Luckmann (1966) explored the importance of face to face interaction, language and interpretations of meaning. Face to face interaction is an example of the flexibility inherent in developing an unfolding reality as people in conversation co-construct a picture of their reality. Language plays an important part in this since 'language…is the most important sign system in human society' (Berger and Luckmann 1966, p.51).

Although the theoretical concepts of the social constructionist approach have been around for some time it is only more recently that the ideas have really influenced mainstream therapies. Parton (2009) suggests that 'it is only in the last twenty years that postmodern and social constructionist perspectives have been drawn upon to think about, analyse and directly contribute to social work practice' (p.220). Social constructionist thinking is also related to some of the emerging ideas from the systemic based family therapy approach. Minuchin and Fishman (1981) considered the earlier emphasis on understanding families from a problem focused perspective. They commented that the 'orientation of family therapist toward "constructing a reality" that highlights deficits is therefore being challenged. Family therapists are finding that the exploration of strengths is essential to challenge family dysfunction' (p.268). This was a shift in thinking for counsellors and family therapists. The notion that through discussing problems we may be contributing to a negative reality for clients was beyond the scope of systemic theories. It may have been inevitable that systems thinkers with roots in sociology rather than psychology looked to the study of the social rather than the psychological for some inspiration. Burr (2003) says that

> social constructionism can be thought of as a theoretical orientation which to a greater or lesser degree underpins all of these newer approaches which are currently offering radical and critical alternatives in psychology and social psychology as well as in other disciplines in the social sciences and humanities. (p.1)

This chapter will consider social constructionist theory while keeping in mind the connections between systems theories and radical theories. We have looked at the notion of shifting ways of thinking away from a focus on the individual and on to the social. One way to think about social constructionist theory is to look at it as a shift away from belief in the certainty of science to a curiosity about the uncertainty of human nature. Gergen (1973 cited in Burr 2003) talked about knowledge being specific to time (history) and culture. This means that the shift in thinking made in social constructionist theory could only have happened in a particular place and time. The time was what we now call the post-modern era. So the place to start is with postmodernism. Burr (2003) says that 'the cultural and intellectual backdrop against which social constructionism has taken shape, and which to some extent gives it its particular flavour, is what is usually referred to as postmodernism' (p.10). Franklin and Jordan (1999) comment that an important group of postmodernists are the social constructionist Berger and Luckmann 1966, Gergen 1985, and McNamee and Gergen 1992.

Postmodernism

We are interested in postmodernism because the term 'is often used to describe the range of "post" theories, yet there are substantial differences among these theories' (Healy 2005, p.197). This chapter is focusing on social constructionist theory which is yet another theoretical framework. However we are going to explore social constructionist thinking from the perspective that it fits into a post-modern world rather than a modern world. Burr (2003) makes the distinction between the modern world which was concerned with a search for rules and structure. This world believed in 'grand theories' which offered ways of understanding the entire social world based on certainty and 'established' principles. The post-modern world does not believe that such certainty is possible. It wants to take apart these principles and certainties and find out what is really going on. One of the frameworks for taking apart these certainties is social constructionist theory. It is at risk of becoming a 'grand' theory itself if it is used to claim that only social constructionists really know what's going on (p.11).

With this cautionary note in mind let us look some more at the post-modern world that is trying to embrace uncertainty. Postmodernism is concerned with understanding the ways in which we construct meaning. It is interested in exploring the ways in which language, power, social factors, and history shape our views about reality truth and knowledge (Hollinger 1994). 'For example, postmodern perspectives urge us to recognise the different discourses, like biomedicine and consumer rights, construct "client needs" rather than view one of these perspectives as more accurate that the other' (Healy 2005, p.194). These notions of constructing meaning and privileging some discourses more than others are consistent with the social constructions world view. One might say that social constructionist theory is a post-modern theory.

Since the concept of postmodernism obviously implies something that comes after modernism we should first mention what we understand by modernism. A most simplified explanation of modernism is that it is a view that certainty is possible and desirable. It is founded in a positivistic world view where science and truth are valued and privileged. Parton (2009) says that that the term 'modernity is seen to refer to a cluster of social, economic and political systems that emerged in the West with the Enlightenment in the later eighteenth century' (p.221). He (Parton 1994, cited in Parton 2009) identified 'two crucial elements of modernity... the progressive union of scientific objectivity and politico economic rationality' (p.222). Parton (2009) comments that 'in fact, the modern approach, rather than being humanitarian, progressive and emancipatory, is seen as invariably exploitative and repressive because of its failure to recognise difference and its reliance on totalising belief systems' (p.223).

Postmodernism then refers to a transformation or paradigm shift where it was recognised that truth is relative not objective. Parton (2009) claims that this transformation has been characterised in terms of: globalisation, the increased significance of the media and the widening networks of information technology, which transform and transmit knowledge, the changes in modes of consumption and production and the increased awareness of risk and uncertainty.

According to Walsh (2006) 'postmodernists assert, following the ideas of Foucault (1966) that any generalisation about people and societies serves to reinforce positions of power among groups rather than represent objective truth' (p.251). You can see that these ideas about power and influence can also be related to the radical ideas we looked at earlier. However postmodernism has been criticised for being too concerned with the 'small'. It views language and discourse as important for understanding. Postmodernism is sometimes criticised by social activists for ignoring social problems and de-emphasising collective action (Lengermann and Nierbrugge 2000 in Walsh 2006). The postmodern view is that there are no absolute truth claims and that, rather, the utility of theories should be judged within specific practice contexts (Healy 2005).

Social constructionism

One of the classic books on social construction was published in 1966 by Berger and Luckmann. This was a sociological text which discussed the social construction of reality. They believed that 'all human knowledge is developed, transmitted, and maintained in a social situation and through social institution' (p.3). Ideas about the importance of social interaction and social context in constructing knowledge and meaning have been around for some time. Franklin and Jordan (1999) connect social constructionism with phenomenology and ethnomethodological research based in sociology. They view social constructionism as a method of post-modern discourse. Since one of the aims of this book is to distinguish between theory and method this comment is somewhat confusing. It seems more consistent to view social constructionism as a theory that only makes sense thorough a postmodernist world view. The methods that are associated with this theory or are informed by this theory are generally agreed to be narrative therapy, reflective practice, collaborative therapy and solution focused work. We will engage more with solution focused work later in this chapter.

Summarising the main ideas in social constructionism Teater (2010) suggests that it emphasises the influence of the use of language within interpersonal relationships in creating one's reality as well as the influence of history, society and culture while social constructivism emphasises one's biology, developmental processes and cognitive structures.

Social constructivism

More simply social constructionism focuses on the sociological aspects that influence and help shape or create reality for a person (more on the influences of nurture) and constructivism focuses on the psychological aspects of the individual and how these assist and create reality for the person (more of an influence from nature). Social constructivism acknowledges that the psychological and sociology aspects work in combination (Teater 2010).

Burr (2003) in identifying some of the debates in social constructionism points to the fact that there is a connection between this theoretical framework and attempts to understand some aspects of oppression and discrimination that were a feature of the radical approach. She says (2003) 'social constructionist theory and research has been taken up in a variety of ways by those wishing to challenge oppressive and discriminatory practices, for example, in the areas of gender and sexuality, disability and race' (p.20).

Key concepts in social constructionist theory

Language

Since we are now considering the social construction of our realities it is important to start with one of the central 'building blocks' of that construction process that is language. Parton (2009) tells us that 'language does not simply reflect or mirror objects, events and categories existing in the social and natural world – it actively constructs those things' (p.224). The writings of philosophers such as Foucault and Derrida are important influences on this approach to seeing the world. This emphasises the importance of languaging ideas and recognises how this can be a powerful process. Sets of language or language systems can then form discourses.

van Dijk (1997) clarifies that

> language users actively engage in test and talk not only as speakers, writers, listeners or readers, but also as members of social categories, groups, professions, organisations, communities, societies or cultures... they interact as women and men, blacks and whites, old and young, poor and rich, doctors and patients,

teachers and students, friends and enemies... and mostly in complex combinations of these social and cultural roles and identities. (p.3)

Discourse

'Discourses are structures of knowledge claims and practices through which we understand, explain and decide things... a discourse is best understood as a system of possibilities for knowledge and agency that makes some actions possible while precluding others' (Parton 2009, p.224). There is no one discourse but among the range of discourses some may be more powerful and/or hold more influence than others. One example of such a discourse would be medical discourse. It is not unlike the older idea of jargon in that you had to be 'in the know' to participate in a conversation and use of jargon facilitated identifying those who did not belong. Likewise a medical discourse would be a conversation in which medicalised language, terms and 'jargon' dominate. The discourse adds weight to the view proffered about what is happening, the medical view may be said to be privileged. In some situations this may seem appropriate as we become dependent on medical expertise to 'save us'. But if you consider that now we are more aware of the distinction between Western medicine and Eastern medicine it could be said that medical discourse is being challenged by the discourse of alternative medicines.

Discourse can be a very powerful thing. It can as Parton (2009) describes construct 'a reality' by supporting particular views and dismissing or ignoring others. Supporting a particular view may simply mean employing language that has created terms for the aspects of the situation that are considered relevant or important while simply not identifying or naming other aspects at all. The notion of privileging some point of view or discourse or interpretation conveys this idea that we as a society give preference to some forms of knowledge or some constructions that are created to explain realities. In post-modern thinking 'the creation of particular discourses creates contingent centres of power' (Parton 2009, p.224).

Healy (2005) also reminds us that it is possible to have competing discourses, as in the example of Western and Eastern medicine. So too in working with families it is possible to have a resilience discourse and a pathologising discourse. Each language system performs a version of the same situation but tells it with different and often competing emphasis... the family has issues but overall it is surviving or the family is surviving but only just. Even the same words can be used differently to support a resilience or failure discourse.

Political discourse offers an interesting example of the use of language. Terms connected to the use of the language of left and right create different meanings. We can accept the attribution of left and right in political discourse and yet both have very powerful connotations. Right implies such things as: righting a wrong, right meaning correct, accurate, precise, right on (being correct and cool), right hand (right hand man meaning the most helpful/useful/important), right and wrong, right up front, rightful, even righteous. Left is used to convey such things as: left (absent, gone, missing, not here, abandoned), left out (marginalised), left aside (not important), left over (unwanted), left behind (slower or not as able), left sided, left handed. Then we have the left and right in politics. Interesting to consider which term you would choose for your own brand of politics if you had the choice. Perhaps left wing does describe a concern for the left out and left aside but what is right trying to say?

Power

Healy (2005) says that 'if we want to understand power in any context, we need to analyse how discourses operate to construct identity, knowledge and power within that specific context' (p.202). She (2005) quotes Foucault's work on power and highlights a number of his ideas: his shift in focus from those who possess power to the consideration of how power is exercised; and his argument that we analyse power from the local to the structural taking account of the fact that a focus on macro-processes of power is not particularly useful in understanding the micro politics of power in local contexts and finally, his position that we must not get distracted form the fact that while power can be repressive it can also be productive. This adds a further dimension to the concept of empowerment we looked at in the last chapter. We may need to take account of ways in which clients exercise power even if they do not possess power.

Non expert

Hoffman (1992) in discussing the more traditional aspects of systems bases therapies said that 'about ten years ago, I found myself increasingly haunted by the paradoxes of power that beset the traditional methods of family therapy. They all seemed based on secrecy, hierarchy and control' (p.15). These types of concern led to a shift in position within therapies informed by social constructionist thinking. This shift was from the expert to the non expert position. In line with accepting the lack of certainty that is consistent with the post-modern view it is appropriate that the worker operationalises that view by stepping back from being the expert with the answers. Two main ideas 'replace' if you like the expert. One is that we work with the client as the expert. While the client may be in difficulty he remains the expert in terms of his own life, his goals and abilities. The second notion is that in place of expert the worker adopts a stance of 'curiosity'. Being curious in a respectful manner allows the worker to engage with the client in a more open way and allows for possibilities previously undiscovered or unconsidered to be explored.

Narratives

Beels (2009) recounts a personal journey with psychotherapy beginning in the modernist 1950s. Beels sees 'this history in three phases: (1) the reign of psychoanalysis then, and the succeeding waves of (2) family and (3) narrative therapy that followed.' Although Beels observed that family therapy did break with the orthodoxy of the psychoanalytic dominance it did retain some of its 'master therapist' ideas. 'The power of defining and interpreting the problem continued to reside in the therapist. Narrative work took this change a crucial step further. It aimed to shift power from the expert professional therapist or teacher toward the beneficiaries of the process, thus changing the character of both therapy and training' (Beels 2009, p.364). Beels (2009) recommends Anderson's chapter in the *Handbook of Family Therapy* (Anderson 2003) for an excellent history of narrative work as an outcome of ideas and concepts that originated in post-modern criticisms of literature and philosophy.

Deconstruction

Since we are exploring a world which has been socially constructed it is inevitable that one of the techniques we need to employ to make sense of the world is to deconstruct it. Deconstruction means taking apart what seem like accepted 'truths' and discovering what lies behind them. The technique can be applied to anything from a body of knowledge to a specific term. Payne (2009) offers a very helpful definition of the concept: 'deconstruction involves taking apart ideas so that we can see where the power conventional assumptions and acceptance of normative generalisations are leading us to see as inevitable things that we could have a go at changing' (p.96).

Burr (2003) reminds us that

our ways of talking about and representing the world through written texts, pictures and images all constitute the discourses through which we experience the world... the way that discourses construct our experience can be examined by 'deconstructing' these... taking them apart and showing how they work to present us with a particular vision of the world, and thus enable us to challenge it. (p.18)

Deconstruction is a central activity in social constructionist approaches to working with people. It underlies that important belief that there are many versions of the client's life story. Some of the versions may emphasise the failures and problems therefore pathologising the client. Others (including this approach) will attempt to draw out the stories of strength, courage and striving that have been forgotten, ignored or simply gone unnoticed because of the volume and intensity of the problem stories.

This activity of deconstructing ideas and given 'facts', is also important from the point of view of best practice in the counselling and helping professions. Payne (2009) ties this in with the importance of reflective practice to ensure that workers do take the time to question both themselves and the given knowledge which informs their decisions.

Metaphors and externalising

Metaphors are figures of speech where we try to explain one experience by using words or terms that we usually associate with something different. It is one way of representing our world to others and to ourselves. The idea is that associating say being upset with I cried a bucket of tears, it will be easier to understand what we are saying. Metaphors may be very regional so that people living in one area have ways of expressing themselves (colloquialisms) that are only understood by their own group/s. Other metaphors are more universally understood at least within a specific language world. These terms or phrases can be very powerful. A client describing himself as a 'waste of space' or 'on the scrap heap' is generating a powerful negative image of himself. Rather than simply challenging the metaphor it might be useful if we try to understand it and what it means to the client. Parton and O'Byrne (2000) recommend that

it is always worthwhile listening to these and joining them, for in joining we create for ourselves the possibility of influencing the metaphors when it contains a virus of impossibility, and of putting in its place a virus of possibility or a frame of new metaphors. (pp.80–81)

One of the methods associated with social constructionism is narrative therapy. This form of therapy tries to work with metaphors. It may be possible to deconstruct the negative metaphor or to create alternative meanings by developing the metaphor. White (1995) developed one of the best known ways of working with metaphors and/or negative life stories, a technique he called externalising. By helping clients to think of the problem or issue in their lives as something outside of themselves it creates a distance between the client and the problem. This distance can be used as a space to create or co-create alternative stories. When we externalise the issue/story/metaphor then shift away from allowing the problem to take over our lives. Parton and O'Byrne (2000) explain that the problem can be seen as the oppressor, and the self as the heroic resistance fighter. These ideas really only make sense in a world of therapy where clients are viewed as a resource and workers value the clients' resilience.

Problem saturation versus resilience

Walsh (1998) is quoted by Greene *et al.* (2005) as having defined resilience as 'a person's ability not only to cope with, survive, and bounce back from difficult and traumatic experiences and situations but also to continue to grow and develop psychologically and emotionally' (p.66). Think about a client telling his story. The social context is often that he is seeking help and so it is perhaps inevitable that he will want to convey as clearly as possible the extent of his difficulties and why he needs or deserves help. This story or narrative is constructed in a way that highlights need and edits out resilience. To focus on resilience or ability might undermine the request for help (we may even have created social services that supports declarations of deficiency as a pre-requisite to being allocated scare resources).

Think about a worker, she probably sees her role as helping others. In other theoretical frameworks this may involve learning as much as possible about what has gone wrong for the client in order to be able to complete an assessment and develop a plan for helping. So with two parties focusing on the deficits and problems the story becomes problem saturated, it's all about what is not working. But this is only a socially constructed story developed between a help seeker and a help giver. If one of the parties, and due to issues of power over scare resources, it probably needs to be the worker, decides to explore the whole story then she may access information about some things that are going OK. The things that are going OK are part of the resilience story. We will look at this in applying a solution focused perspective to crisis intervention. Social constructionist theory helps us to recognise that there are indeed many sides to a story. If we create a social context which demands a portrayal of failure then people will have to focus on that portrait of themselves. They will focus on an identity which is organised around their shortcomings. If we facilitate the creation of a more balanced story without penalties then that story will include examples of strengths and resilience.

Change

The social constructionist view of change is somewhat different as you might expect. We have looked at ideas that suggest that change is difficult, that change is unusual, it only happens in response to extreme pressure or crisis, that it is difficult to maintain change, that change is often only superficial. In a social constructionist world 'change is endless, constant and inevitable' (Parton and O'Byrne 2000, p.59). Change is happening all the time. It may go unnoticed but that does not mean it does not exist only that we do not have the tools or lens to spot it. Changes both small and large are constant. We have to make adjustments constantly in our everyday life. There are road works on your way to work so you have to take a different route; your child has to stay home from school so you have to make alternative arrangements. Sometimes these changes happen with little effort and sometimes these changes can prove difficult.

Problems, solutions and strengths

Franklin and Jordan (1999) in describing solution focused work comment that the method was developed from a practice base, guided by a philosophical position rather than based on empirical research. But it is nonetheless consistent in many ways with social constructionist thinking. 'Consistent with social constructionism, solution focused therapists believe that a client's interpersonal and social reality evolves out of a social context, or in transaction with other people' (p.108). Franklin and Jordon suggest that 'because solution focused therapy seeks to change language, narratives, and cognition in a process that leads to behavior change, it has been closely associated with the social construction theory' (p.108).

Susan and Jake: A social constructionist perspective/story

In general terms social constructionist theory would look at not just the crisis event but the precursors to the event. By this it means trying to understand what picture Susan has already constructed of herself and her circumstances. This theory would direct us to listen carefully to her 'languaging' of the event but also to listen to ourselves as we contribute to the discourse around women, parenting and coping with such events.

Susan was in her late teens when she discovered she was pregnant. This was an unplanned pregnancy and she and her boyfriend were shocked and very distressed. The pregnancy was experienced by them as a crisis. Pregnancy can become a crisis in many different circumstances. Usually the concept of crisis pregnancy is used to refer to an unplanned teen pregnancy but this is only one type of 'crisis pregnancy'. For Susan she was frightened about her future and how she would cope with a baby. She was able to talk to her parents who offered support and decided to continue the pregnancy and keep the baby.

The conventional notion of teen pregnancy as a crisis can be disputed from the social constructionist framework. The application of social constructionist thinking will involve considering how society has constructed the concept of crisis pregnancy. A pregnancy can result in a crisis for many reasons but being unplanned is often an element. The unplanned nature of the pregnancy can elicit a shock that temporarily makes a woman feel out of control. This may be accompanied by a more persistent sense of being at risk. The sense of risk is usually related to the perception of the consequences that are likely to ensue.

The consequences associated with unplanned pregnancy vary and are to a large extent socially defined. For example a society can either directly or indirectly sanction teen pregnancy by imposing a range of consequences from stigmatisation, limited access to resources and supports, exclusion from continuing education and or employment opportunities. These are social sanctions that operate as a disincentive. In the UK the Social Exclusion Unit (2006) clearly acknowledged that becoming a teenage parent was not only related to social exclusion but could contribute to or even be the cause of social exclusion.

Studies have shown the link between disadvantage, poverty and becoming a teenage mother (McLeod 2001) and their perception of those links (Loughran and Richardson 2005). Austerberry and Wiggins (2007) in a discussion of social exclusion and teen mothers quote Giddens (1998) who highlighted that any society had a choice to focus on 'investing' in human and social capital (in this case investing to ensure participation by teen mothers in work and or education) rather than providing direct provision of economic maintenance. They argue that policy on combating social exclusion is dominated by a discourse of integrating the 'excluded' into a skills-based economy through their participation in education and training. This is a one dimensional approach and 'feeds into an inconsistent government strategy towards motherhood and employment that has extended rights and promoted flexibility for middle class women, while prescribing that mothers living in poverty seek paid employment' (Austerberry and Wiggins 2007, p.3). Compare this to a society where women are encouraged to establish a career and to delay pregnancy, even where this may have more risks.

Lawlor and Shaw (2002) suggest that 'the management of reproduction and childbirth has, in most countries and most cultures been the province of women' (p.552). But they go on to propose that this has changed and that biomedicine has contributed to a situation where women's bodies and reproduction are seen as legitimate subjects for social control. Teenage pregnancy is now languaged as a public health problem. This has happened in spite of the fact that research is inconclusive about the risks associated with teenage pregnancy. Lawlor and Shaw (2002) point out that 'studies report that once maternal socioeconomic position and smoking are taken into account young age is actually associated with better outcomes' (p.552). So the view that teenage pregnancy is a problem in itself is socially constructed. That is not to suggest that teen parenting is desirable but it is also not saying that those who find themselves pregnant and young should be categorised as a problem or suffer social sanctions as a result. The point here is that our response to teen pregnancy is socially constructed and not necessarily based on factual or medical concerns.

What did all this mean for Susan? The socially defined parameters for successfully managing the crisis of her pregnancy and parenting her son demanded that she remain in education and/or employment. The provision of the state was insufficient to allow this without the continued support of her parents. Susan therefore found herself in a prolonged state of dependence on her parents. Her recent decision to become more independent and take on the financial responsibility of renting her own flat meant that she was feeling financially vulnerable. Even a small additional expense may have significant consequences. She knows that as a single mother she is at risk as she has already experienced disadvantage and so the flood has potentially much more serious repercussions for her.

Aside from the discourse around teen pregnancy as a crisis that is associated with disadvantage and restriction of access to choices in society there are other aspects of young motherhood that may be influenced by for example the socially constructed dominant discourse about gendered roles. If the dominant discourse is the paternalistic version of events where men take care of the technical problems and women display distress rather than resilience then this may impact on Susan's version of her story, unless there is a competing discourse such as self sufficiency, independence, and coping (the problem saturated story or the resilience story). Often in the beginning both these sides of the interpretation of events are evident and then the risk is that the helping process supports one and not the other.

You can probably see some of the similarities with cognitive theory earlier. In this theory while interpretation and perception are important it is viewed that these mechanisms are influenced by the social. What the cognitive thinker might view as simply a thought or belief the social constructionist thinker would view as the internalisation of some socially constructed position. So the social remains an important consideration even when it seems the individual has adopted a position/set of beliefs/way of seeing the world because these things are all constructed in a social and cultural context and through the face to face interaction of people in that context. The meaning attributed to an event can be constructed and conveyed through language. This is not to say that the individual is at the mercy of some 'social' dictum because the social constructionist does see the individual as playing a part in the construction process. This is sometimes presented as a criticism of the theory that too much attention is given to the individual in the construction process at the expense of incorporating an understanding of structural determinants in the problem story.

It is a crisis

Susan has internalised a social construction of identity which fortifies a story that she is a vulnerable mother living alone with her son. The narrative is about coping alone, the risk of loneliness and the challenge of getting through each day having to deal with the pressures of work, the heavy responsibilities of parenthood and the value of having a male support person who will deal with domestic difficulties. In some ways this was a crisis waiting to happen. Susan talked to her friends about her inadequacy when dealing with household responsibilities. She often framed this in a narrative about appreciating her parents and what they had done for her. She would regularly say things like: I don't know how I would cope without them, they really are my crutch, I lean on them all the time. Discussion with her friends on the topic of her work and life balance would usually be in terms of: how difficult it must be for you, how do you do it, I couldn't, you have done a great job with Jake but it's such a sacrifice you can't really have a life of your own, it's so hard being alone. Another possible conversation might be if only Jake was older, then he might be able to sort these things for me.

This draws on the gender based division of labour discourse where the male can cope with these practical problems and the female cannot. These conversations tend to highlight the challenges of her life and not her achievements. As was mentioned earlier here lies one of the risks in social constructionist thinking. What if Susan just adopts a new narrative? Could it be that simple? Of course it's not simple. There is a complex interplay between Susan and her world through which some version of her reality emerges. The good news is that it is just one version of the story, the more problematic news is that the version that dominates may be supported by all sorts of social discourses that Susan alone cannot overcome. She can begin to reject some of the story and tell other tales of achievement, satisfaction, happiness, learning and growing.

This is a crisis because the narrative supports the meaning of the event as an inevitable outcome of trying to go it alone, the price of making a mistake or even of being irresponsible as a teenager. It is about her identity as a mother struggling to cope, not a mother adapting and changing with every experience. Susan understands the flooded home as an outcome of her inadequacy and the risk of trying to go it alone. It is consistent with the dominant view that you need a man for these situations.

It is not a crisis

Susan comes home to the flooding. She turns off the main water supply, realises that there may be an electrical risk due to the water damage, leaves her home with Jake, talks to some other people living in the building and compares damages, finds out that no-one is blaming her, checks that the appropriate people have been contacted and accepts a neighbour's offer of a cup of tea while she waits for the next stage in sorting out the mess. She has internalised the view that this is part of living alone and she is capable of dealing with the problem. She knows how this type of thing is handled in work so she is confident about the steps to take. She was prepared for life as the sole responsible adult in the home and looked forward to embracing all that it offered, including opportunities to learn new skills and develop even more independence.

She talked about moving into her new home as an adventure, exciting, something she looked forward to for ages, a new opportunity for Jake and herself. Her parents also talked about the move in a positive way and her friends told stories about Susan being a competent and self sufficient person who would enjoy her new living arrangements. This side of the story did not detract form the 'supportive parents' narrative but allowed for the 'self sufficient' mother to emerge as well. This sense of identity influenced how she sees the current situation and in particular will play an important part in how she tells the story of the event first to herself and then to others.

Even how the flood gets recorded is important since this has implications for the future. The non crisis story is something like: what a mess, the place needed a complete clean out but everyone helped out and I realised I had some great neighbours. The landlord was very helpful too since it was a faulty machine that caused the problem so he let me pick what I wanted to replace the damaged furniture, now I really feel the place is mine.

The crisis story which may be the basis for future experiences of crisis might be: the place was a mess, even though the landlord said I could replace the damaged furniture I had no time to sort it out, I could not cope with this again, maybe living alone is a bit too much for me right now.

This is not just about how Susan thinks about the situation (that fits with the cognitive theory); this is emphasising how she interacts with others and creates an identity for herself through that face to face conversation. The language used contributes to the meaning inferred from the event. But it is also about how the others in her life and even a professional helper talk about the event, not just the flood but the context for the event that relates to living alone with Jake.

Case example: Nina, Roy and domestic violence

Nina and Roy have been together for 12 years. They first met when Nina was 23 and Roy 31. Nina had been in a relationship with Henry whom she had known since she was 14. He had decided to leave home to travel abroad and did not ask Nina to go with him. At the time she was heart broken and so when she met Roy, who seemed a bit older and more settled she felt she could make a life with him.

In the beginning of their relationship Roy seemed to be jealous of Nina's relationship with Henry even though they had no contact. She thought that was a sign of how much Roy liked her and so she was relieved and flattered. Within a very short time Roy asked Nina to move in with him. She moved in and within a couple of months she was pregnant with their son Paul.

Roy was a few years older than Nina and from the start she saw this as one of the good things in her relationship. She felt she could rely on him and that he was always there to take care of her. He was very attentive and while they went out with friends a lot in the beginning Nina soon began to think they had a better time when they went out alone. Roy thought some of her friends didn't like him because he wasn't Henry. He felt that Nina should start a new life with him. When she got pregnant Nina agreed that they would get married, move to a new area and start their lives together with their new baby. Nina had been working as a receptionist in a doctor's surgery and knew she would get a similar job easily enough. Roy was a sales man for a large food company and so he was able to continue working in the same job.

Twelve years later, Nina (35) and Roy (43) have three children; Paul 11, Stacy 10 and Lily 5 years old. They have few friends and a limited social life. Nina would say that Roy can feel intimidated and out of place in social situations. This came as a surprise to her as when she met him he seemed to be very sociable and of course his work involves meeting new people all the time. Nina got pregnant with Stacy very soon after Paul was born and so her plan to return to work was postponed. Then when Stacy was going to school Lily arrived and so Nina stayed home. Recently Nina decided she wanted to return to work and found out about a re-training course. She had been worried as Roy was often in a bad mood and he blamed this on the pressure of being the 'only worker' in the home. However he didn't think she needed to go out to work and they had several rows about it. Nina had seen Roy lose his temper a number of times in their relationship and so knew when to back off and let him cool down.

In fact the first time Roy really lost it was when Nina was pregnant with Paul and she when out with some friends for a goodbye night out. Roy was waiting up for her when she got home and said he had been worried sick about her. He was angry that she had been drinking when she was pregnant and shouted at her that she was so irresponsible with their child, in the heat of the moment he hit her across the face and knocked her into the armchair. The next day Roy was horrified that he had hit her but reminded her that he was worried for her and the baby. He became even more attentive and agreed that this would never happen again. Nina too felt guilty even though she had not in fact been drinking but she agreed that she had been out of line and so decided that since she was a bit younger than Roy maybe he was right. She could not believe he had hit her; she had never had such a thing happen to her before but she was committed to Roy and decided it was all sorted now.

They moved to a new town and things settled down. Nina felt she was dependent on Roy because she had no friends and her family were no longer living nearby. They got into a pattern of Roy going out to socialise with some people from work while Nina stayed home with Paul and later Stacy. She realised quickly that it was better not to complain about this as Roy would accuse her of wanting to meet other men if she expressed an interest in going out. She enjoyed her children and was often exhausted at the end of the day and was happy to just stay home. There were a couple of what Nina thought of as minor rows where Roy would get worked up for some reason, maybe Paul getting into trouble in school or Nina spending too much money. She would acknowledge that once or twice this may have ended up with Roy shaking or pushing her and even on one occasion locking her into the bathroom. Later it came out that he had sometimes punched her and once in the more recent past he had actually kicked her when she fell down. Roy often commented that she was not the woman he married; she had lost her figure when she had the children and he sometimes commented that she should look after her appearance a bit better. Nina came to believe that this was part of married life. Roy was a good provider and it was not every mother who could give her time to her children full time so she was grateful for this.

When Lily started school Nina decided it was time for her to contribute more financially to the family. Lily had a friend who lived on the same street and the friend's mother Jo often chatted to Nina when they brought the kids to school. Jo and Nina had recently agreed to share the school collection. When Nina talked to Roy about her plan to start helping out with finances he completely lost his temper, he shouted and began to punch her and scream that she wanted to leave him. On this occasion Paul heard noise and came to the top of the stairs, Nina got hysterical and Roy stormed out. The next day she was very bruised and thought she might have a broken nose. Jo called to the house to collect Lily and insisted that Nina see her doctor.

Domestic violence, theories and crisis intervention

Crisis intervention with cases of domestic violence is well documented in the literature. A number of authors have written about dealing with crisis and domestic violence from different perspectives. For example Aguilera (1998) focuses on domestic violence as a situational crisis, Roberts and Roberts (2005) focus specifically on a limited aspect of domestic violence, that is, the actual physical violence often referred to as battering and apply Roberts's seven stage model, Roberts (2006) developed a classification of battering, Hamberger and Holtzworth-Munroe (2007) using cognitive behavioural crisis intervention, and McLeod, Muldoon and Hays (2010) deal with the broader definition of domestic violence that includes emotional abuse and power issues.

Although the concept of battering is now considered to be too limiting both in terms of describing and understanding domestic violence it is useful to comment on Roberts's (2006) five level classification of women battering. Each level differs in terms of the severity and duration of the battering. Short term: one year or less involving mild to moderate intensity; Intermediate: several months to two years; involving moderate to severe injury; Intermittent long term: long periods without violence but severe and intense episodes; Chronic and predictable: frequent, severe, repetitive, often associated with alcohol or drug use; Homicidal: violence escalates to life threatening injuries or murder.

Nina and Roy fit in with the intermediate level in terms of severity of injuries but the pattern extended into a long term period. Two factors may have contributed to the longer duration of the violence, Nina's compliance in the face of Roy's abuse and absence of family. In Roberts's intermediate category the presence of a caring support system usually precipitated an end to the relationship. In this case it was many years into the marriage before someone was close enough to discover the violence and offer Nina support.

Allen (2008) reports on a study conducted in 1995 by Kelleher and O'Connor. They identified a number of risk factors for domestic violence. They found that risk was increased by: being female, being young, having children, being isolated, having parents who were abusive to each other and not being allowed to make decisions about money. Nina met all but one of these over the time of her relationship.

This book has explored different theories to help in our understanding of crisis. Each theoretical framework places emphasis on different aspects of the crisis. The same is true of theories about the other issues we have considered including domestic violence. McLeod, Muldoon and Hays (2010) summarise some of the theories of intimate partner violence (IPV), the term they use for domestic violence. They include the notion of the cycle of violence (Walker 1979) which looked at domestic violence as having a tension building and acute battering incident and a honeymoon phase. They attribute the learned helplessness approach to Seligman (1975) which explains that survivors of abuse learn to believe they cannot control the situation and become passive. They note that there is much argument about theories of domestic violence and one such alternative is offered by constructivist theorists who 'argue that the decision to stay with an abusive partner could result from a rational decision-making process based on weighing the costs and benefits of ending the relationship' (McLeod *et al.* 2010, pp.139–140).

Crisis therapies, domestic violence and social constructionist theory

The main focus of this section will be considering some crisis therapies informed by social constructionist thinking. However we will first look in brief at how a social constructionist might view domestic violence as a phenomenon. In applying some of the key ideas of social constructionist theory one of the first things to consider is the term domestic violence. Language and discourse are fundamental to a social constructionist understanding. Meaning is conferred and constructed through language and discourse. Domestic violence can only be acknowledged as a reality because it is now something we recognise and attempt to take account of. Prevalence data demonstrates that domestic violence occurs and that it is a serious problem.

A US study (Tjaden and Thoennes 2000) suggests that about one quarter of all women are thought to experience intimate partner violence at some point in their lives. There have been various attempts to define domestic violence since its earlier iteration as the battered wife syndrome. Whether we talk about an issue and then how we talk about issues is something that is socially constructed. For example Murray and Powell (2009) acknowledge the importance of the decision to 'break the silence' about domestic violence as an important step in developing policy and service responses to domestic violence. Mehrotra (1999) in reviewing the social construction of wife abuse says 'despite the historic prevalence of abuse, the terms wife abuse and battered women were coined only in the 1970s (Kelly 1988; Loseke 1992). That is women's experiences of abuse was labelled as a social problem only about two decades ago' (p.619). Mehrotra (1999) attributes this progress to a feminist discourse which began politicising the personal experiences of women in violent relationships.

The debate about terminology continues. Allen (2008) gives an account of some of the debate which refers to battering, spouse abuse, violence against women, domestic violence and intimate partner violence. Each term constructs a different picture of the violence. Battering emphasises physical violence but not the emotional or psychological, wife abuse confines its interest to legally married women, spouse abuse widens that to married couples. Forgey and Badger (2006) note that while the term adult intimate abuse deals with some of the definitional problem it does not deal with the 'directionality' of the abuse. It does not reflect the dominance of male to female violence.

Domestic violence and intimate partner violence (IPV) seem to be the currently popular terms. From a social constructionist perspective one could suggest that the word domestic is used as another term for tame. One could question if the use of the term demonstrates ambivalence about the violence, is domestic violence a tamer, less dangerous violence because it is in a relationship? Is it not still a physical assault or intimidation? Even IPV draws attention to the intimate nature of the relationship when there is nothing intimate about the abuse that occurs. The term intimate may serve to blur the facts as there may be some suggestion of reciprocity in the use of intimate partner.

A social constructionist view might ask why even in the face of uncontroversial evidence that physical, emotional and psychological violence takes place, predominantly from men to women, are we still conjecturing about reciprocity and responsibility?

Apart from how we confer meaning on the events that we will refer to as IPV there are other challenges from the social constructionist framework. McLeod, Muldoon and Hays (2010) in their definition of IPV refer to 'the intent of establishing power and control over the abused partner' (p.135). These issues of power and control extend earlier ideas about IPV which focused predominantly on causal explanations of stress, poor communication and inability to deal with emotions and/or control aggression. These newer ideas about IPV raise questions about intention and control not spontaneity or loss of control. Muehlenhard and Kimes (1999) discuss the point that 'what counts as violence is socially constructed, has varied over time and reflects power relationships' (p.234). They raise questions about who is now deciding if violence has occurred, what actually counts as IPV and look to the role of gender in defining domestic and sexual violence. Roberts (2006) addresses the place of poverty as a risk factor with women in lower socio-economic situations being more at risk.

The questions raised about IPV in a social constructionist analysis are not necessarily new. Some have been discussed in other contexts by feminists and sociologists who were interested in expanding the understanding of IPV beyond the personal to the socially defined and socially contextualised problem that it is. Allen (2008) presents a more extensive discussion referencing: Dobash and Dobash's (1979) review of the history of patriarchy and its impact on our interpretation of domestic violence in terms of gender roles, specifically the place of women in a male dominated society; Kirkwood's (1993) feminist analysis of battering as an expression of the institutional oppression of women and Birns, Cascardi and Meyers' (1994) sex role socialisation of men and women and its contribution to IPV.

Social constructionist theory challenges how we attempt to explain IPV and also how we intervene therapeutically in cases of IPV. Divergent views of women as helpless victims or provocateurs who incite the violence continue to be debated. These views influence the interventions offered to women. Responses to incidents of IPV continue to reflect this ambivalence. Services in response to IPV can often mean that the victim has to leave home and abandon their lives in order to ensure their safety and that of their children while the perpetrator remains in the family home. The view that a woman should just leave is widespread yet we know that women are most at risk when they decide to leave. Hence therapy drawing on a social constructionist framework which looks to understand not just the victimisation of women but also their resilience in the face of danger takes a different position on intervention.

There are a number of therapeutic interventions that emanate from the social constructionist framework. These include Wade's (1997) resistance therapy, White's (1989, 1995) and White and Epston's (1990) narrative therapy, and de Shazer's (1985, 1988, 1991) solution focused therapy. We will explore the approach to domestic violence taken in solution focused work.

Domestic violence and solution focused work

Solution focused work is informed by a social constructionist perspective. It was developed by de Shazer who was influenced by the ideas of problem focused work. He reacted against the problem saturated aspect of therapies of the time and decided that such approaches were missing the opportunities to construct a different picture of the client's problems. The difference that makes a difference as de Shazer (1991) called it. The difference was that instead of talking about the problems he wanted to talk about what was happening when the problem was not happening (de Shazer 1985). He developed ideas such as looking for these exceptions to the problem, exploring stories about clients' strengths and resilience, engaging in conversation about ways in which clients had already found solutions to their problems. Instead of trying to understand the past and the cause of problems de Shazer looked to the future. He and his colleague and partner Insoo Kim Berg (DeJong and Berg 1997) developed strategies for helping clients to set goals for the future, goals that would serve as motivation for the client. The two key goal setting strategies they employed were the miracle question and scaling questions.

According to George, Iveson and Ratner (1999), de Shazer thought that solution focused work was the same no matter what the problem. Lethem (1994) disagrees. She takes the view that when working with domestic violence solution focused therapists need to 'adjust their usual approach. It is not ethical to take a neutral approach to clients' goals in such cases. The goals of non violence by the man and the safety of the women have to be a pre condition of therapy' (p.80).

But what happens in the case of a crisis? One question that we might ask which we considered in the introduction chapter is: who is in crisis?

Roy is in crisis

Employing a social constructionist view it is likely that the crisis related to a loss or threatened loss of power and control. In this sense Roy is in crisis. He may fear that his control over his wife is slipping and her involvement in a workplace may have terrible consequences for him (with regard to that power). This means that he may be very motivated to prevent that outcome.

Roy is not in crisis

Roy thinks he has control over the situation. Since the first time he 'lost his temper' and became violent Nina has shown no sign of leaving him. He is confident that she won't leave him or cause any problems. Roy has successfully undermined Nina's self-esteem and self-confidence. He tells her that no-one else would have her and he thinks she believes that message. He is confident in his role as master of his home.

Nina is not in crisis

Nina on the other hand may have become so accustomed to Roy's violence that it does not represent a crisis as we think of it. Violence from Roy although never acceptable is becoming more expected. It is not a crisis because she has found ways of coping with Roy's violence, although she is not always able to keep herself safe. She has accepted her role as dependent economically and emotionally on Roy and has made a decision to deal with it by remaining in her home with her children. Alternatively Nina knows she has few options since there is little chance that she can be protected in her home and she has no place else to go. She is trapped not just by Roy but also by her social position and role in life.

Nina is in crisis

While the above position may be true for Nina this time is different. She has not been able to keep this a secret. Now someone else is aware of Roy's violence and Nina does not know how far that information will go. She may consider that some social services or even police involvement is now inevitable. She thinks that Roy will be even more violent in anticipation of such intervention in his life. The fact that her secret is out may precipitate a crisis and the thought that Roy may get worse because of this is terrifying. Alternatively she is in crisis because she feels she can no longer cope with Roy's violence. She is growing more concerned that the children are being affected and that is not something she can accept.

The neighbour is in crisis

The neighbour is terrified. While she wants to help she realises that Roy may not stop at being violent to Nina and she is becoming more and more distraught that she and her family may also be at risk. She has no emotional investment in Roy and so wants to report him. Nina will not agree and since Roy has done nothing to her Jo does not know what to do. She can't sleep at night and is afraid to go out on her own in case she meets Roy on the street.

A solution focused approach to domestic violence

Social constructionist thinking opened up new options for re-considering the notions of problems and vulnerability. Instead of focusing concern on problem resolution and vulnerability the social constructionist thinker can appreciate that problems have solutions and even the vulnerable have strengths. Hence the understanding of a crisis situation and the response to that crisis can look only at the deficit model of the old problem solving and pathologising approaches to assessment or it can place an emphasis on the strengths and resilience that a client demonstrates in the face of the crisis. The story of the crisis is created not just by the event itself but also in how the event is described and how the response to the event is depicted by the people involved in that event and subsequently by the 'worker' who attempts to hear the story of the events retold by the participants. All these players contribute to the final narrative that tells the story of distress or triumph in the face of extreme stress or crisis.

Greene *et al.* (2005) applied the principles of a solution focused approach to crisis intervention. Table 8.1 shows the connections and different emphases of the solution focused approach and the seven stage model.

Table 8.1: Solution focused approach and Roberts's seven stage model

Greene *et al.* (2005) A solution focused approach to crisis	Roberts (2005) Seven-stage crisis intervention model
	Plan and conduct a crisis assessment
Joining	Establish rapport and establish relationship
Defining problems	Identify major problems
	Deal with feelings and emotions
Setting goals	Generate and explore alternatives
Identifying solutions	
Develop and implement an action plan	Develop and formulate an action plan
	Establish follow up plan and agreement

In looking at this case it is useful to consider two elements. The first is the development of an appreciation of the social construction of 'domestic violence'. Remembering the importance of language we need to consider how we language domestic violence. The term domestic violence/intimate partner violence (IPV) could be said to reflect society's ambivalence about the phenomenon. Who decides that the violent act should be prefaced with the language of domesticity or intimacy? Why not simply use the term assault in the way violence acts between others would be defined?

The second element is to consider the choice of a therapeutic model to be employed in the case. Consistent with social constructionist thinking we will look at a solution focused model of interventions in the crisis of 'intimate partner violence'.

Working with Nina in crisis

Most approaches to domestic violence are very unambiguous about the importance of seeing the individuals in the couple separately. While the same holds true for the most part in solution focused work the option of talking to the couple together is not totally dismissed. For example with Roy and Nina this would *only* happen if or when the worker was satisfied that Roy had completely accepted the invitation to take full responsibility for his abusive behaviour and is acting on this commitment (Lethem 1994). It is unlikely that this could be established at the time of a crisis but it may be something for a later stage when adopting a solution focused approach. Solution focused (SF) work with crisis as with other approaches must place the safety of the victim as the priority. This depends on the ability of those who meet with Nina at the time of the crisis actually to recognise what is happening as IPV. Roberts and Roberts (2005) highlight the importance of front line health care workers, police and others knowing what IPV looks like. With Nina it is essential that her GP recognised that she has been the victim of violence otherwise the opportunity to access some help for Nina may be lost.

As with other approaches to IPV it is important to develop some trust between the worker and Nina. SF work acknowledges the power imbalance inherent in IPV. Their approach respects the wishes of women who wish to stay with their partners who have been violent to them, rather than implicitly criticising or blaming them as do approaches which seek to influence women to leave, and does not criticise or blame Nina for staying with Roy. Roberts (2005) says that 'battered women are often motivated to change their lifestyle only during the crisis or post-crisis period' (p.478). This means that it is vital that the GP and any other professional helper working with Nina while considering the opportunity of change associated with the crisis must also be aware that she is most at risk when she is thinking about or planning to leave Roy. This may be related to Roy's sense of heightened threat which may make him more dangerous at this time. In an SF approach to crisis in IPV ensuring clients' safety is viewed not as a separate step but as a theme continuing throughout the crisis work.

An SF crisis approach matches many of the steps in Roberts's crisis approach as depicted in Table 8.1. What may be different is the focus on setting goals and defining solutions based on clients' strengths and past success in dealing with the problem. If this incident of IPV has reached a crisis level for Nina it may be that her strategies for coping are now depleted and she needs help with developing new strategies, or it may be that the crisis has disrupted her coping because she has responded to many similar crises and over time this has just returned things at home to a stability which incorporates rather than excludes Roy's violent episodes. At some stage a crisis will arise that cannot be resolved by a return to the 'normal' IPV situation. It is possible that Nina's current crisis may create a situation where Nina decides to do something differently. SF work in IPV is clear in its view that Nina is the victim, however it equally wants to respect her and her decisions so far. In an SF approach to IPV the goal of the worker is to ensure safety. The worker will explore to what extent safety is possible even if the client remains with the perpetrator. Safety may be more compromised in a time of crisis because the threat to Roy may make him even more volatile than usual. According to Greene *et al.* (2005) SF work has had some success in working with IPV offenders and their partners (Lee, Sebold and Uken 2002, 2003).

SF work in the crisis will be concerned with re-establishing Nina's already successful ways of keeping safe; it will also begin to address her level of confidence so that she can remain safe in the future. Even if safety is not on Nina's agenda the SF worker will make it a priority (use of a scaling question might assist in accessing Nina's confidence about keeping safe or her techniques of keeping safe). As a crisis gives rise to possibilities for change it allows for the opportunity for Nina to consider a preferred future (elicited by a miracle style question). SF offers a template for this conversation while affirming Nina's strengths and resilience to date. It allows her the chance to consider change in a safe setting without any pressure to act on it immediately. This means that it may be possible to make use of the momentum of the crisis to consider an 'exit strategy' without creating immediate further risk for Nina.

No matter what approach is taken we do know that getting out of a violent relationship is not easy. Apart for the heightened risk when planning to leave there is evidence that even in separating the risks may remain. Some women choose to remain because they feel they cannot cope with the continued and unpredictable risk once they leave. SF crisis work helps to focus not just on leaving but on creating a plan to stay safe while staying if that is what Nina decides.

While the main aim of the SF crisis work is to address solutions for safety other aspects of the crisis will also be of concern. Nina has suffered not just physical abuse. Given her situation she is likely to have constructed a very negative image of herself as a wife and mother and as a woman. The SF conversation will attempt to be affirming of her and her coping with a difficult situation, it will take the opportunity to help her to identify her strengths and resilience. The SF approach can also assist in helping Nina to consider views that may have been imposed on her such as you must stay in your marriage, separation will hurt the children, you are a failure if you leave, what about the stigma of letting people know you are an abused woman.

Developing a plan of action may be more about helping Nina to reconsider her view of herself even before she deals with the possibility of leaving Roy. Whatever the objective though the SF helper will attempt to have a plan in place to maximise Nina's safety if she chooses to return to Roy, even if it is only for now.

One of the concerns with any crisis is that if unresolved it may develop into a longer term and even more serious problem. This is a possibility with victims of IPV since they often remain in the violent situation and have to deal with multiple incidence of crisis. The crises are often resolved only through a return to the unsatisfactory stability of IPV. Sometimes such women can suffer from post traumatic stress disorder (PTSD). PTSD will be discussed in the following chapter.

Chapter 9

Post Traumatic Stress Disorder (PTSD)

Introduction

This chapter on post traumatic stress disorder differs for the preceding chapters in that it does not deal with a theory about crisis rather it is focusing on one outcome of exposure to crisis. The subject of post traumatic stress has become one of the growing areas in crisis work. This is evidenced by its inclusion in many of the crisis intervention texts. These contributions will be discussed in this chapter. PTSD has many characteristics that are outside the remit of traditional crisis interventions. It does however fit within the wider conceptualisation of crisis therapies proposed in this work.

A brief history of PTSD

The diagnosis of PTSD first appeared as a defined psychiatric disorder in the *Diagnostic and Statistical Manual of Mental Disorders* (DSM-MD) in 1980. Since that time there has been much discussion and debate about the exact nature of the disorder. From the start PTSD has attracted controversy and scepticism (Mezey and Robbins 2001).

In the 1980s mental health professionals in the US were struggling to deal with the many issues that arose for the soldiers returning from the Vietnam war. Unlike other veterans the soldiers returning from Vietnam were not returning to a heroes' welcome. The incidence of soldiers returning from Vietnam who were experiencing some mental health problems exceeded anything seen among previous veterans. Kukla *et al.* in a report published in 1990 estimated that up to 26 per cent of the Vietnam veterans experienced some form of PTSD. Summerfield (2001) has suggested that

> PTSD was invented as a new diagnosis, which became a successor to the older diagnosis of battle fatigue and war neurosis. The new diagnosis was meant to shift the focus of attention from the details of a soldier's background and psyche to the fundamentally traumatogenic nature of war...Vietnam veterans were to be seen... as people traumatised by roles thrust on them by the US military. (p.95)

Summerfield (2001) argues that the invention of PTSD was 'a powerful and an essentially political transformation' (p.95) while Mezey and Robbins (2001) argue that the diagnosis is both useful and valid as a psychiatric category. They (Mezey and Robbins 2001) accept that the disorder may indeed have been constructed out of sociopolitical ideas rather than psychiatric ones as Summerfield suggested but contend that many conditions reflect this type of influence. Mezey and Robbins (2001) hold that

> the diagnosis of PTSD was developed partly as an attempt to normalise the psychological, cognitive, and behavioural symptoms observed in many traumatised people. It redefined the symptoms of the disorder as a normal response to an abnormal event rather than a pathological condition. (p.561)

Some of the difficulties with the diagnosis of PTSD may lie in the fact that it is often defined in very broad terms. McFarlane (2005) presents the following clarification:

> Post-traumatic stress disorder is triggered by psychologically traumatic events outside the usual range of human experience. Such events include a serious threat to a person's life or physical integrity (for example, rape, motor vehicle accident, or violent assault), destruction of a person's home or community (for example, through a natural disaster or fire), or seeing another person who is mutilated, dying or dead. (p.69)

He (2005) further adds that 'one need not be too rigid in the definition of a traumatic event because a person's perceptions of the danger or threat posed by the event depend on a range of factors, such as past experience' (p.69).

Rechtman (2004) proposes that PTSD has been reformulated since its first iteration in 1980. He suggests that PTSD in its earlier form held onto a notion of psychological trauma that related back to the pathology found in traumatic neurosis. The shift in thinking which Rechtman (2004) dates from the 1990s placed more emphasis on the traumatic nature of 'the event' and so avoids any suspicion of the victim.

> The new definition of the traumatic event as being outside the normal range of human experience and of PTSD as being a response possible in almost anyone...are direct consequences of the desire to get rid of the moral suspicion attached to the theoretical framework of traumatic neurosis. (p.914)

McFarlane (2005) commented on the point that in developing the concept of PTSD with its origins in the battlefield experience, problems arose with issues of cowardice and moral inferiority becoming confused with vulnerability.

> In World War II and the Korean War 'combat fatigue' (the earlier understanding of PTSD) was treated as a psychological disturbance. The treatment approach was best conducted as quickly as possible and as close to the battle lines as possible. The idea was to facilitate a quick return to active duty. (James 2008, p.126)

McFarlane writing about PTSD in a 2005 edition of a text on crisis intervention reminds us that an 'ongoing debate has questioned whether the trauma or individual vulnerability is the central etiological variable in PTSD' (2005, p.71). So while some progress has been made in protecting victims of trauma from the suspicion that they were in some way responsible for their distressed response (PTSD) difficulties do remain. We still cannot explain why some people who experience 'traumatic events' will develop PTSD and others do not. Nor can we predict with any certainty what type of event will educe PTSD or indeed if there is any event that will always result in this type of ongoing distress.

Everly (2000) quotes figures from the US Department of Health and Human Services (2000) which state that 9 per cent of those exposed to a traumatic stressor will develop PTSD. This figure may in part represent the effectiveness of preventative interventions based on the crisis intervention principle we have been considering. If a person experiencing a crisis is given sufficient support and help in the early stages of the crisis then this may act as a preventative measure against the development of the more severe symptoms of PTSD in the longer term. However it may also be indicative of the fact that we are still unclear about what factors contribute to one person developing PTSD while another does not. The shift in emphasis away from considering the unique qualities of the individual has helped to focus on the traumatic event and has assisted in protecting the individual from 'blame' but the shift in emphasis should not necessitate professionals ignoring the factors in clients' lives that may be protective for them in dealing with traumatic events. We still need to understand some of the same issues that have been highlighted in connection with the crisis response. Factors such as social networks, past experiences and current and past mental health may act as contributory or protective factors in the development of PTSD:

> For most individuals, crises are immediate, transient, and temporary. For other individuals, however, the temporary nature of crisis may lead to years of upset. Their life crisis may become part of a posttraumatic stress that is long term and chronic. (Dattilio and Freeman 2007, p.3)

PTSD and mental health problems

The fact that 'other diagnoses such as anxiety or major depression were found to be directly linked to trauma' (Rechtman 2001, p.915) further complicates the matter. James (2008) also comments on this difficulty. He quotes examples in the field that highlight the fact that PTSD is often seen with other disorders. For example, according to the American Psychiatric Association (2000) it is not uncommon for those who suffer from PTSD to have companion diagnoses of anxiety, depressive, organic mental, and substance abuse disorders. McFarlane (2005) references a number of studies that suggest that PTSD is associated with another psychiatric disorder in 50 per cent of individuals (Davidson *et al*. 1985 and Escobar *et al*. 1983).

Aguilera noted the connection between PTSD and substance abuse (1998). She identifies the possibility that people with the disorder may be self medicating to control the symptoms of PTSD by using alcohol and/or other drugs. For the person in a helping role whatever their background the co-morbidity of PTSD with complex mental health issues makes assessment of the trauma and the traumatised response very challenging. McFarlane (2005) adds a different dimension to this debate. He looks to the research in the field to see if there is support for the fact that traumatic life events were a potential cause of mental and physical illness. He concludes referencing Quarantelli's (1985) work in which he argued that there was little evidence to support the view that life events such as disasters have an enduring negative effect on mental health. Pinpointing the reasons for developing PTSD may be further complicated because we tend to incorporate a broad array of trigger events to include traumatic events, crisis situations, natural and man-made disasters. Often these terms are used interchangeably.

Perhaps this is a good time to consider the other aspect of PTSD that may cause confusion. While suggesting those terms such as trauma, and disaster are at times used interchangeably there is still little clarity about distinguishing terms used to describe *responses* to these events. Terms such as stress, distress, crisis, and trauma are used to describe responses to the trigger events. Earlier chapters have dealt with definitions of stress and crisis. We will now explore the definition of post traumatic stress disorder by identifying the key symptoms of the disorder.

Disasters

It is fair to say that in the earlier ideas about trauma the concept was associated with major events such as disasters both natural and man made. The concept of trauma has expanded over time to incorporate the impact of a wider range of events. It is perhaps this inclusiveness that has detracted from a sense of clarity about what is a trauma versus what is a crisis or even just a stressful situation. In the midst of this fluidity about the use of the terms there has developed a particular interest in the importance of responding to the 'disaster'. Planning and responding to disasters have become important activities. This may be in response to the apparent increase in disasters and probably more accurately because of the increase in information and media reporting about such disasters. 'The implication of the term "disaster" in its current usage at least, is that of a calamity or misfortune which goes beyond personal suffering' (Thompson 1991, p.85).

Disaster work may be more closely related to crisis than PTSD. Crisis work and disaster work are based on the immediacy of response with a view to preventing any ongoing or long term negative effects. PTSD by definition is concerned with those who, for whatever reasons, do suffer long term or delayed effects from crisis, disaster, or traumatic events. Thompson (1991) argues convincingly that there is a strong connection between crisis theory, crisis intervention and working with disasters. Disaster work incorporates the ideas of being proactive in response to the situation, providing support and encouraging the natural recovery process while identifying high risk factors that may demand further intervention to prevent ongoing problems. Disaster work encompasses the possibilities of opportunity and fostering resilience that are also part of crisis work.

However disaster work differs from crisis work because of the magnitude of the situations involved (Thompson 1991). Writers (James 2008; Thompson 1991; O'Hagan 1986) in the area of responding to disasters have highlighted that the risk to workers, often both physical and psychological, means that responding to disasters places a particularly heavy burden on workers. Disasters are usually situations that are out of the control of victims, workers, service providers and even governments. This aspect makes work in the field particularly onerous. It often means that workers have to respond in very difficult circumstances with minimum access to support from their agencies. As highlighted previously there is no evidence that shows that experience of such disasters inevitably leads to long term mental health problems. The resilience of people, services and nations can play an important role in mediating the impact of the disaster on the individual. Inevitably some may experience PTSD and it is important to note that workers may be among those to experience the disorder.

Critical incident stress

Critical incident stress is yet another variation of the multifaceted concept of crisis. Alongside the 'disaster planning and response' movement the notion of 'critical incident stress' has developed. A critical incident refers to a traumatic event experienced by an individual. Originally the concept was devised to describe the experiences of people who respond to traumatic events in their capacity as 'helpers'. According to James (2008) critical incident stress debriefing was developed by a fire-fighter named Mitchell in response to his own experiences in dealing with fires, accidents and other events. The idea was to offer an opportunity to those working with 'trauma' or 'critical incidents' to talk about their experiences. This 'debriefing' was proposed as a preventative measure against the subsequent onset of PTSD. James (2008) comments that 'probably no emergent technique in crisis intervention had created more controversy that debriefing procedures' (p.613).

There are a number of studies that are critical of the Mitchell and Everly (1995) critical incident stress debriefing (CISD) formula. The notion of a one-off debriefing is criticised on a number of points primarily the lack of research to support the effectiveness of CISD (James 2008; Roberts et al. 2009). However CISD was reformulated as 'Critical

Incident Stress Management' (Everly and Mitchell 1997, 1999). In a discussion of emergency responses McGlothlin *et al.* (2010) considered the impact of CISM. They reviewed work by Castellano and Plionis (2006) who found that CISM was successfully implemented to augment established individual counselling. The place of CISD or CISM may be disputed but it offers a useful example of the diverse ways in which ideas about crisis and responding to crisis have been applied even where there is little empirical research support.

The main symptoms of PTSD

Some of the continuing questions about PTSD have already been highlighted. In spite of the debate over who is most likely to suffer from PTSD and why, there is relative agreement about the symptoms. The APA did include PTSD in the 1980 edition of its diagnostic manual (DSM-III) as we have seen. In subsequent editions some of the features of the disorder have changed. For example in DSM-IV (1994) PTSD and Acute Stress Disorder (ASD) were placed in two different categories (Aguilera 1998). She offers a summary of the main symptoms associated with the disorder:

> Individuals suffering from PTSD often have an episode when the traumatic event 'intrudes' into their current life. This can happen in sudden, vivid memories that are accompanied by painful emotions. Sometimes the trauma is 're-experienced'. This is called a flashback, a recollection that is so strong that the individual thinks he is actually experiencing the trauma again...re-experiencing may occur in nightmares. The re-experiencing may come as a sudden painful onset of emotion, seemingly without cause. (1998, p.63)

James (2005) states that PTSD is a complex and diagnostically troublesome disorder. He discusses the DSM-IV-TR (APA 2000) conditions and symptoms of PTSD. He mentions a number of important points raised by the APA:

- First the person must have been exposed to a trauma in which he or she was confronted with an event that involved actual or threatened death or serious injury, or a threat to self or others' physical well being... The person's response to the trauma was intense fear, helplessness or horror, as a result he or she has persistent symptoms of anxiety or arousal that were not evident before the traumatic event.

- The person persistently re-experiences the traumatic event (intrusive distressing recollections, nightmares, flashbacks, distress on exposure to cues that resemble an aspect of the event).

- Avoidance of thoughts, feelings associated with the trauma, often resulting in feeling numb or detached.

- The duration of the symptoms must be for more than one month.

(James 2005, pp.128–129)

Aguilera (1998) in differentiating between PTSD and ASD suggests that the symptoms should last beyond a three month period to fit with a diagnosis of PTSD. However she does note that the symptoms may not develop for months or even years after the experience of the traumatic event.

Treatment of PTSD

For the most part the treatment of PTSD approximates what we have been discussing in relation to crisis interventions. Key features of a treatment include developing a relationship with the person, helping the individual to accept the traumatic experience without being overwhelmed, offering support and safety and facilitating family and friends in attempts to provide necessary support. Beyond these basic steps it is important that the individual be helped in developing coping strategies which will include methods for addressing the re-experiencing of the trauma (flashbacks) and easing emotional distress (James 2008; Aguilera 1998). What may be different is the approach to the use of medication to assist in dealing with some of the symptoms. With crisis intervention because the crisis response is immediate and short term there is an emphasis on helping the individual to deal with the stress, distress, or crisis though behavioural, cognitive and systemic strategies discussed in earlier chapters.

In the case of PTSD it may be seen as necessary to supplement the psychotherapeutic interventions with appropriate use of prescribed drugs. Treatment for PTSD may involve long term engagement with medical and other support services. Herman (1992) quoted in Aguilera (1998) states that 'these medications, as part of an integrated treatment plan, can help prevent the development of long term psychological problems in traumatised individuals' (p.68). The use of medication may be contested as some believe that the symptoms exhibited by people experiencing crisis or even trauma are a natural response albeit an extreme response to their situation. The goal of treatment should be to support the individual to develop healthier responses. Medication may have the effect of suppressing an individual's emotional response and exposing her to the risk of possible drug dependence and so should only be offered under expert medical supervision.

PTSD and crisis

While we have dated crisis intervention from the 1940s, PTSD is a relative newcomer. However PTSD is often included in texts dealing with crisis therapies, for example Aguilera (1998), Parad and Parad (2005a) and James (2008) have all addressed the disorder. The relationship between crisis, crisis intervention and PTSD remains unclear. For this reason it seemed important to consider the place of PTSD in understanding crisis therapies.

This book is about crisis therapies and as such it is important to explore the connections between the brief intervention that is crisis intervention and the more long term diagnosis of PTSD. The aim of including PTSD is not to offer an in-depth knowledge base for diagnosis of and intervention with PTSD. If you are involved in providing a service for people with PTSD then the service should and will have developed clearly defined guidelines for assessment of the status of potential clients as well as a procedure for treatment. Some crisis services will work with short term crisis intervention strategies as well as longer term PTSD. What has been offered is a brief account of the development of PTSD.

PTSD does not fit with the brevity and immediacy of crisis intervention but it is suggested here that it highlights the need to expand the notion of crisis intervention to encapsulate a broader range of activities in relation to crisis work. The notion of crisis therapies has been proposed as an alternative construct which will be discussed in the context of the integrative framework for practice in the next and final chapter.

PTSD is relevant to the understanding of crisis therapies for a number of reasons: PTSD may develop when crisis intervention strategies implemented at the time of the impact of the crisis are not effective in helping to resolve the crisis; PTSD may in fact be a totally different phenomenon from those we are exploring in crisis therapies; PTSD and crisis therapies may run along a continuum of responses to crisis situations.

We will consider these issues later in the discussion. What is important for now is to raise the fact that there is continuing debate about where distress, crisis and trauma responses intersect and so accurate assessment of the needs of clients continues to offer a challenge to professionals in the field.

Kolb (1987) in exploring PTSD and ASD made the case that the disorders should be classified into different levels of severity from mild, moderate to severe. The assignment to one level would correlate to the severity and extent of the symptoms. There is a case to be made for a similar categorising of the range of crisis and stress responses. This might assist in distinguishing between short and long term problems and also between intense and less intense exposure to crisis or traumatic events.

Some key points for consideration when attempting to distinguish between PTSD and crisis which could be included are identified in Table 9.1. Drawing on work by James (2008), McFarlane (2005) and Aguilera (1998) this identifies key questions about an event and about symptoms that will help to distinguish PTSD from crisis with the more extreme events, longer duration, and higher intensity being more associated with PTSD.

Table 9.1: Factors to consider in distinguishing PTSD and crisis

The event	The symptoms
The nature of the event (threat to self, threat to others, directly engaged in event, witness to event, interpersonal/public/national)	**The onset of symptoms** (within days of the event/years after the event)
The duration of exposure to the event (once off/repetitive, short/long term exposure)	**The duration of the symptoms** (hours/days/months/years)
The intensity of the event (limited/chaotic)	**The intensity of symptoms** (mild/moderate/severe)
The immediacy of the event (recent or not)	**The intrusiveness of symptoms** (rare/continuous)
The interpretation /meaning of the event (meaning of event to individual, including their sense of culpability or blamelessness)	**The persistence of symptoms** (lasting minutes/hours/days/weeks/months)

It is important not to over simplify what are indeed very complex phenomena. However differentiating between the event and the symptoms may be a useful place to start unravelling some of the intricate aspects of both PTSD and crisis responses. The items included in the event category may not offer a clear indication about the likelihood of early resolution of the crisis response or delayed resolution leading to PTSD. It would be too simplistic to say that the more extreme the event the more likely it will result in PTSD. The intervening factors play such a significant role in determining the outcome of any crisis or traumatic event. It may be that duration and intensity of the event would be significant in terms of evoking particular responses. It seems logical to assume that the longer exposure and more intense event would be more indicative of the onset of PTSD but there is no evidence to prove that these features of the event are reliable predictors.

However understanding the event gives the worker some important insights into the experiences of the individual. The purpose of the dual categorisation is to acknowledge the event while also highlighting the significance of the symptoms in helping to identify the difference between a crisis response and PTSD. In terms of the symptoms category it is helpful to consider that the mild end of the spectrum is most likely to reflect a crisis response while the more severe is consistent with PTSD. The term mild does not refer to the nature of the event which may in fact have been very severe but rather draws attention to the fact that the features of the symptoms as outlined in the table and the severity of the event are not necessarily going to be the same.

Stress, distress, grief, upset, trauma, shock, anxiety are all terms that describe the response to difficult situations we may encounter. Crisis, emergency, disaster, tragedy are terms that we use as descriptions of those events. We complicate matters by referring to traumatic events and crisis responses so that by combining a descriptor of the event with a descriptor of a response we create multiple terms for what is essentially the combination of event and response. This may prove confusing and definitely makes discussion of the phenomena more cumbersome. But the availability of multiple terminologies is preferable to the inadequate language that existed prior to the pioneering work of Lindemann and Caplan. A cautionary note for professionals working in the field: these terms which we associate with describing difficult life situations are used in multiple ways to describe very different experiences. Language is just that, it is not a precise science. Meaning is constructed by two people in conversation as they attempt to convey and understand messages and life stories. It is important to clarify what an individual means when they use the term stressed, or in crisis. It may have different meanings for the individual and the worker.

PTSD is an important contribution to the growing understanding of the impact of stress on individuals. It fits with the individual focus explored in earlier chapters. It also fits with the medical discourse that has dominated many aspects of working with individuals. In attempting to make sense of PTSD and its relationship to crisis and crisis interventions it may be that the key lies in this medical discourse. When Lindemann first identified the grief reactions he observed in the Coconut Grove tragedy he was able to make a case for the need to help people in similar circumstances. Through his work he created an awareness and acceptance of the impact of crisis on individuals and families. He was able to establish guidelines that informed workers about what they might witness as they worked to help those in crisis. It was 40 years before PTSD was categorised as a disorder in the diagnostic manual for mental health (APA 1980).

It seems that while PTSD is a useful medical categorisation of a set of symptoms associated with the experience of trauma it may be open to misuse as suggested by Summerfield (2001). PTSD legitimates the experience of stress which results in long term problems. It gives the experience a medical label. That label offers the individual a diagnosis which is recognised and which serves to protect the individual from suspicion or blame. All of these are useful attributes. The difficulties lie in the over use of the diagnostic label to cover experiences that are legitimate but may not fall into the category of a disorder. What about a natural or normal response to crisis?

Natural or normal response to crisis

Often the natural or normal response to crisis is and should be upset, distress, and/or stress. Such a reaction does not necessarily mean that the individual has a disorder. To categorise reacting to crisis as a disorder has the potential to undermine natural coping mechanisms and resilience. Everly (2000) cautioned against the risk of intervening too early in response to crisis reactions, what he called premature crisis intervention. This premature intervention might result in interfering with the natural resilience for processing such events. It may be useful to take a step back from PTSD and recognise the place of post traumatic stress. Kolb

(1987) did address this when he suggested that PTSD and ASD should be viewed as a continuum of responses. In order to achieve a legitimate place in psychiatric parlance the term disorder seems to be required. Yet for many they do not suffer any disorder in the sense of mental ill health. They may suffer disorder in terms of disorganisation because of the crisis event but that is not necessarily a mental health disorder. There needs to be legitimation of the various levels of reactions to crisis or trauma and not just the more severe spectrum which is deserving of the mental health diagnosis of PTSD.

Susan and Jake

Since we have looked at the case of Susan in relation to each of the theoretical approaches considered in earlier chapters it might be useful to look at the case in the context of PTSD. In the first place the basic event of moving into new accommodation and experiencing the disruption caused by a domestic flood does not really meet the criteria of a traumatic event. In other chapters we have adjusted the story to illustrate how the event may create a crisis reaction for Susan. In order to generate a PTSD the event would probably need to have a number of added dimensions.

For example the event itself: Susan came home to discover the flood in her kitchen. She was attempting to discover the source of the flood when a neighbour came running to her door shouting at her to leave the building. The flood was just the first sign that there was a major defect in the structure of the building. Within minutes of being alerted by her neighbour Susan and Jake were assembled outside the building and a gas explosion occurred that started a major fire in the building. The apartment was not at the centre of the explosion but the fire destroyed most of the building before the fire services got it under control.

The initial reaction: Susan was in a state of shock and was unable to respond when asked what had happened. She was clinging onto Jake and crying hysterically when her father arrived at the scene. Susan returned home with her parents and was supported by them through the following weeks. Because of the terrible shock Susan's parents encouraged her to stay with them for several months. She returned to work and seemed to be coping well.

Three months later: When Susan decided it was time to start looking for new accommodation she began to have sleepless nights. She kept checking on Jake and on a number of occasions woke up screaming for everyone to get out fast. She avoided looking for a place in the same area she had been living in at the time of the explosion even though it was very central and made the most sense in terms of her living arrangement. Her parents noticed that she was becoming more and more distant and even observed that she was emotionally cutting herself off from Jake, not responding to his demonstrations of affection and snapping at him on and off.

PTSD: The combination of the traumatic nature of the event and her subsequent long term reactions, physical, psychological and emotional might be indicative of PTSD. Susan was referred to her local health services and began to see a counsellor on a weekly basis. She undertook a course in cognitive behaviour therapy which helped her to become desensitised to the anxiety she was experiencing, helped her to gain control of her emotional reactions and facilitated the development of new coping skills. She was also able to recognise her own resilience in the face of the traumatic event. The support of family and friends became an important aspect of her ongoing coping and successful re-engagement with her life goals.

Conclusion

Perhaps the easiest way to understand PTSD and crisis is to consider PTSD as part of the continuum of stress responses to trigger events that challenge coping behaviours. For the most part as we have already discussed individuals respond to challenging situations in a resourceful and resilient way. Even when faced with more difficult situations that may be categorised as traumas, crises or disasters many people do manage their stress reactions. Sometimes the initial expression of anxiety, shock, and crisis is mitigated by time, personal coping strategies and/or external social supports. In some cases the sense of being in crisis lasts for a number of weeks in others the sense of crisis diminishes more quickly.

> The range of reactions people exhibit when confronted with interpersonal loss or violent events has led to considerable controversy regarding people's capacity to cope with such experiences… Of particular note is the growing awareness that many – often the majority – endure even horrific events without experiencing significant disruption in functioning. (Mancini and Bonanno 2006, p.972)

For a number of people the stress response becomes more accentuated, more enduring and may lead to a diagnosis of PTSD. This may happen because there were no opportunities to intervene at an early stage of the crisis or because a crisis intervention strategy was insufficient for the needs of that individual. We really do not know why some are more vulnerable to PTSD but this chapter has identified some of the factors that appear to be important. Whatever the reason it is important to recognise that for some people dealing with traumatic events becomes a more long term struggle and may demand not just the range of counselling options associated with crisis intervention approaches but also may involve medical intervention including medication and even hospitalisation. It is important to remember as well that many, maybe most people *do* cope without any formal or professional intervention.

Roberts *et al.* (2009) report in their findings of a meta-analysis intervention following trauma that there was no evidence to support the implementation of routine psychological interventions following a traumatic event. Well informed professional judgement and assessment concerning risk and resilience are central to responding effectively to crisis. This includes supporting resilience and the natural process of coping where more intensive intervention may be experienced as counterproductive or undermining. This raises one of the ongoing problems with crisis interventions as with other counselling approaches and that is the difficulty in conducting research which can demonstrate that success or crisis resolution can be attributed exclusively to the crisis intervention strategy employed. It is difficult to exclude the spontaneous recovery of the individual as an important factor in dealing with crisis. These are often referred to as the common factors in the therapeutic process (Asay and Lambert 1999) where the client or participant is acknowledged to make the major contribution to the success of any treatment or therapeutic process.

Chapter 10

An Integrated Theoretical Framework for Practice in Crisis Work

Introduction

Crisis as a risk

Crisis as a way of life

Crisis as an opportunity

These are very challenging questions about crisis for both the clients and the workers. While clients may struggle to face the immediate impact of a crisis we must consider both the immediate risk and the opportunity for change. It is easy to underestimate or misjudge the relationship between the impact of the crisis and the resulting momentum it can create for change.

Understanding crisis therapies starts with identifying the key aspects of the crisis therapy interaction. This means understanding the nature of crisis (or at least the theories we have so far about the nature of crisis), therapy, the worker or helper and most important the person or people in crisis. It is fair to say that developing such understanding is not a simple task. In fact it is an ongoing process which has been unfolding for almost a century. What is perhaps important is that interest in developing our understanding has been sustained over that time. This in itself seems to support the view that the experience of crisis and the attempts to resolve these crisis experiences is of widespread interest.

As mentioned in the introduction approaches to dealing with crisis have been among the most versatile and adaptable of all therapeutic interventions. Each emerging theory has addressed the notion of crisis giving rise to the multiple views that we have explored.

In discussing the various ways of understanding crisis some latitude has been taken in terms of outlining a timeline of theoretical ideas that have shaped our understanding of crisis. The aim of working from a historical perspective from the 1920s to the present day was to provide some organisational framework rather than to suggest any preference for the most recent developments. In fact the aim of this final chapter is to consider the implications of the accumulation of what we know so far and to consider how we can utilise this in the best interests of the clients we serve.

Looking at the historical development of our understanding of crisis also helps to demonstrate that there are few 'facts' and little indisputable knowledge in this field. Each theory offered a different perspective on human experiences in general and we were able to track how that informed the experience of crisis in particular. Given that some of these theories have been around longer than others there may be an element of some having a more established place as accepted explanations. The more recent, often referred to as post-modern ideas certainly suggest that some ways of explaining what we observe and experience are more privileged than others. It may be that the more traditional ideas have simply gained credibility because they have survived or perhaps they have a resonance that rings true to professionals in the field. Other possibilities may be that training in more traditional ways is well established and that professionals like the clients we work with may have some difficulties with adapting to and incorporating change.

Probably one of the main influences on how we see the therapy world today is the dominance of the evidence based directive. The danger here is that if something cannot be proven to be effective then it is not considered either effective or therapeutic. This is a much disputed position and contrary to the concurrent growth in the post-modern position that acknowledges that it is unhelpful to apply quantitative measures only to what works in therapy. Really understanding what works demands paying attention to not just measurable outcomes but also to understanding the process of helping. While acknowledging this debate it is not the focus of our attention here. What is the focus is developing an appreciation of the myriad of ideas that can, if we are willing, inform our thinking about crisis events and how they impact our clients.

What we have then are ideas or concepts that when assembled together form a set of interrelated ideas or theory. The theory then sets out a way of observing the world and a way of making sense of what we observe. This we often refer to as a theoretical framework as it operates in a way that includes some things within the frame and excludes others, it may also serve to draw our attention to some aspects of the picture more than others and to focus our attention on particular qualities or aspects of the events we are observing. The method we then adopt to work with what we observe is contingent on what it is we have been able to observe. In other words if we see only vulnerability then we need to respond to that whereas if we see both vulnerability and resilience in the same person then it opens up a different set of possible responses.

Again if we look to the past to provide the information we think important to understand the problem we may get a very different picture than if we look to the present or even the future to explain what is happening for the client. Each of the theories we have explored then adds to our repertoire of understanding of what is a crisis and what it might mean to the individuals involved in dealing with a crisis. Each theory also indicates what the priority is in terms of helping to resolve the crisis. For example we considered the cognitive theory that prioritised what we think, our attitudes and values, while radical theory considered action outside of the individual to address social inequity that has contributed to the crisis.

What we have then are multiple ways of understanding the nature of crisis and also multiple ways of interpreting what the crisis means to the client. It might be easy to get overwhelmed ourselves in all this theory but if we consider that all can contribute to a more comprehensive appreciation of the clients' experience then it is important to take account of the possibilities. That is not to say that this eclectic approach is the only approach. Many people think that it is better to have a thorough understanding of one theoretical framework than an incomplete grasp of many theories. The risk in this one dimensional approach is that we might miss something that has important implications for the client. At a minimum it is essential that as professionals and helpers we have a sufficient awareness of our preferred ways of seeing the world so that when our way is not working for the client we do not blame the client and we can explore alternative possibilities.

The experience of crisis is most often a time of intense distress. It is not a time when someone in crisis can easily contradict those around who may be misinterpreting what is going on. It is therefore important to have an open mind and consider many possible options for assessing the crisis. Figure 10.1 helps to draw together a way of considering the main ideas that are found in the range of theories we have explored. It is important to be cautious that we do not oversimplify the crisis event and distil it down to one acceptable explanation. The integrative theories model should be viewed with this caution in mind. It offers a guide to sets of ideas that may be important in developing a comprehensive picture of what the crisis is and what the crisis means to the client.

The model starts at the centre with the individual and draws attention to the theoretical ideas that address such issues as the unconscious, cognitive, emotional and behavioural (skills) aspects of defining a crisis and also of attempting to understand the experience of such a crisis for the individual concerned. The model however clearly situates all these individual aspects of crisis within a framework that takes account of the world outside the individual, the world in which the individual must live and deal with the crisis. This broader picture includes family, community and ultimately culture. All of these elements are then bounded by the influences of the social, political and economic world in which they are situated.

Crisis intervention as a brief intervention or longer term therapy

The integrated model outlined here illustrates the richness derived from diversity. It is interesting that in spite of the diversity demonstrated in the exploration of the various theoretical perspectives on crisis they all seem to have accepted the central belief that crisis is a time limited experience. Caplan (1964) clearly placed crisis intervention in the realm of brief therapy when he stressed this time limiting nature of crisis. Some form of resolution will happen within a few weeks of the crisis because a person cannot sustain or endure the level of stress, distress, and intense discomfort that accompanies the crisis experience.

This central belief about crisis had been retained despite the influence of multiple ways of defining and understanding what makes an event a crisis and what is considered the best approach to working with crisis. One aspect of the debate about the therapeutic response to crisis hinges on the question of the duration of the crisis and by association the duration

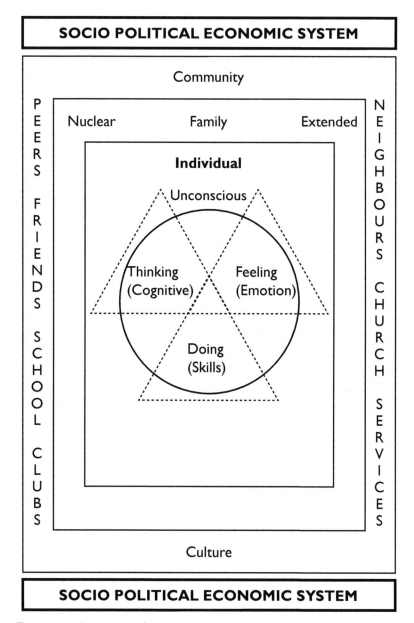

Figure 10.1: An integrative theoretical framework for understanding crisis

of the intervention. There has been debate about the exact nature of crisis intervention in relation to other brief therapies (Stuart and MacKay 1977; Parad and Parad 2005a). Stuart and Mackay (1977) in differentiating what they call short term therapy from crisis intervention suggested that in crisis interventions the emphasis is on the quick resolution of the stress induced by the crisis while short term therapy is concerned with the person and his symptoms and behaviour patterns. Given the developments in crisis therapies this argument seems somewhat limited.

Aguilera (1990) while offering an approach to crisis that is consistent with the earlier ideas of Caplan goes on to distinguish what can be considered as two levels to crisis intervention. She addresses the immediacy issue by suggesting that some relief of the symptoms was necessary in the first level of work with clients. She promoted the view that some relief would be required in order to restore previous functioning and allow a client to understand what had led to the crisis and to get support from others to deal with the crisis. In this conceptualisation of crisis intervention making connections to past crisis and developing new ways of thinking and coping were tasks for a second level intervention. The model of two levels of intervention is a way of addressing the different needs that may arise immediately the crisis hits and over the following weeks.

In the discussion of PTSD it became clear that there was potentially some conflict between including PTSD in crisis therapy and this attribute of crisis work as a brief approach. For the most part there was agreement that PTSD was a reaction to a traumatic event where the reaction has lasted longer than the crisis reactions otherwise deemed to be appropriate for crisis work. This indicates that in some situations a crisis response has long term implications for clients and demands longer term therapy. The criteria for this longer term approach may be still in dispute but it seems there is some agreement that the event must be traumatic and that negative reactions are sustained over a more extended period of time, at least several months. In discussing PTSD in an earlier chapter it was proposed that the differences were sufficient to warrant dealing with PTSD outside of a crisis intervention framework but that it could be encapsulated in an expanded crisis therapies formula or paradigm (see Figure 10.2).

A crisis therapies paradigm: Crisis intervention and crisis therapies

Throughout this discussion we have used crisis intervention and crisis therapies as more or less interchangeable constructs. This is perhaps misleading and should be clarified. Crisis intervention of course refers to the original development of the concept by Lindemann in 1944 and to subsequent theorists who have built on his ideas. Here I am suggesting that given the development of our understanding of the complex nature of crisis and the diversity of theoretical contributions that we have explored, the concept of crisis intervention which implies an agreed single and unified approach to crisis is no longer sufficient. Crisis intervention has developed into a more expansive field of therapy with a range of options for interpreting problems and informing the worker or helper's response. Crisis intervention is more correctly then a range of therapies that offer different options for dealing with crisis situations. Crisis therapies also incorporate therapeutic interventions which are referred to here as strategic crisis therapies, these utilise crisis to enhance motivation and engagement with change and go beyond actions which simply offer immediate relief from the stress educed by a crisis event.

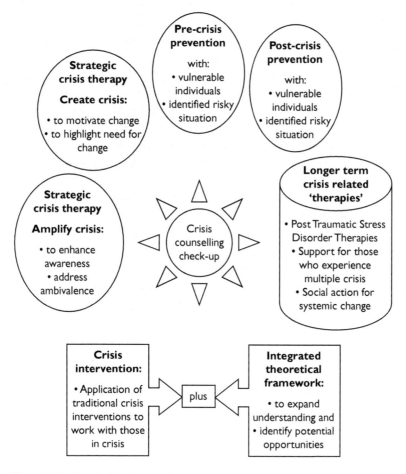

Figure 10.2: A crisis therapies paradigm

Maybe we are then looking at a range of interventions that are linked together by some relationship to a crisis event. Figure 10.2 illustrates some of the elements of a broader interpretation of crisis related therapies. It is worth noting of course that in some cases a crisis leads to a spontaneous or natural resolution and so no intervention is required, in others the crisis is such that the individual, family or community in crisis need immediate and direct intervention. In still another formulation those in crisis will be helped sufficiently by a restoration of the pre-crisis homeostasis or equilibrium. This would be helpful in cases where the level of functioning pre-crisis was good. There are however many incidences of crisis where the pre-crisis functioning was in itself instrumental in precipitating the current crisis. This can happen where the individual, family or community has been subjected to previous crisis and where the resolution achieved from that earlier crisis left those involved in a more vulnerable state.

Sometimes we think of these as individuals or families who are chaotic... moving from one crisis to another. The cumulative effect of multiple crises renders the brief therapeutic approach of traditional crisis intervention insufficient and the reinstatement of the pre-crisis functioning only will serve to guarantee the onset of a future crisis. These cases are not suitable for crisis intervention alone. They may demand a long term support strategy in conjunction with a response to the trigger crisis event yet they can be included in the expanded crisis therapies construct.

We also mentioned situations where for example families are in crisis because of the actions of one family member but that person does not see there is any crisis. The development of therapies informed by motivational interviewing highlights that crisis work can be useful not just in helping someone to deal with a crisis as he actually experiences it but that it may be important to have strategies to help someone recognise that there is a crisis. The strategy of amplifying ambivalence is one example that fits with this use of crisis to motivate change.

The traditional crisis interventions in their various formulations that have been developed and expanded over the timeline as discussed in the introduction are of course central to any consideration of crisis work. In this summary these are enhanced by employing the integrated theoretical framework in Figure 10.1 to maximise our options for understanding the crisis as experienced by individuals, families and communities. This framework also acts as a reminder that people are resilient and that it is crucial not to undermine this resilience or to interfere with their natural resolution where this is likely to be beneficial to them. It also serves to underline that not all spontaneous resolution results in a return to pre-crisis coping or improved coping. In such cases without help the intensity of the crisis can be abated but the seeds of the next crisis are already in place and resources depleted by the earlier crisis will be unable to sustain the individual, family and community through another crisis event.

Post traumatic stress has been discussed at some length. The longer term nature of both the experience of trauma and the recovery process associated with PTSD is not consistent with a core element of crisis intervention with its brief approach. However PTSD is often incorporated into a crisis intervention model because of its close links with crisis events. It seems more useful to reconstruct our understanding of crisis related events and the necessary responses to those events by adopting a crisis therapies paradigm. This can allow for the inclusion of PTSD while still acknowledging that the needs of those experiencing PTSD are not the same as those in other crisis situations. We can use our expanded understanding of crisis work to assist in the ongoing work of developing empathic and effective therapeutic responses to PTSD.

A crisis therapies paradigm must also include recognition that when crises have a social dimension this must be addressed. The over emphasis on the individual and families in crisis intervention may serve to camouflage the underlying systemic predicators of crisis. On the continuum of change transformative change is difficult for anyone to achieve. It is perhaps even more difficult to achieve in the sociocultural-political and economic systems within which individuals, families and communities are attempting to cope. The social action required to bring about such change demands long term and sustained work. Many do not consider this to be part of a therapeutic paradigm. Failure to, at a minimum, take account of these systemic factors and preferably to target them for change is a disservice to the individual and families who cannot successfully resolve their crisis with transformative change unless the system in which they are living changes to support them more effectively.

Social action can be discredited as the business of extremists but we are all living within the constraints of social and economic policies that are not always crisis sensitive and certainly not always sufficiently responsive to those who are marginalised by disadvantage. What could be more therapeutic than working to improve the quality of life of the clients we work with beyond what they can achieve through individual effort alone? One step in this direction is the acknowledged effectiveness of group responses to crisis situations. Moving beyond the individual to harness the power of group action is one step toward addressing the need for social action. This was perhaps most evident when we discussed natural disasters. When awarded with an Emmey for his work with disasters George Clooney highlighted that it was all very well to respond to the immediate needs in a time of natural disaster such as Katrina in the US but five years later people are still struggling – their crisis is not over. These are long term issues.

Finally crisis therapies can also include the aspect of 'helping' which attempts to equip those we work with to achieve a transformative change in response to crisis. Such change will help to prevent future events resulting in the overwhelming distress that accompanies crisis. Post-crisis prevention and pre-crisis prevention may be very closely related. They both identify potential vulnerability. Pre-crisis looks to our understanding and knowledge of characteristics in individuals, families and communities that may leave them open to crisis events. Post-crisis attempts to assimilate new information about what factors contributed to this crisis now for this individual, family or community and attempts to prevent the reoccurrence of similar crises through strengthening protective factors and tackling risk factors or characteristics. This post-crisis prevention work should also include continued work on addressing systems related risk factors.

Immediate relief, motivation and the impetus to change

Aguilera's (1998) view of crisis resolution is very focused on the restoration of equilibrium and refers to factors that bring the person back into a balanced state. If the aim of the intervention is equilibrium then it fits with the continuum of change proposed in the introduction. One interpretation of the Aguilera (1998) model is that it places emphasis on stability and later the possibility of augmentation of skills. It is not clear how this approach conceptualises the other end of the change continuum that indicates a transformative change.

This issue highlights another interesting point about crisis intervention and that relates to the extent to which the worker or helper should intervene in a direct or even directive way. This is perhaps one of the most challenging aspects of crisis work as it calls for the worker or helper to weigh up the risks and benefits of taking direct action to resolve the crisis versus giving the crisis time to impact on the person as an impetus or motivation for change. Roberts (2005) emphasises the need for comprehensive assessment when he warns 'if we don't assess, we are likely to engage in well intentioned but misguided and potentially harmful action' (p.149). The integrative theoretical framework serves as a guide to the key concepts to be considered in crisis work. Drawing on this framework I have developed a crisis counselling check-up (Figure 10.3) to serve as a summary reminder of some of these key ideas that may be useful to keep in mind while conducting an assessment.

A crisis counselling check-up

One aim of this book is to help develop an understanding that crisis therapies have a complex knowledge base. It stresses that an appreciation of the different theoretical perspectives can enhance our ability to both understand the client's experience of crisis and offer us a range of options with regard to our response to the crisis situation. It is important not to underestimate the skill required to integrate the possibilities generated by the various theoretical frameworks and then to make professional decisions about what needs to be done. There is however some agreement about some basic skills required whichever approach to crisis is adopted. These are presented here with a cautionary reminder that they have been developed as a quick reference guide and reminder and do not and should not replace the need to work on the more in depth theories and concepts discussed in the earlier chapters. First we will consider this guide or check up on aspects of assessment (Figure 10.3).

The notion of a crisis counselling check-up was developed to help practitioners consider aspects of assessment drawn from the range of theoretical perspectives on crisis discussed in earlier chapters. It attempts to encompass the key aspects of understanding the crisis and draws attention to the central place of assessment in dealing with crisis work. It is not meant as a replacement for other assessment tools that may be established as part of a particular agency protocol nor does it replace some of the specialised assessment tools mentioned earlier which focus on for example assessment of depression or suicide risk. This check-up is a broad based reminder of what might be worth considering as we attempt to develop a comprehensive understanding of the client's position.

Figure 10.3 represents the main elements of the assessment factors which help to establish where the client is in terms of the crisis. It is designed to be used in conjunction with the integrative theoretical framework which gives guidance about the underlying ways of understanding and interpreting the crisis experience. Any assessment is an attempt to measure or make a judgement about facts of the issue that have been identified as significant. The check-up highlights eight different aspects of the crisis situation which should be considered in the assessment process. The eight aspects are placed together in pairs to draw attention to the interconnectedness between particular concerns. In reality all eight of the factors are of course interrelated and the level of presence or absence of any one of them has implications for the remaining factors and so has implications for the strategy that emerges from the assessment.

The check-up is conceptualised as four sets of factors: risk and opportunity, vulnerability and resilience, stability and change and finally individual and systems. These represent the pairs of variables that are presented here as interrelated in the crisis experience.

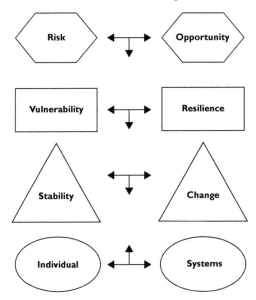

Figure 10.3: Crisis counselling check-up

Risk and opportunity

There is much agreement that the assessment of risk, sometimes referred to as lethality is a core activity in crisis intervention. There is no dispute about the importance of assessing and addressing risk. The check-up reminds us of the centrality of this concern but places risk on a continuum with opportunity. These two elements of an assessment can be viewed as interrelated. It is too simplistic to say that if you have risk you do not have opportunity. The idea of placing the factors on a continuum is to emphasise the relationship between them. The priority is always to ensure safety in so far as it is possible. Placing opportunity in the same range as risk reminds us that crisis is also opportunity. It may be useful to attempt to assess risk in relation to opportunity. It may be that the greater the risk the more attention we must pay to that risk and in doing so we may have to be less attentive to the opportunity created by the crisis. Of course this suggests that sometimes we underestimate the opportunity aspect of the crisis. The judgement on where the client sits in relation to the risk–opportunity continuum is also connected to the remaining sets of attributes.

Vulnerability and resilience

It is important to assess levels of vulnerability but it is also important to consider resilience. These factors, as with risk and opportunity, are not mutually exclusive. The idea behind the check-up is that most clients, families and communities will have risk and opportunity as well as vulnerability and resilience. The check-up again serves to remind us to look for both. Whatever decision we reach on the question of risk and vulnerability will have consequences in terms of the type of approach we take and the model of intervention we select. If we are unsure of the levels of risk but think that the client has other vulnerabilities then the combination of the two may suggest that the emphasis in the intervention should be more directive or direct and securing safety is the priority. The third set of attributes will also influence decision making and intervention planning.

Stability and change

At the centre of crisis intervention is the notion that crisis can give an impetus to change. In considering some of the debate about change presented in earlier chapters it is clear that change in the form of transformative change is not always possible or even desirable. Sometimes restoration to pre-crisis stability is a sufficient goal. But that is not always the case. Sometimes restoration to pre-crisis stability may represent simply a temporary hold on the crisis and even the smallest upset may regenerate the crisis. An assessment should indicate which is the most desirable goal, stability or more extensive change. More often than not the most helpful outcome would be both the restoration of pre-crisis stability and from there the initiation of changes that would be the basis of a transformation or long term change. You can of course see how this is tied up with the other factor sets. If the impetus for change is powered by the crisis then resolution of the crisis event at pre-crisis stability may result in limiting the change opportunity. Decisions about achieving pre-crisis stability do not lie only with the worker; the client, family or community, when they understand the nature of the crisis experience may themselves choose to optimise the change opportunity presented through the crisis. Higher levels of resilience are also likely to shift the balance in favour of change.

In an assessment where there is high risk, high vulnerability and a strong indication that stability is urgently needed then the opportunity for change may be limited, or may need to be sacrificed in order to address a more immediate need for safety. On the other hand where there is evidence of resilience and the risk is adjudged to be less significant then it may be possible to enhance change opportunities. The check-up is simply a tool to alert us to consider the interrelatedness of these factors in the assessment process.

Individual and social

The final set of factors that are included in the check-up relate specifically to the frameworks that challenge the individualisation of crisis. They suggest that it is always important to ask questions about the social aspects of crisis situations. (Refer to the chapters on systems and radical perspectives for reminders of these concerns.) That is not to say that it is always possible to address the social aspects of the crisis. In the immediacy of a crisis it may be difficult enough to deal with the individual or individuals directly involved in the crisis. However, the argument about who needs to change to ensure that the crisis is not repeated does draw attention to the way in which we conceptualise the crisis.

If we consider the crisis only in terms of those individuals directly affected we will lose sight of the greater social systems that may have contributed to the onset of the crisis. In doing this we limit our ability to redress the crisis and ensure transformative change.

If we focus on the individual we may also underestimate the power of the social systems in which he lives. These systems may be very significant in developing coping and support strategies for clients who experience crisis. The check-up therefore suggests that we should always think both of the individual and the social perspective in assessing crisis.

The comprehensive crisis approach presented is an attempt to encapsulate the main ideas from the wide range of ideas about crisis presented in the earlier chapters. It is an integrative approach and is an attempt to draw together what we know so far. The tools presented in this chapter have been developed as a guide to practitioners and helpers to assist in their task of understanding and employing the widest range of ideas we have to respond to crisis events experienced by individuals, families and communities.

The final tool developed here illustrates the type of skills required in crisis helping. These are conceptualised as elements of a crisis conversation (Figure 10.4). The three essential elements of a crisis conversation are summarised: calming, coping and changing. Each of these refer to skills and actions that can play a role in helping in a crisis whether the crisis is one experienced by an individual, family or community.

The 3 Cs of crisis conversations: Calming, coping and changing

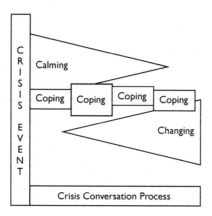

Figure 10.4: The 3 Cs of crisis conversations – calming, coping and changing

Calming

This element is represented as a triangle which is directly connected to the crisis event. This demonstrates the need to employ calming skill strategies immediately the event occurs or is known to have occurred. The largest side of the triangle is in contact with the event which indicates that this early conversation may be more about calming than either of the other elements. The triangle illustrates that as time elapses calming skills may be less central to the conversation, when a trusting relationship has been established that in itself may suffice to support the client's ability to retain composure and handle the most debilitating aspects of distress.

Coping

This element is represented by a series of blocks. The blocks are of different sizes to indicate that the coping skills conversation may vary over time. It may be more useful in working alongside the calming conversation near the start of the process which is connected to the event (although the worker must be careful not to appear dismissive of the crisis or condescending about coping). Later coping conversation is undulating or flexible and is dependent on the workers' assessment of its usefulness. It is another element of the crisis conversation that demands skilful application and should not be underestimated.

Changing

The tip of the triangle does not make contact with the event but the triangle's broadest side appears at the later stages of the crisis conversation. This illustrates that while changing conversation may not be appropriate in the immediate shock of the crisis event it may be possible to introduce and expand on this element of the conversation as time goes by. In some cases conversation about change may have to happen immediately where some change in behaviour and/or thinking is necessary as an immediate response to risk in the crisis.

The elements of the conversation are not all of equal importance in every conversation. If you consider the three elements as ingredients in a conversation the decision about the amount of each to be used should be determined by the worker or helper in response to the assessment of the client's needs which differ in every situation. An alternative depiction of the three Cs is shown in Figure 10.5. Here the different measures of each element are illustrated by different sized circles. The circles are interconnected but differ in size as dictated by the assessment of the priorities in each specific crisis case.

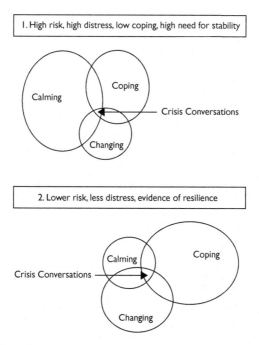

Figure 10.5: The 3 Cs of crisis conversations – calming, coping and changing (not in equal measure)

The illustration of a crisis conversation has been developed to help summarise some of the important aspects of crisis work. The sets of skills and actions that are incorporated into each of the three elements are expanded on in Table 10.1. The table is not designed to be exhaustive but is set out to help link the generic skills of all professional helping relationships with skills and actions that are seen as useful in a therapeutic response to crisis. Alongside the skills and actions is a listing for some things to watch out for as potential mistakes or 'traps' in crisis therapies. The final listing connects the skills, actions and errors to the literature on crisis work.

Table 10.1: Calming, coping and changing – skills and actions

Calming	Watch out for!	Related to
• Build relationship	• Not establishing relationship	*Miller and Rollnick (2002)*
• Develop trust	• Going too fast for client	• Phase one strategies in motivational interviewing
• Be respectful and genuine	• Missing important clues (especially when worker is feeling stressed)	• open questions
• Engage in active listening and empathic responses	• Viewing assessment as procedure instead of integral part of therapeutic experience	• reflection
• Open questions	• Giving unrealistic reassurances	• affirming
• Reflective responses	• Appearing to be condescending	• Empathic listening *Roberts (2005)*
• simple reflections	• Acting on own interpretation of what the crisis is without checking with client	• Plan and assess
• reflect content		• Establish rapport and rapidly establish relationship
• reflect feeling	• Creating further stress by taking too much control	• Identify major problems and deal with feelings and emotions
• Clarify your role	• Not taking enough control	*James (2008)*
• Acknowledge fears and other feelings	• Failing to balance directive and non directive helping	• Assessing
• Assess	• Not understanding the nature of the crisis – insufficient knowledge base on the issue involved	• Listening
• immediate safety of clients and worker	• Allowing stress to affect non verbals for example: body language, tone of voice, appearing to be rushed	• defining the problem
• what is the crisis?		• ensuring client safety
– the client's view		• proving support
• what is the crisis?		*Puleo and McGlothlin (2010)*
– the worker's view		• Contextualise and triage symptoms
• consider need for short term goal/s		• Employ directive, non directive or collaborative approach
• Inspire confidence		• Identify client's strengths and protective factors
• Act competently		
• Be supportive		
• Work in collaboration with client and other workers		

• Give realistic reassurance
• Be informative
• Answer questions
• Be directive and/or non directive as required
• Congruent non verbals:
  • use calm tone of voice
  • nod
  • make eye contact (when appropriate)
	• Eye contact is not always calming; sometimes it is experienced as challenging or even disrespectful
	• Be cautious about even limited physical contact – it may be misconstrued
	  • holding hands or touching shoulder/ back may be acceptable in some situations but not all
	  • hugging – while it may seem comforting it may be invasive for some
		Daughhetee and Bartlett (2010)
		• Coordinate response to crisis
		• Mitigate further suffering of client
		• Generate safe environment for worker
		• Work collaboratively
		Berg (1994)
		• Joining
		Dattilio and Freeman (2007)
		• Develop relationship, identify specific problems

Table 10.1: Calming, coping and changing – skills and actions *cont.*

Coping	Watch out for!	Related to
<ul><li>Continue with calming skills as necessary</li><li>Define further the extent of the crisis</li><li>Identify client coping attempts</li><li>Focus on strengths</li><li>Amplify coping that has been helpful</li><li>Reframe other skills as useful in coping</li><li>Address fears</li><li>Assess and engage resources</li><li>Begin to consider appropriate coping response to crisis<ul><li>plans and possible actions</li><li>who needs to be involved in plan</li><li>what resources are available</li><li>client's preferences</li><li>worker's assessment</li></ul></li><li>Continue to balance directive, non directive and collaborative moving more towards empowering client</li><li>Apply specialised knowledge about what is important/effective in dealing with this specific type of crisis</li><li>Maintain your professional role</li><li>Assess readiness to change<ul><li>client's ability to change</li><li>willingness to change</li><li>need to change</li></ul></li><li>Who/what needs to change</li><li>Explore alternatives</li></ul>	<ul><li>Too much coping talk may seem dismissive of fears/sense of threat</li><li>Overenthusiastic reframing or identification of coping may be unrealistic/unhelpful</li><li>Suggesting coping without any evidence that it actually exists…it may be questioned and rejected and impact on the trusting relationship</li><li>Timing of introduction of planning alternatives… this is the start of talk about changing and needs to be done when there is some calm but still openness to thinking about alternatives</li><li>Appearing to be 'too expert' when attempting to apply your specialised knowledge</li><li>Not being expert enough and so undermining trust</li><li>Being too fixed about who needs to change, in particular not taking account of the social context</li><li>Being too fixed on what needs to change, following your preferred alternatives</li><li>Undermining or underestimating natural/normal recovery from crisis</li></ul>	*Saleebey (2002)*<ul><li>Everyone has strengths, these when supported can lead to transformational change</li></ul>*de Shazer (1985, 1988, 1991), DeJong and Berg (2001), Greene et al. (2005)*<ul><li>Exploring strengths</li><li>Finding exceptions</li><li>Amplifying</li><li>Coping questions</li><li>Compliments</li></ul>*Aguilera (1998)*<ul><li>Identify situational supports and coping mechanisms</li></ul>*Roberts (2005)*<ul><li>Generate and explore alternatives</li></ul>*James (2008)*<ul><li>Examine alternatives</li></ul>*Bandura 1997*<ul><li>Self-efficacy</li></ul>*Miller and Rollnick (2002)*<ul><li>Support self-efficacy, exploring the problem</li></ul>*Hohman, Kleinpeter and Loughran (2005)*<ul><li>Normalise the difficulties and validate concerns</li></ul>*Dattilio and Freeman (2007)*<ul><li>Assess and mobilise client's strengths and resources</li></ul>

Changing	Watch out for!	Related to
• Continue with calming and coping as appropriate	• Overlooking opportunities for longer term change and settling for stability which may be short lived	*Miller and Rollnick (2002)*
• Assess timing for moving on to talk about changing	• Restoration of stability without sufficient change to prevent another crisis	• First and second stage strategies including: self motivating statements, engaging in change talk, use of complex reflections, decisional balance, and developing a change plan
• Work towards balancing talk about change with positive input about coping and a sufficient degree of calm to allow thinking through planning change	• 'Blaming' the victim: pressure on the victim to change but not addressing need for other change	*de Shazer (1985, 1988, 1991), DeJong and Berg (2001), Greene et al. (2005)*
• Depending on assessment consider options for	• Unrealistic plan which will generate further stress and possible crisis	• Goal setting, connecting exceptions to solutions
• return to pre-crisis stability	• Lack of engagement with services/ supports leaving the client vulnerable and isolated	• Identify, amplify and reinforce what is working
• augmentation of coping	• Unclear about how plan will result in improvements	*James (2008)*
• opportunities for transformative change	• Lack of follow up support to help continued commitment to change	• Make plans
• social change/ action	• The change/s being prescribed by worker are not sought by client	• Obtain commitment
• Facilitate consideration of options rather than panic driven change	• Failing to consider post-crisis coping as a preventative strategy	*Roberts (2005)*
• Weigh up options for short term and longer term change		• Develop and formulate an action plan
• Consider motivation for change accentuated by the crisis		• Establish follow up plan and agreement
• Engage social networks/systems in supporting and facilitating change		*Bartlett and Daughhetee (2010)*
• Establish links with		• Compliance with treatment
• specialised support services		*Golan (1978)*
• mutual help		• Contracts
• crisis response services		*Dattilio and Freeman (2007)*
• ongoing counselling		• Work jointly to develop plan
• Obtain commitment to change		• Test new ideas and behaviours
• Plan post-crisis coping		

Crisis therapies and the problems of an evidence base for practice

The evidence base for crisis therapies is limited due to a dearth of research about what works in practice in crisis therapy (Walsh 2006, Roberts and Everly 2006, and Corcoran and Roberts 2000). In their meta-analysis of crisis intervention Roberts and Everly (2006) comment on this problem about research, 'the relative effectiveness of in-person, in-home, and/or telephone crisis intervention had not been systematically and rigorously studied' (p.16). They caution that crisis intervention is not always appropriate and recommend that good diagnostic criteria are necessary in using crisis therapies. They conclude that intensive in-home crisis intervention and critical incident stress management approaches are effective.

Earlier discussion presented the disputed ideas about the effectiveness of critical incident stress debriefing as a crisis approach. Given that the concerns raised about that approach resulted in a reformulation of the interventions it is important that we consider the need for further research into crisis therapies in general. There are several problems with such research. Some of these have been addressed within other therapeutic schools of thought but some barriers remain. With crisis therapies it would be difficult to develop a randomised experimental study. This might raise ethical issues about possible withholding of a response to some in order to establish a control group; it would be difficult to create a random sample since the experience of crisis is as we have seen a very personalised issue. It would not be a true test of a crisis approach simply to select all who had a similar crisis event since that would not have the same impact on the participants; as with other counselling models it is difficult to accurately attribute all or any success in outcome exclusively to the intervention method employed. Walsh (2006) raised some of these points in connection to the evidence for effectiveness in crisis work. He mentioned the fact that every crisis is different, in the nature of the crisis and in the client's perception of the crisis and the client's resources.

Life for clients' families and community does go on and it is not possible to take account of all the possible influences which may impact on an individual, family or community as they struggle with the crisis experience. It may be difficult to attribute all or even some of the successful resolution to a specific approach or intervention strategy.

The debate about evidence based practice is a very contentious issue. Castonguay and Beutler (2006) outline the 'common factors' to be considered in research in the field of therapy: the participants, the therapeutic relationship and the techniques employed. It is important to be able to evaluate the effectiveness of our practice yet it is an oversimplification to look at outcomes without taking account of process. Asay and Lambert (1999) support the notion that there are 'common factors' to be considered in evaluating the effectiveness of therapy. Kim, Wampold and Bolt's (2001) research supports the fact that the therapist is important. In counselling in general we have some indication that the counselling process is in itself important. For example we know that the therapeutic relationship, building a trusting relationship based on respect is key. Lambert and Barley (2001) found that up to 30 per cent of patient improvement was attributable to the therapeutic relationship.

The research that we have points to the fact that psychotherapy does work (Lambert and Olges 2004; Howard *et al*. 1986, 1996; Lambert and Bergin 1994). Reisner (2005) commented that

> although […] psychotherapy in general is effective, and […] common factors may account for most of the change, there are areas wherein one therapy may have received more scientific study than another, or it may have demonstrated greater effectiveness in circumscribed areas (p.388).

We have some evidence that the specific approach adopted by the worker or helper is less important than this relationship and the workers' competence in whatever approach they employ (Norcross 2001). Project MATCH (1998) found little variation in outcome when comparing three different approaches to therapy in substance misuse.

More recently there has been evidence that the belief in the importance of talking about trauma is not well founded in research. There has even been some discussion that reliving a trauma by recounting your story may be counterproductive. This information is very important if we are to be able to assist people in crisis. In counselling we are at a minimum trying to ensure that we do no harm and at best that we can facilitate the clients to do the best they can in whatever challenging situations they face. The more we can learn about what actually works for clients the more effective a service we can offer. But this means not looking just at limited outcome measures at the expense of understanding the helping process.

References

Adams, R. (2008) *Empowerment, Participation, and Social Work*. London: Palgrave McMillan.

Adams, R. and Payne, M. (2009) 'Ethical Tensions and Later Life: Choice, Consent and Mental Capacity.' In R. Adams, L. Dominelli and M. Payne (eds) *Critical Practice in Social Work* (2nd edition). Basingstoke: Palgrave.

Aguilera, D. (1980) *Crisis Intervention: Theory and Methodology* (1st edition). St Louis, MO: C.V. Mosby Company.

Aguilera, D. (1986) *Crisis Intervention: Theory and Methodology* (5th edition). St Louis, MO: C.V. Mosby.

Aguilera, D.C. (1990) *Crisis Intervention: Theory and Methodology* (6th edition). St Louis, MO: C.V. Mosby.

Aguilera, D. (1998) *Crisis Intervention: Theory and Methodology* (8th edition). St Louis, MO: C.V. Mosby.

Aldridge, D. (1998) *Suicide: The Tragedy of Hopelessness*. London: Jessica Kingsley Publishers.

Allen, M. (2008) *Journey to Safety: The Construction of Identity and Meaning in Women's Resistance to Intimate Partner Violence*. Unpublished PhD thesis. Dublin: University College Dublin.

American Psychiatric Association (1980) *Diagnostic and Statistical Manual of Mental Disorders* (3rd edition). Washington, DC: APA.

American Psychiatric Association (1994) *Diagnostic and Statistical Manual of Mental Disorders* (4th edition). Washington, DC: APA.

Anderson, H. (2003) 'Postmodern Social Construction Therapies.' In T. Sexton, G. Weeks and M. Robbins (eds) *Handbook of Family Therapy: The Science and Practice of Working with Families and Couples*. New York: Brunner-Routledge.

Ansbacher, H.L. and Ansbacher, R.R. (1956) *The Individual Psychology of Alfred Adler: A Systematic Presentation in Selections from his Writings*. New York: Basic Books.

Asay, T. and Lambert, M. (1999) 'The Empirical Case for the Common Factors in Therapy.' In M. Hubble, B. Duncan and S. Miller (eds) *The Heart and Soul of Change: What Works in Therapy*. Washington, DC: American Psychological Associations.

Austerberry, H. and Wiggins, M. (2007) 'Taking a pro-choice perspective on promoting inclusion of teenage mothers: Lessons from an evaluation of the Sure Start programme.' *Critical Public Health 17*, 1, 3–15.

Bandura, A. (1969) *Principles of Behavior Modification*. New York, NY: Holt, Rinehart and Winston.

Bandura, A. (1997) *Self-efficacy: The Exercise of Control*. New York: W.H. Freeman.

Bartlett, M. and Daughhetee, C. (2010) 'Intervention with Clients: Suicide and Homicide.' In L. Jackson-Cherry and B. Erford (eds) *Crisis Intervention, and Prevention*. Boston, MA: Pearson.

Beck, A. (1976) *Cognitive Therapies and Emotional Disorders*. New York: Penguin Books.

Beck, A. and Freeman, A. (1990) *Cognitive Therapy of Personality Disorders.* New York: Guilford Press.

Beels, C. (2009) 'Some historical conditions of narrative work.' *Family Process 48,* 363–378.

Bellack, A. and Hersen, M. (1985) 'General Considerations.' In M. Hersen and A. Bellack (eds) *Handbook of Clinical Behavior Therapy with Adults.* New York: Plenum Press.

Berger, P. and Luckmann, T. (1966) *The Social Construction of Reality: A Treatise in the Sociology of Knowledge.* London: Penguin.

Bibring, E. (1954) 'Psychoanalysis and the dynamic psychotherapies.' *Journal of American Psychoanalytic Association 2,* 745–770.

Bindman, J. and Flowers, M. (2008) 'Practical Psychosocial Interventions.' In S. Johnson, J. Needle, J. Bindman and G. Thornicroft (eds) *Crisis Resolution and Home Treatment in Mental Health.* Cambridge: Cambridge University Press.

Birns, B., Cascardi, M. and Meyers, S. (1994) 'Sex roles, socialization: Developmental influences on wife abuse.' *American Orthopsychiatry Association 64,* 1.

Bowen, M. (1959) 'The family as the unit and study of treatment: Family psychotherapy' *American Journal of Orthopsychiatry 31,* 40–60.

Bowen, M. (1978) *Family Therapy in Clinical Practice.* Northvale, NJ: Jason Aronson.

Breslau, N. (1998) 'Epidemiology of Trauma and Posttraumatic Stress Disorder.' In R. Yehuda (ed.) *Psychological Trauma.* Washington, DC: American Psychiatric Press.

Bridgett, C. and Gijsman, H. (2008) 'Working with Families and Social Networks.' In S. Johnson, J. Needle, J. Bindman and G. Thornicroft (eds) *Crisis Resolution and Home Treatment in Mental Health.* Cambridge: Cambridge University Press.

Brown, L., Shiang, J. and Bongar, B. (2003) 'Crisis Intervention.' In G. Stricker and T. Widiger (volume eds), I. Weiner (ed. in chief) *Handbook in Psychology, Volume 8: Clinical Psychology.* Hoboken, NJ: Wiley.

Burke, B. and Harrison, P. (2009) 'Anti-oppressive Approaches' In R. Adams, L. Dominelli and M. Payne (eds) *Critical Practice in Social Work* (2nd edition). Basingstoke: Palgrave.

Burr, V. (2003) *Social Constructionism* (2nd edition). London: Routledge.

Camilleri, P. (1999) 'Social Work and its Search for Meaning: Theories, Narratives and Practices.' In B. Pearse and J. Fook (eds) *Transforming Social Work Practice.* London: Routledge.

Caplan, G. (1961) *An Approach to Community Mental Health.* New York: Grune and Statton.

Caplan, G. (1964) *Principles in Preventive Psychiatry.* New York: Basic Books.

Capra, F. (1996) *The Web of Life.* New York: Anchor and Doubleday.

Carter, B. and McGoldrick, M. (eds) (1989) *The Changing Family Life Cycle: A Framework for Family Therapy* (2nd edition). Boston, MA: Allyn and Bacon.

Castellano, C. and Plionis, E. (2006) 'Comparative analysis of three crisis intervention models applied to law enforcement first responders during 9/11 and Hurricane Katrina.' *Brief Treatment and Crisis Intervention 6,* 326–336.

Castonguay, L. and Beutler, L. (2006) 'Principles of therapeutic change: A task force on participants, relationships, and techniques factors.' *Journal of Clinical Psychology 62,* 631–638.

Clemen-Stone, S. (2002) 'Foundations for Family Interventions: Families under Stress.' In S. Clemen-Stone, S. McGuire and D. Eigsti (eds) *Comprehensive Community Health Nursing: Family, Aggregate and Community Practice.* St Louis, MO: Mosby.

Collins, B. and Collins, T. (2005) *Crisis and Trauma Developmental-Ecological Intervention.* Boston, MA: Houghton Mifflin/Lahaska Press.

Corcoran, J. and Roberts, A. (2000) 'Research on Crisis Intervention and Recommendations for Future Research.' In A. Roberts (ed.) *Crisis Intervention Handbook* (2nd edition). New York: Oxford University Press.

Corey, G. (1996) *Theory and Practice of Counselling and Psychotherapy* (5th edition). Belmont, CA: Brooks/Cole.

Cottingham, J., Stoothoff, R. and Murdoch, D. (1988) *Descartes: Selected Philosophical Writings.* Cambridge: Cambridge University Press.

Crain, W.C. (1985) *Theories of Development* (2nd edition). Upper Saddle River, NJ: Prentice Hall.

Darbonne, A.R. (1967) 'Crisis: A review of theory, research and practice.' *Psychotherapy: Theory, Research and Practice, 4*, 2, 49–56.

Dattilio, F. and Freeman, A. (eds) (2007) *Cognitive-Behavioral Strategies in Crisis Intervention.* New York: Guilford.

Davidson, J., Swartz, M., Storck, M., Krisnan, R. and Hammett, R. (1985) 'A diagnostic and family study of post-traumatic stress.' *American Journal of Psychiatry 142*, 90–93.

DeJong, P. and Berg, I.K. (1997) *Interviewing for Solutions* (1st edition). Pacific Grove, CA: Brooks/Cole.

DeJong, P. and Berg, I. (2001) *Interviewing for Solutions* (2nd edition). Pacific Grove, CA: Brooks/Cole.

de Shazer, S. (1985) *Keys to Solutions in Brief Therapy.* New York: Norton.

de Shazer, S. (1988) *Clues: Investigating Solutions in Brief Therapy.* New York: Norton.

de Shazer, S. (1991) *Putting Differences to Work.* New York: Norton.

Dobash, R.E. and Dobash, R. (1979) *Violence Against Wives: A Case against the Patriarchy.* New York: Free Press.

Dominelli, L. (1988) *Anti-racist Social Work.* Basingstoke: Macmillan.

Dominelli, L. (2002) *Anti-oppressive Social Work Theory and Practice.* Basingstoke: Palgrave Macmillan.

Dryden, W. and Yankura, J. (1995) *Developing Rational Emotive Behavioural Counselling.* London: Sage.

Durkheim, E. (1951) *Suicide: A Study in Sociology* (Spaulding Simpson translation). New York: Free Press.

Eisler, R. and Hersen, M. (1973) 'Behavioral techniques in family orientated crisis intervention.' *Archives of General Psychiatry 28*, 10, 111–116.

Ellis, A. (1962) *Reason and Emotion in Psychotherapy.* Secaucus, NJ: Lyle Stuart.

Ellis, A. (1969) 'Rational emotive therapy.' *Journal of Contemporary Psychotherapy 1*, 2, 82–90.

Ellis, A. (1995) 'Rational Emotive Behaviour Therapy.' In R. Corsini and D. Weddings (eds) *Current Psychotherapies* (5th edition). Itasca, IL: FE Peacock.

Ellis, A. and Blau, S. (1998) *The Albert Ellis Reader: A Guide to Well-Being Using Rational Emotive Behaviour Therapy.* Secaucus, NJ: Citadel Press.

Erikson, E. (1950) *Childhood and Society.* New York: Norton and Co.

Erikson, E. (1959) 'Identity and the life cycle.' *Psychological Issues* (Monograph No.1). New York: Norton and Co.

Erikson, E. (1980) *Identity and the Life Cycle.* New York: Norton and Co.

Escobar, J., Randolph, E., Pruente, G., Spiwak, F., Asamen, J., Hill, M. and Hough, R. (1983) 'Post-traumatic stress disorder in Hispanic Vietnam veterans.' *Journal of Nervous and Mental Disease 171,* 585–596.

Everly, G. (2000) 'Five principles of crisis intervention: Reducing the risk of premature crisis intervention.' *International Journal of Emergency Mental Health 2,* 1, 1–4.

Everly, G. and Mitchell, J. (1997) *Critical Incident Stress Management.* Ellicott City, MD: Chevron.

Everly, G. and Mitchell, J. (1999) *Critical Incident Stress Management* (2nd edition). Ellicott City, MD: Chevron.

Ferguson, I. (2008) *Reclaiming Social Work: Challenging Neo-Liberalism and Promoting Social Justice.* London: Sage.

Ferguson, I. and Woodward, R. (2009) *Radical Social work in Practice: Making a Difference.* Bristol: The Policy Press.

Flavell, J. (1971) 'Stage-related properties of cognitive development.' *Cognitive Psychology 2,* 421–453.

Flavell, J. (1982) 'On cognitive development.' *Child Development 53,* 1–10.

Fook, J. (1993) *Radical Casework: A Theory of Practice.* Sydney: Allen & Unwin.

Fook, J. (2002) *Social Work: Critical Theory and Practice.* London: Sage.

Forgey, M. and Badger, L. (2006) 'Patterns of intimate partner violence among married women in the military: Type, level directionality and consequences.' *Journal of Family Violence 21,* 6, 369–380.

Franklin, C. and Jordan, C. (1999) *Family Practice: Brief Systems Methods for Social Work.* Pacific Grove, CA: Brooks/Cole.

Franks, C.M. (1969) *Behavior Therapy: Appraisal and Status.* New York: McGraw Hill.

Freire, P. (1970) *The Pedagogy of the Oppressed.* New York: Continuum International Publishing Group.

Freud, S. (1900) *The Interpretation of Dreams.* New York: Wiley.

Freud, S. (1912) 'The Dynamics of Transference.' In G.P. Bauer (ed.) *Essential Papers on Transference Analysis* (1994). Northvale, NJ: Jason Aronson.

Freud, A. (1966) *The Ego and Mechanisms of Defence.* New York: International University Press.

George, E., Iveson, C. and Ratner, H. (1999) *Problems to Solutions.* London: BT Press.

Gergen, K. (1973) 'Social psychology as history.' *Journal of Personality and Social Psychology 26,* 309–320.

Gergen, K. (1985) 'The social constructionist movement in modern psychology.' *American Psychologist 40,* 266–275.

Germain, C. and Gitterman, A. (1996) *The Life Model of Social Work Practice: Advances in Theory and Practice* (2nd edition). New York: Columbia University Press.

Giddens, A. (1998) *The Third Way: The Renewal of Social Democracy.* Cambridge: Cambridge University Press.

Glick, R.A. and Meyerson, A.T. (1980/1981) 'The use of psychoanalytic concepts in crisis intervention.' *International Journal of Psychoanalytic Psychotherapy 8,* 171–188.

Golan, N. (1978) *Treatment in Crisis Situations.* New York: Free Press.

Greene, G., Lee, M., Trask, R. and Rheinscheld, J. (2005) 'How to Work with Clients' Strengths in Crisis Intervention: A Solution-Focused Approach' in A. Roberts (ed.) *Crisis Intervention Handbook: Assessment, Treatment and Research* (3rd edition). New York: Oxford University Press.

Goldenberg, I. and Goldenberg, H. (2004) *Family Therapy: An Overview*. Pacific Grove, CA: Thomson Brooks/Cole.

Granvold, D. (2005) 'The Crisis of Divorce: Cognitive-Behavioral and Constructivist Assessment and Treatment.' In A.Roberts (ed.) *Crisis Intervention Handbook: Assessment, Treatment and Research* (3rd edition). New York: Oxford University Press.

Gray, M. and Webb, S. (eds) (2009) *Social Work Theories and Methods*. Los Angeles, CA: Sage.

Haley, J. (1980) *Leaving Home*. New York: McGraw Hill Books Co.

Hall, G.S. (1912) *Founders of Modern Psychology*. London: Appleton.

Hamberger, L. and Holtzworth-Munroe, A. (2007) 'Spousal Abuse.' In F. Dattilio and A. Freeman (eds) *Cognitive-Behavioral Strategies in Crisis Intervention*. New York: Guilford.

Harmon-Jones, E. (1999) 'Toward an Understanding of the Motivation Underlying Dissonance Effects: Is the Production of Aversive Consequences Necessary?' In E. Harmon-Jones and J. Mills (eds) *Cognitive Dissonance: Progress on a Pivotal Theory in Social Psychology*. Washington, DC: American Psychological Association.

Harris, M., Kalish, B. and Freeman, E. (1963) 'Precipitating stress: An approach to brief therapy.' *American Journal of Psychotherapy 17*, 465–471.

Healy, K. (2005) *Social Work Theories in Context: Creating Frameworks for Practice*. Basingstoke: Palgrave MacMillan.

Hedges, F. (2005) *An Introduction to Systemic Therapy with Individuals: A Social Constructionist Approach*. Basingstoke: Palgrave Macmillan.

Herman, J. (1992) *Trauma and Recovery*. New York: Basic Books.

Hester, R. and Miller, W. (1995) (eds) *Handbook of Alcoholism Treatment Approaches: Effective Alternatives* (2nd edition). Boston, MA: Allyn and Bacon.

Hick, S. and Murray, K. (2009) 'Structural Social Work.' In M. Gray and S. Webb (eds) *Social Work Theories and Methods*. Los Angeles, CA: Sage.

Hill, R. (1949) *Families under Stress*. Westport, CT: Greenwood Press.

Hill, R. (1958) 'Social stresses on the family: Generic features of families under stress.' *Social Casework 39*, 139–150.

Hoffman, L. (1981) *Foundations of Family Therapy: A Conceptual Framework for Systems Change*. New York: Basic Books.

Hoffman, L. (1992) 'A Reflexive Stance for Family Therapy.' In S. McNamee and K. Gergen (eds) *Therapy as a Social Construction*. London: Sage.

Hohman, M., Kleinpeter, C. and Loughran, H. (2005) 'Enhancing Motivation, Strengths, and Skills of Parents in the Child Welfare System.' In J. Corcoran (ed.) *Building Strengths and Skills: A Collaborative Approach to Working with Clients*. New York: Oxford University Press.

Hollinger, R. (1994) *Postmodernism and the Social Sciences*. Thousand Oaks, CA: Sage.

Howard, K., Kopta, S., Krause, M. and Orlinsky, D. (1986) 'The dose-effect relationship in psychotherapy.' *American Psychologist 41*, 159–164.

Howard, K., Moris, K., Brill, P., Martinovick, Z. and Lutz, W. (1996) 'Evaluation of psychotherapy: Efficacy, effectiveness, and patient progress.' *American Psychologist 51*, 10, 1059–1064. Special Issue: Outcome assessment of psychotherapy.

Jack, G. and Jack, D. (2000) 'Ecological Social Work: The Application of Systems Model of Development in Context.' In P. Stepney and D. Ford (eds) *Social Work Models, Methods and Theories: A Framework for Practice.* Lyme Regis: Russell House.

Jackson-Cherry, L. and Erford, B. (2010) *Crisis Intervention, and Prevention.* Boston, MA: Pearson.

Jacobson, G.F, Strickleer, M. and Morley, W.E. (1968) 'Generic and individual approaches to crisis intervention.' *American Journal of Public Health 58,* 2, 338–343.

James, R. (2008) *Crisis Intervention Strategies* (6th edition). Brooks/Cole Belmont, CA: Thomson.

Jehu, D., Hardiker, P., Yelloly, M. and Shaw, M. (1972) *Behaviour Modification in Social Work.* London: Wiley-Interscience.

Jerry, P.A. (1998) 'Dynamic change in crisis intervention.' *American Journal of Psychotherapy 52,* 4, 437–449.

Jobes, D., Berman, A. and Martin, C. (2005) 'Adolescent Suicidality and Crisis Intervention.' In A. Roberts (ed.) *Crisis Intervention Handbook: Assessment, Treatment and Research* (3rd edition). New York: Oxford University Press.

Johnson, K. (1979) 'Durkheim revisited: Why do women kill themselves?' *Suicide Life-Threatening Behavior 9,* 145–153.

Johnson, S., Needle, J., Bindman, J. and Thornicroft, G. (eds) (2008) *Crisis Resolution and Home Treatment in Mental Health.* Cambridge: Cambridge University Press.

Kanfer, F.H. and Phillips, J.S. (1970) *Learning Foundations of Behaviour Therapy.* New York: Wiley.

Kelleher, P. and O'Connor, M. (1995) *Making the Links.* Dublin: Women's Aid.

Kelly, L. (1988) 'How Women Define their Experiences of Violence.' In K. Yllo and M. Bograd (eds) *Feminist Perspectives on Wife Abuse.* Newbury: Sage.

Kfir, N. (1989) *Crisis Intervention Verbatim.* New York: Hemisphere Publishing Corporation.

Kim, D., Wampold, B. and Bolt, D. (2006) 'Therapist effects in psychotherapy: A random effects modeling of the NIMH TDCRP data.' *Psychotherapy Research 16,* 161–172.

Kirkwood, C. (1993) *Leaving Abusive Partners.* London: Sage.

Klein, M. (1927) 'The psychological principles of infant analysis.' *Journal of Psychoanalysis 8,* 25–37.

Kohlberg, L. (1981) *Essays on Moral Development, Vol. I: The Philosophy of Moral Development.* San Francisco, CA: Harper and Row.

Kolb, L. (1987) 'A neuropsychological hypothesis explaining post traumatic stress disorder.' *American Journal of Psychiatry 144,* 8, 989–995.

Kukla, R., Schlenger, W., Fairbank, J., Hough, R., Jordan, B. and Marmar, C. (1990) *Trauma and the Vietnam War Generation: Report of Findings from the National Vietnam Vertners Readjustment Study.* New York: Brunner/Mazel.

Kushner, H. and Sterk, C. (2005) 'The limits of social capital: Durkheim, suicide, and social cohesion.' *American Journal of Public Health 95,* 7, 1139–1143.

Kutak, R. (1938) 'The sociology of crises: The Louisville flood of 1937.' *Social Forces 1,* 66–72.

Lambert, M. and Barley, D. (2001) 'Research summary on the therapeutic relationship and psychotherapy outcome.' *Psychotherapy 3,* 4, 357–361.

Lambert, M. and Bergin, A. (1994) 'The Effectiveness of Psychotherapy.' In A. Bergin, and S. Garfield (eds) *Handbook of Psychotherapy and Behavior Change* (4th edition). New York: Wiley.

Lambert, M. and Olges, B. (2004) 'The efficacy and effectiveness of psychotherapy.' In M. Lambert (ed.) *Handbook of Psychotherapy and Behavior Change.* New York: Wiley.

Langan, M. and Lee, P. (1989) 'Whatever Happened to Radical Social Work?' In M. Langan and P. Lee (eds) *Radical Social Work Today.* London: Unwin Hyman.

Lawlor, D. and Shaw, M. (2002) 'Too much too young? Teenage pregnancy is not a public health problem.' *International Journal of Epidemiology 31,* 552–554.

Lee, M., Sebold, J. and Uken, A. (2002) 'Brief solution focused group treatment with domestic violence offenders: Listening to the narratives of participants and their partners.' *Journal of Brief Therapy 2,* 1, 3–26.

Lee, M., Sebold, J. and Uken, A. (2003) *Solution Focused Treatment of Domestic Violence Offenders: Accountability for Change.* New York: Oxford University Press.

Lethem, J. (1994) *Moved to Tears, Moved to Action: Solution Focused Work with Women and Children.* London: BT Press.

Lindemann, E. (1944) 'Symptomatology and management of acute grief.' *American Journal of Psychiatry 101,* 141–148.

Lindemann, E. (1956) 'The meaning of crisis in individual and family.' *Teachers College Record 57,* 310–315.

Loseke, D. (1992) *The Battered Woman and Shelters: The Social Construction of Wife Abuse.* Albany, NY: State University of New York Press.

Loughran, H. (2002) *A Study of Alcohol Problems and Marriage from a Treatment Perspective.* Unpublished thesis. Dublin: University College Dublin.

Loughran, H. and Richardson, V. (2005) *Mixed Methods Adoption Research, Crisis Pregnancy Agency Report No. 13.* The Adoption Board, Dublin. Dublin: Crisis Pregnancy Agency.

McCubbin, H. and Patterson, J. (1982) 'Family Adaptation to Crisis.' In H. McCubbin, A. Cauble and J. Patterson (eds) *Family Stress, Coping, and Social Support.* Springfield, IL: Charles C. Thomas.

McFarlane, A. (2005) 'Post-traumatic Stress Syndrome Revisited.' In H. Parad and L. Parad (eds) *Crisis Intervention Book 2: The Practitioner's Sourcebook, for Brief Therapy.* Tucson, AZ: Fenestra Books.

McGlothlin, J., Jackson-Cherry, L. and Garofolo, M. (2010) 'Emergency Preparedness and Response.' In L. Jackson-Cherry and B. Erford (eds) *Crisis Intervention, and Prevention.* Boston, MA: Pearson.

McLeod, A. (2001) 'Changing patterns of teenage pregnancy: Population based study of small areas.' *British Medical Journal 323,* 199–203.

McLeod, A., Muldoon, J. and Hays, D. (2010) 'Intimate Partner Violence.' In L. Jackson-Cherry and B. Erford (eds) *Crisis Intervention, and Prevention.* Boston, MA: Pearson.

McNamee, S. and Gergen, K. (1992) *The Social Construction of Therapy.* London: Sage.

Maier, H. (1988) *Three Theories of Child Development* (3rd edition). New York: University Press of America.

Malan, D. (1979) *Individual Psychotherapy and the Science of Psychodynamics.* London: Butterworths.

Mancini, A. and Bonanno, G. (2006) 'Resilience in the face of potential trauma: Clinical practices and illustrations.' *Journal of Clinical Psychology 62,* 8, 971–985.

Mehrotra, M. (1999) 'The social construction of wife abuse: Experiences of Asian Indian women in the United States.' *Violence Against Women 5*, 6, 619–640.

Mezey, G. and Robbins, I. (2001) 'Usefulness and validity of post-traumatic stress disorder as a psychiatric category.' *British Medical Journal 323*, 561–563.

Miller, P.H. (2002) *Theories of Developmental Psychology* (4th edition). New York: Worth.

Miller, W. (1983) 'Motivational interviewing with problem drinkers.' *Behavioural Psychotherapy 1*, 147–172.

Miller, W. and Rollnick, S. (1991) *Motivational Interviewing* (1st edition). New York: Guilford Press.

Miller, W. and Rollnick, S. (2002) *Motivational Interviewing* (2nd edition). New York: Guilford Press.

Minuchin, S. (1974) *Families and Family Therapy.* Cambridge, MA: Harvard University Press.

Minuchin, S. and Fishman, H. (1981) *Family Therapy Techniques.* Cambridge, MA: Harvard University Press.

Mitchell, J. and Everly, G. (1995) *Advanced Critical Incident Stress Debriefing.* Ellicott City, MD: International Critical Incidents Stress Foundation.

Muehlenhard, C. and Kimes, L. (1999) 'The social construction of violence: The case of sexual and domestic violence.' *Personality and Social Psychology Review 3*, 3, 234–245.

Mullaly, R. (1993) *Structural Social Work: Ideology, Theory and Practice.* Toronto: McClelland and Stewart.

Murdock, D. and Barker, P. (1991) *Basic Behaviour Therapy.* London: Blackwell Scientific Publications.

Murray, S. and Powell, A. (2009) 'What's the problem?: Australian public policy constructions of domestic violence.' *Violence Against Women 15*, 5, 532–552.

Myer, R. and Moore, H. (2006) 'Crisis in context theory: An ecological model.' *Journal of Counselling and Development 84*, 2, 139–147.

Norcross, J. (2001) 'Purposes, processes, and products of the task force on empirically supported therapy relationships.' *Psychotherapy 38*, 4, 345–356.

O'Hagan, K. (1986) *Crisis Intervention in Social Services.* Basingstoke: MacMillan.

Orme, J. (2009) 'Feminist Social Work.' In M. Gray and S. Webb (eds) *Social Work Theories and Methods.* Los Angeles, CA: Sage.

Palazzoli, M.S., Boscolo, L., Cecchin, G. and Prata, G. (1980) 'Hypothesizing-circularity-neutrality: Three guidelines for the conductor of the session.' *Family Process 19*, 3–12.

Paolino, T. and McCrady, B. (1977) *The Alcoholic Marriage: Alternative Perspectives.* New York: Grune and Stratton.

Parad, H.J. (1971) 'Crisis Intervention.' In R. Morris (ed.) *Encyclopedia of Social Work* (Volume 1). New York: National Association of Social Workers.

Parad, H.J. and Caplan, G. (1960) 'A Framework for Studying Families in Crisis.' In H.J. Parad (ed.) (1965) *Crisis Intervention: Selected Readings.* New York: Family Service Association of America.

Parad, H. and Parad, L. (2005a) (eds) *Crisis Intervention Book 2: The Practitioner's Sourcebook, for Brief Therapy.* Tucson, AZ: Fenestra Books.

Parad, H. and Parad L. (2005b) 'Crisis Intervention: An Introductory Overview.' In H. Parad and L. Parad (eds) *Crisis Intervention Book 2: The Practitioner's Sourcebook, for Brief Therapy.* Tucson, AZ: Fenestra Books.

Parton, N. (2009) 'Postmodern and Constructionist Approaches to Social Work.' In R. Adams, L. Dominelli and M. Payne (eds) *Critical Practice in Social Work* (2nd edition). Basingstoke: Macmillan.

Parton, N. and O'Byrne, P. (2000) *Constructive Social Work: Towards a New Practice.* Basingstoke: Macmillan and New York: St. Martin's Press.

Payne, M. (1997) *Modern Social Work Theory* (2nd edition.). Basingstoke: Macmillan.

Pearse, B. (2009) 'From Radical to Critical Social Work: Progressive Transformation or Mainstream Incorporation?' In R. Adams, L. Dominelli and M. Payne (eds) *Critical Practice in Social Work* (2nd edition). Basingstoke: Palgrave.

Piaget, J. (1950) *The Psychology of Intelligence.* New York: Harcourt Brace.

Portes, A. (1971) 'On the emergence of behaviour therapy in modern society.' *Journal of Consulting and Clinical Psychology 36*, 303–313.

Prochaska, J. and DiClemente, C. (1982) 'Transtheoretical therapy: Toward a more integrative model of change.' *Psychotherapy: Theory, Research and Practice 19*, 276–288.

Project MATCH (1994) *Volume 2 – Motivational Enhancement Therapy Manual.* NIH Pub. No. 94-3723.

Project MATCH (1995a) *Volume 1 – Twelve Step Facilitation Therapy Manual.* NIH Pub. No. 94-3722.

Project MATCH (1995b) *Volume 3 – Cognitive-Behavioral Coping Skills Therapy Manual.* NIH Pub. No. 94-3724.

Project MATCH (1998) 'Matching alcoholism treatments to client heterogeneity: Project MATCH three year drinking outcomes.' *Alcoholism: Clinical Land Experimental Research 22*, 6, 1300–1311.

Puleo, S. and McGlothlin, J. (2010) 'Overview of Crisis Intervention.' In L. Jackson-Cherry and B. Erford (eds) *Crisis Intervention, and Prevention.* Boston, MA: Pearson.

Quarantelli, E. (1985) 'An Assessment of Conflicting Views on Mental Health: The Consequences of Traumatic Events.' In C. Figley (ed.) *Trauma and its Wake: The Study and Treatment of Post-traumatic Stress Disorder.* New York: Brunner/Mazel.

Racker, H. (2001) *Transference and Counter-transference.* Madison, CT: International Universities Press.

Rapoport, L. (1962) 'The state of crisis: Some theoretical considerations.' *The Social Service Review 34*, 2, 211–217.

Rapoport, L. (1965) 'The State of Crisis: Some Theoretical Considerations.' In J. Howard and H. Parad (eds) *Crisis Intervention: Selected Readings.* New York: Family Service Association of America.

Rechtman, R. (2004) 'The rebirth of PTSD: The rise of a new paradigm in psychiatry.' *Social Psychiatry Psychiatric Epidemiology 39*, 913–915.

Reid, W. (2004) 'Contribution of Operant Theory to Social Work Practice and Research.' In H. Briggs and T. Rzepnicki (eds) *Using evidence in Social Work Practice: Behavioral Perspectives.* Chicago, IL: Lyceum Books.

Reisner, A. (2005) 'The common factors, empirically validated treatments, and recovery models of therapeutic change.' *The Psychological Record 55*, 3, 377–400.

Roberts, A. (1991) 'Conceptualizing Crisis Theory and the Crisis Intervention Model.' In A. Roberts (ed.) *Contemporary Perspectives on Crisis Intervention and Prevention.* Englewood Cliffs, NJ: Prentice-Hall.

Roberts, A. (ed.) (2005) *Crisis Intervention Handbook: Assessment, Treatment and Research* (3rd edition). New York: Oxford University Press.

Roberts, A. (2006) 'Classification typology and assessment of five levels of women battering.' *Journal of Family Violence 21*, 521–527.

Roberts, A. and Everly, G. (2006) 'A meta analysis of 36 crisis intervention studies.' *Brief Treatment and Crisis Intervention 6*, 1, 10–21.

Roberts, A. and Yeager, K. (2005) 'Lethality Assessment and Crisis Intervention with Persons Presenting with Suicidal Ideation.' In A. Roberts (ed.) *Crisis Intervention Handbook: Assessment, Treatment and Research* (3rd edition). New York: Oxford University Press.

Roberts, A. and Yeager, K. (2009) *Foundations of Evidence Based Social Work Practice.* New York: Oxford University Press.

Roberts, N., Kitchiner, N., Kenardy, J. and Bisson, J. (2009) 'Systematic review and meta-analysis of multiple-session early intervention following traumatic events.' *The American Journal of Psychiatry 166*, 3, 293–301.

Rodgers, C. (1957) 'The necessary and sufficient conditions of therapeutic personality change.' *Journal of Consulting Psychology 21*, 2, 95–103.

Rodgers, C. (1980) *A Way of Being.* Boston, MA: Houghton Mifflin.

Rosenthal, E. (1999) 'Suicides reveal bitter roots of China's rural life' *New York Times*, 24 January, p.1.

Saleebey, D. (2002) *The Strengths Perspective in Social Work Practice* (3rd edition). New York: Longman.

Satin, D. (1984) 'Lindemann as Humanist, Scientist, and Change Agent. *American Journal of Community Psychiatry 12*, 5, 519–527.

Satir, V. (1964) *Conjoint Family Therapy.* Palo Alto, CA: Science and Behavior Books.

Scott, M. (1989) *A Cognitive-Behavioural Approach to Clients' Problems.* New York: Routledge.

Selby, L.G. (1963) *Social Work and Crisis Theory.* Los Angeles, CA: University of Southern California, School of Social Work.

Seligman, M. (1975) *Helplessness: On Depression, Development and Death.* San Francisco, CA: Freeman.

Sheldon, B. (2000) 'Cognitive Behavioural Methods in Social Care: A Look at the Evidence.' In P. Stepney and D. Ford (eds) *Social Work Models, Methods and Theories: A Framework for Practice.* Lyme Regis: Russell House.

Simon, G. (2004) 'An examination of emotionally focused therapy.' *The Family Journal 12*, 3, 254–262.

Skinner, B.F. (1953) *Science and Human Behaviour.* New York: Macmillan.

Skynner, R. and Cleese, J. (1984) *Families and How to Survive Them.* New York: Oxford University Press.

Smith, R. (2008) *Social Work and Power.* Basingstoke: Palgrave.

Stepney, P. and Ford, D. (2000) *Social Work Models, Methods and Theories: A Framework for Practice.* Lyme Regis: Russell House.

Stevens, A. (1994) *Jung: A Very Short Introduction.* Oxford: Oxford University Press.

Stuart, M. and Mackay, K. (1977) 'Defining the differences between crisis intervention and short term therapy.' *Hospital Community Psychiatry 28*, 527–529.

Summerfield. D. (2001) 'The invention of post-traumatic stress disorder and the social usefulness of a psychiatric category.' *British Medical Journal 322*, 95–98.

Talbott, J.A. (1980–1981) 'Crisis intervention and psychoanalysis: Compatible or antagonistic?' *International Journal of Psychoanalytic Psychotherapy 8*, 189–201.

Teater, B. (2010) *Applying Social Work Theories and Methods.* Maidenhead: Open University Press.

Thompson, N. (1991) *Crisis Intervention Revisited.* Birmingham: Pepar Publications.

Thompson, N. (1997) *Anti-Discriminatory Practice* (2nd edition). Basingstoke: Macmillan.

Tjaden, P. and Thoennes, N. (2000) 'Prevalence and consequences of male to female and female to male intimate partner violence as measured by the National Violence Against Women Survey.' *Violence Against Women 6*, 142–161.

UK Social Exclusion Unit (2006) *Young People, Pregnancy and Social Exclusion: A Systematic Synthesis of Research Evidence to Identify Effective, Appropriate and Promising Approaches for Prevention and Support.* London: Social Science Research Unit and Institute of Education, University of London.

US Department of Health and Human Services (2000) 'Mental health: A report of the Surgeon General.' Rockville, MD: US Department of Health and Human Services.

van Dijk, T. (ed.) (1997) *Discourse as Social Interaction.* London: Sage.

Wade, A. (1997) 'Small acts of living: Everyday resistance to violence and other forms of oppression.' *Journal of Contemporary Family Therapy 19*, 1, 23–40.

Waelder, R. (1936) 'Principle of multiple function.' *Psychoanalytic Quarterly 5*, 45–62.

Walker, L. (1979) *The Battered Woman.* New York: Harper & Row.

Walsh, F. (1998) *Strengthening Family Resilience.* New York: Guilford.

Walsh, J. (2006) *Theories for Direct Social Work Practice.* Belmont, CA: Thomas Brooks/Cole.

Warren, K., Franklin, C. and Streeter, C. (1998) 'New directions in systems theory: Chaos and complexity.' *Social Work 43*, 4, 357–372.

Watson, J. and Rayner, R. (1920) 'Conditioned emotional reactions.' *Journal of Experimental Psychology 3*, 1–14.

Watzlawick, P., Weakland, J. and Fisch, R. (1974) *Change: Principles of Problem Formation and Problem Resolution.* New York: Norton.

Weiss, A. (2001) 'The no suicide contract: Possibilities and pitfalls.' *American Journal of Psychotherapy 55*, 414–419.

White, M. (1989) *Selected Papers.* Adelaide: Dulwich Centre Publications.

White, M. (1995) *Re-authoring Our Lives.* Adelaide: Dulwich Centre Publications.

White, M. and Epston, D. (1990) *Narrative Ends to Therapeutic Means.* New York: Norton.

Woods, M.E. and Hollis, F. (2000) *Casework – A Psychosocial Therapy* (5th edition). Boston, MA: McGraw Hill.

Worden, J. (2002) *Grief Counselling and Grief Therapy: A Handbook for the Mental Health Practitioner* (4th edition). New York: Guilford Press.

World Health Organization (2007) 'Suicide prevention (SUPRE).' Available at www.who.int/mental_health/prevention/suicide/suicideprevent/en, accessed on 9 March 2011.

Yalom, I. (1970) *The Theory and Practice of Group Psychotherapy.* New York: Basic Books.

Yates, A. (1970) *Behavior Therapy.* New York: Wiley.

Yates, A. (1975) *Theory and Practice in Behavior Therapy.* New York: Wiley.

Yeager, K. and Gregoire, T. (2005) 'Crisis Intervention Application of Brief Solution-focused Therapy in Addictions.' In A. Roberts (ed.) *Crisis Intervention Handbook: Assessment, Treatment and Research* (3rd edition). New York: Oxford University Press.

Subject Index

Author Index

Lightning Source UK Ltd.
Milton Keynes UK
UKOW04f0952250816

281458UK00002B/191/P